SIMPLE GIFTS

SIMPLE GIFTS

A life in the theatre

George Ogilvie

*Macquarie
Regional Library*

CURRENCY HOUSE

First published in 2006 by
Currency House Inc.
PO Box 2270
Strawberry Hills NSW 2012 Australia
www.currencyhouse.org.au
info@currencyhouse.org.au

National Library of Australia Cataloguing-in-Publication Data:
Ogilvie, George.
    Simple gifts : a life in the theatre.
    ISBN 978 0 97573 017 1.
    ISBN 978 0 97573 018 8 (pbk.).
    ISBN 0 9757301 7 7.
    ISBN 0 9757301 8 5 (pbk.).
    1. Ogilvie, George. 2. Theatrical producers and directors – Australia – Biography.
    3. Motion picture producers and directors – Australia – Biography. 4. Actors
    – Australia – Biography. I. Title.
    792.092
Front cover photograph shows George Ogilvie, Paris, c.1962. (Photo in possession of the
author)
Cover design by Kate Florance
Typeset in Revival 565 BT 11.5 / 15.5
Index by Garry Cousins
Printed in China through Printciple Source

HELMUT BAKAITIS

It seems strange to be introducing a book by my dearly beloved friend and teacher, George Ogilvie, to a new generation of theatre lovers and practitioners, if only because our lives have been so closely interconnected over the last forty years. What can I add that George has not already written?

When I first met George at the Melbourne Theatre Company in 1965, he had just staged a brilliant production of *War and Peace* at the Russell Street Theatre. I was a Young Elizabethan Player at the time, touring regional arts institutes and school halls all over the southern States. I do not exaggerate when I say that, at that time, it was the dream of every actor in Melbourne to work under Ogilvie. Already he was known as 'the actor's director'.

For the next five years, I was a member of the MTC 'family' doing shows back-to-back. The pattern was usually a show with John Sumner, followed by a show with George. Apart from the joy of being treated not just as an actor but as a collaborator in George's landmark productions, the greatest joy of all was his continuing workshop classes with the Company. George introduced us to his unique amalgam of Lecoq exercises, *commedia dell'arte* and Celtic mysticism.

It was George who first nurtured my love for working with young people in theatre arts. It was George who told me I was a director. It was George who encouraged me to create a new form of youth theatre in Australia, founded on Brechtian principles. And it was George who invited me, along with Rodney Fisher, to form the Directorate of the South Australian Theatre Company.

Our paths separated for a few years, as he became increasingly involved in the arcane world of film, television and Siddha Yoga, but eventually our professional lives reconnected—when I was artistic director at Penrith's Q Theatre. As if by magic, George was then available on a freelance basis. The production budgets I offered him were tiny, compared with his other projects, but his productions shone like jewels in our repertoire. His *Twelfth Night* with Jacqueline McKenzie remains one of the highlights of my years at the Q. Just as my acting career had really begun with George's legendary production of *The Three Sisters* at the MTC, so it came to a perfect conclusion with George's production of *King Lear* at the Q and at the Sydney Theatre Company.

During the time I have been Head of the Directing Course at NIDA, George has been a living treasure; and he continues to share his knowledge with my students. His profound passion for the art of the theatre, his total commitment to the sharing of knowledge, continues to make him a great teacher. To watch him at play with young people is to see him become a child himself.

When George told me that he had received a Keating creative fellowship to write his story, I was overjoyed. It has taken a considerable amount of time and required a great deal of encouragement as well as criticism to get him to finish it. But it is an important story for the arts in this nation. Reading through the manuscript, I am astonished to realise in how many areas of Australian theatre history George was a pioneer. So much of the history of its development has been lost to us and this book is invaluable in the way it has been able to give an insider's view of our theatre from beginnings with the Australian Elizabethan Theatre Trust to the State companies, the rise of our choreographers and scene designers and the rebirth of the film industry. That is why George's book is so important. His journey chronicles the time when theatre in Melbourne and Sydney was stepping out of its post-colonial phase and taking its first steps to assert a kind of modernity and continues to the present day. A long and remarkable life.

Most of George's theatre work is lost to us—that's the nature of theatre; but his films and TV series are still around and, just as his work in theatre was a kind of Golden Age, so too was his apprenticeship with George Miller and Byron Kennedy, producing work with a regularity and of a calibre that has never been equalled.

I am proud to be a part of his story.

Contents

Subscribers

Currency House Inc. expresses its thanks to the patrons and supporters who assisted in the publication of this book:

The Australian Ballet
Kennedy Miller
State Theatre Company of
    South Australia

Antonia Barnard
John Bell
Frederick Blackwood
Katharine Brisbane
Al Clark
Patricia Conolly
Russell and Danielle Spencer
    Crowe
Vanessa Downing
Graeme Ewer, AM
John Gregg
Jennifer Hagan
Jane Harders
Noni Hazlehurst, AM
Ken and Janet Healey
Edwin Hodgeman
Margaret Leask
Hilary Linstead
Carolyn and Peter Lowry, OAM
Monica Maughan

Rhys McConnochie
Ailsa McPherson
Richard Mills
Karan Monkhouse
Lynne Murphy
Aarne Neeme
Robyn Nevin
Louis Nowra
Dennis Olsen
John Pringle
Gordon and Jacqueline
    Samuels
Maggie Scott
Dr Rodney Seaborn, AO, OBE
Alan Seymour
Barbara Stephens
John Sumner
Dr and Mrs G.M. Tallis
Greig Tillotson
A.E. Tonks
Thea Waddell
Professor Elizabeth Webby
Jo Weeks
George Whaley
Frank Whitten

Illustrations

Unless otherwise indicated the photographs are in the possession of the author.

Acknowledgements

Over the many years of my life in theatre and film, I have worked with and loved many people. My major regret lies in not being able within these pages to give them all their credit. I thank all my fellow actors, singers, dancers and students for a full and grateful life.

I need to thank my two beloved sisters, Jean and Caroline, for their collection of family memorabilia and for their dogged loyalty to collecting mine. For my years in the theatre I must thank my colleague and friend John Sumner for his trust and encouragement; my friend and artistic partner, the late Kristian Fredrikson, for his inspiring creativity; and my friend, the late playwright Nick Enright, who encouraged me to write these memoirs in the first place and pushed me towards their completion.

The great teacher, Jacques Lecoq, disciplined my body and prepared my mind for the future; and two great artists, Margaret Scott and Peggy Van Praagh, opened to me the world of creative dance and movement. Moffatt Oxenbould drew me into the grandeur of opera and George Miller introduced me to the world of film, becoming my mentor and teaching me to love the art and its people.

My close friends Lyndel Rowe, Helmut Bakaitis and Alex Broun kept encouraging my reluctant computer tapping until my friend of forty years Katharine Brisbane, who had begun in my life as a valued critic of my work, took on the task of editing these memoirs.

Finally I would like to thank Siddha Yoga and Swami Muktananda who allowed me to come to see that all work should be created and accomplished for a greater good.

George Ogilvie in the 1980s. (Photo: Branco Gaica)

THE GREEN-ROOM

I guided the old VW through the busy, late afternoon traffic, almost hitting a taxi as I lurched out of a Piscean daydream. It was a summer evening in January 1982 and I was driving down Macquarie Street to the Sydney Opera House. I showed my pass to the security guard at the gate and drove forward, seeking a parking space some hundred yards from the stage door. As I left the car the afternoon sun was playing on the great sails of the building. A momentary wave of nausea swamped me, that sick sensation that always accompanies me on an opening night. My production of Donizetti's opera, *Lucrezia Borgia*, starring Joan Sutherland, was about to open.

This production had originally been staged at the Opera Theatre two years ago. Tonight was its return, set now in the huge Concert Hall and conducted for the first time by Richard Bonynge. I was fifty years old, an actor since the age of twenty-one and a director for the last twenty years; and yet every opening night continued to leave me shivering with apprehension.

There was, however, a further reason for my state of mind tonight. Just as Donizetti's overture filled the Concert Hall, the music of Delibes would begin enchanting the audience of the Opera Theatre as my production of his ballet *Coppelia* took to the stage. And below, in the Drama Theatre, Kaufman and Hart's comedy *You Can't Take It With You* would begin one of its last performances. This great floating dream of a building containing, at this time, three live theatres, would, for a few nights, belong to me.

The security men behind the long counter at the stage door entrance nodded as I hurried past them up the stone staircase to the double doors which opened into the green-room. In this vast waiting room of dreams, artists from every persuasion lingered, chatting over coffee and sandwiches to hide their nerves or their boredom, or sat silently, reflecting on their performance. Young dancers, sprawling over lounge chairs, waved to me, while groups of musicians hurried by, clutching their instruments. A few opera chorus members smiled as they strolled by on their way down the corridors to their dressing rooms. The contralto Olga Sanderson-Smith made a quick detour to give me a hug and a good-luck kiss. The green-room was beginning to come alive as preparations began for the evening performances. I bought a cup of coffee and, nodding to some of the technical staff eating their evening meal, wound through tables to a favourite seat at the far end, close to the window overlooking the harbour.

This building had, over the ten years since its opening, drawn sharply divided opinions. Its external beauty was unchallenged, and the vision it offered of an enormous mythological creature floating free on the harbour. From the artists who worked within it, however, complaints came in their torrents. The main rehearsal room had too low a ceiling for an opera singer's voice; the opera theatre had inadequate wing space; the journey from the dressing rooms to the various stages was complicated and time-consuming; the orchestra had to be squeezed into a tiny space and the task of mounting a theatre production in the Concert Hall was exhausting and limited. The list went on.

Closing my eyes for a long moment I breathed my heart into a quiet rhythm. I was conscious of being at the centre of everything I had ever dreamed of achieving in this life. The dream of a ten-year-old boy had come true.

To understand why opera, ballet and drama had become a natural part of my life, I need to go back to days of childhood, days tempered by World War II. I was born in Goulburn in 1931, moved to Canberra in 1935 and, though living in a country that was dry of opportunity for the young artist, I grew up in a household full of songs, dances and stories. My parents, torn years before from their home in the north of Scotland, continued in exile to celebrate their traditions. Music, dancing and poetry became as intrinsic to my life as the sports field.

The lack of professional performance meant community celebration at home, church and school. I was given an education never to be forgotten. To dance a reel, read a score, sing in church and play drama at school prepared me to pursue a dream and turn it into a reality. Canberra's amateur theatre gave me acting opportunities and instilled in me dreams of Europe and a lifetime love for the classical canon. Ric Throssell, a gentle playwright, actor and director, who was also a diplomat in the Department of External Affairs, became my first mentor.

There were others whom I remember with gratitude. When neither encouragement nor opportunity exists in a country to further the ambitions of the young actor, he must adventure alone. In 1952 I headed for London, the Mecca of theatre, to join a company of touring actors, the last of the old melodramatists, and experienced an apprenticeship unachievable today. Chased back to Australia by the British Army, the apprentice became an actor in the first Australian Elizabethan Theatre Trust Drama Company and a member of the early Union Theatre Repertory Company. Remarkable directors such as Wal Cherry and John Sumner took me in hand and an old Russian refugee, a student of Stanislavski, taught me to love Chekhov.

These mentors thrust me from the role of actor into that of director and together John Sumner and I would transform the old Union Repertory into the Melbourne Theatre Company and build what is remembered by a few as the Golden Years—but not before three intense and transforming years were spent in Paris under the tutelage of that great man of the theatre, Jacques Lecoq. Those years of learning and starvation between 1960 and 1964 laid the foundation of all the direction and teaching I would undertake in the years that followed.

After returning to Australia and the Melbourne Theatre Company and the fulfilling years of the late 1960s, my career as director took another turn. Instead of accepting the invitation of my friend and colleague Leo McKern to return with him to England, the prospect of my own company in a new theatre to be built on the Torrens, sent me on an adventure to Adelaide for four years. From there, an independent life led back to music with the Australian Opera, to direct an ever-growing array of Australian singers under the baton of such conductors as Carlo Felice Cillario, Stuart Challender and Richard Bonynge. Dance caught up with me as Dame Margaret Scott, the brilliant dancer who founded the Australian Ballet School, gave me the chance to work with students like Graeme Murphy; and Peggy Van Praagh swept me into the mainstream and towards this momentous day in my life.

But at the moment these thoughts surfaced, I recalled the judgement of the critics; of 'smug, self-congratulatory smiles' at the curtain calls for *Lucrezia Borgia*; of the 'old fashioned concept of *Coppelia*'; and of the witty young journalist who, after the opening night of *You Can't Take It With You*, wondered if he had seen a rehearsal. And, worst of all, a letter from a man wanting to know, 'if I was so good, why was not I directing in the international arena?' Such barbs go with the territory of anyone who dares to work in the public eye, and the uncertainties they arouse can never quite dispel the good reports and accolades.

How sobering it is that we remember the negative so vividly. I thought of my mother, shaking her head and murmuring in her broad Scots accent, 'It's a sair fecht.' But as the glory and horror collided in my head, the better part of me retained a calm detachment. For this relief I had to thank Siddha Yoga and its teachings.

Meditation had taught me balance, perspective and made me aware that we weave illusions, pushing the 'now' out of focus, leaving us floating in fantasy. Last night had been an important occasion at the ashram to which I belonged. Afterwards, the visiting Swami had gently asked if I might consider becoming a swami myself. Another direction? This was no idle suggestion and I needed time to consider it. The thought of letting go of my present life had been with me for a long time, and particularly quite recently during a visit to Taizé in Burgundy. Now I was given a nudge towards the same mystery by wearing the orange of a Siddha Yoga swami. I already knew that the way of the Christian monk and the Hindu swami were, after all, different tributaries of the same great river.

My thoughts were interrupted by a voice announcing the five-minute calls that brought the artists to the stage and I hurried down corridors to let everyone know I was in for the evening. I was again reminded of the profound differences between the backstage worlds of opera, ballet and drama. With the opera all was easy and full of jokes. No singer can afford to be nervous before a performance, the voice demanded a warm and relaxed body to be at its best. The chorus dressing rooms were full of laughter and welcoming banter. Our easy-going open nature develops great voices. Down the way, principals could be heard testing out the vocal chords for the night. A knock on No. 1 dressing room brought a beaming smile from Joan Sutherland, and in a typical gesture her hand shot out to grasp mine as dressers busied around her headdress.

As I hurried across the green-room to the Opera Theatre stage, actors shouted 'hello' and sped away in the opposite direction. From the wings I watched members of the Australian Ballet warming up behind the curtain. Theirs is a silent world until the music strikes up. The only sound was the murmur of the audience taking their seats. Kelvin Coe, already costumed and made up for the role of Franz, waved to me momentarily, returning to the focus of his body and the concentration of pirouettes. Peggy Van Praagh had given me the chance to re-choreograph *Coppelia*. Plans were already in place to take the production to London and a Royal Command Performance.

They are shyer than the singers, these ballet dancers. Their obsession with their bodies is understandable considering the very few years a dancer's body can bear the astonishing punishment it endures. I loved working with these artists. They have a childlike trust in those who guide them and their pliant bodies become willing instruments for a choreographer. Outsiders do not easily understand the dancer's world; the intense, necessary daily workouts make for a lonely life. As I stood watching young dancers gather on stage, adjusting their costumes, I was reminded that tonight was also special to my long-time friend and colleague, the late Kristian Fredrikson, who had designed all three productions and been a partner in creating them from day one. My friend Anna French had designed the clothes for *You Can't Take It With You*.

Another run across the green-room took me past a host of musicians scurrying to the orchestra pit with their instruments. Here was a world that would always remain a mystery to me. Occasional glimpses of their heads from the stage as I took a dress rehearsal; and listening to them play during an opera *sitzprobe*, when the singers and orchestra come together for the first time, provided me with my only contact. The rituals behind the splendour of their achievement would remain their secret.

I hurried down stone steps into the corridors of the Drama Theatre and a world I had known intimately for thirty years. The large cast for this humane American comedy of the 1930s was in its last week of performances but many actors were still pacing the corridors muttering their lines. Whereas the singer's voice and the dancer's body are the controlling and familiar instruments of their art, actors have to reinvent themselves every night. It becomes a unique preparation that can range from an hour of exercises and meditation to a few minutes of quiet in the wings. This search for the best preparation lasts all their life. Emerging from their dressing rooms Jane Harders and Jim Kemp gave me a hug on their way down to the stage and Carole Raye waved as she followed them. Greeting old-timers like Al Thomas and Margo Lee is always a pleasure. Actors who have been in the profession for many years develop an acute awareness of the fragility of life, combined with a sense of humour that keeps them laughing.

Over the previous two years the Opera House had become my familiar world and the myriad of corridors, lifts and theatres my intimates. About the same time *Borgia* had opened, the Sydney Theatre Company had offered me the chance to work in the Drama Theatre with a production of a great new play by Bob Herbert set in wartime Kings Cross, *No Names… No Pack Drill* starring Mel Gibson and Noni Hazlehurst. The feeling of awe while driving down to this great building for daily rehearsals would sometimes almost engulf me.

The evening passed from interval to interval in a daze of coffees, gossip and leaping thrills of body and voice, and ended in the wings of the Concert Hall as *Lucrezia Borgia* came to its tragic conclusion. The audience erupted as Lucrezia sank to the floor over the body of her dead son. I stood watching as the artists took bow after bow. Suddenly, without warning, Joan appeared beside me like a jewelled figure of myth and, taking me by the hand, swept me on stage. There was no time to protest as I took a bow with her. It was one of the most astonishing moments of my life.

As an actor I had experienced the pleasure of applause and the satisfaction of a warm response from an audience, but this was overwhelming. I was a stranger to most of the audience, but I was standing beside La Stupenda and they went crazy, pouring out their devotion for this great artist. I tried to smile, but the force of the reaction brought my stomach into my mouth and for a moment I felt real terror.

Such applause! Such adulation! It lifts the artist to the gods.

As there was no curtain in the Concert Hall, we left the stage rather formally. I was still caught up in the exhaltation of that applause; Joan gave me a grin and squeezed my hand. She then turned to Margareta Elkins, who had sung the mezzo role and received tumultuous applause herself. The pair at once began discussing domestic arrangements, details of meetings and guests. Suddenly, these two formidable artists were ordinary women again, hurrying off to attend to family matters, leaving behind them an audience still caught up in exhilaration. It was another reminder that great artists do not carry their god-like qualities outside the arena of performance. They see themselves simply as hard-working people among other hard-working people.

I was subdued as I drove home that night. So much seemed to have happened, yet there was still so much to decide upon. And how could I possibly have known that within weeks I would be shot into another career by a simple invitation to lunch?

Joan Sutherland, as Lucrezia Borgia, weeps over the body of her dead son.
(Photo: Branco Gaica)

One

THE DREAMER

Church Music

A gloved hand felt for mine and deposited a large boiled lolly. I grinned at her and filled my mouth; it would make the tedious sermon a little more bearable. My solo was over and I could relax and dream. Now, in my fancy, I flew with the echo of my ten-year-old voice piping out Mozart's *Jubilate* and circled the great ceiling, radiant in my angel robe and wings. I hovered in front of the huge metal plaque attached to the wall on which was inscribed a memorial to the many dead from the Great War. With a magic gesture the young soldiers came alive and we flew together, bonding in a dance that resembled the eightsome reel my parents so loved.

Church was a perfect place for dreaming. The choir, filled with ladies with nice hats and ample bosoms and bespectacled gentlemen with deep sonorous voices, made music every Sunday. Here at St Andrew's Presbyterian Church in Forrest I first heard Handel's *Messiah*. As the entire congregation rose suddenly to its feet at the first ringing chords of the Hallelujah Chorus, my mouth opened and tears ran down my cheeks. I was lifted to heaven.

At the Sunday school I attended every week before church, my twin brother Jim and I were beginning to learn that we Presbyterians could have a direct talk with God. I found this silly and was convinced I was only talking to myself; but from the moment I knew with certainty that music was God's voice, and that Mozart, Handel and Bach were his messengers, it was in music I came to confide. The serenity of their work calmed my terrors. Anger found a voice when I discovered

Beethoven. As I write this, many years later in my small apartment in Paris, Easter is approaching and I look forward as always, to hearing *Messiah*, sung every year in Notre Dame.

The voice of the minister caught my attention as he began to speak of the war that raged on the other side of the world. It was 1942 and many young men from this congregation were fighting in the North African desert. I glanced over the pews to a family I knew whose son had been killed some months ago. They had their heads bowed and seemed as still as statues. A side-glance at my mother took in her tears as she listened to the words. How could one find comfort in death? They were all mad, these adults.

My father was not fighting anywhere and I had felt a little ashamed. So many of my friends' fathers had enlisted. But when he told me that being a baker was part of essential services, the playground of Telopea Park Primary School was filled with my boasting. Bread was the staple of life and every weekend Jim and I would spend time with our father cleaning the pie shells in the bakehouse. I loved to watch his hands moulding and shaping the dough and began to wonder whether the making of a loaf of bread was as much a miracle as music.

Every time I sat on the piano stool at my music teacher's studio I would see on top of the piano a photograph of two hands. They were at rest, one gently folded on the other, as if the master baker had come to rest for a moment after moulding a large loaf of bread. I loved those hands. They had large, strongly veined, powerful fingers; they gave me the feeling that whatever they touched, they commanded. Twice a week I would indulge in a good look at the photograph, before my teacher, Burilda Millet, pulled my attention back to the keys, trying to mould my own small hands into playing scales and exercises before releasing them into a Mozart melody.

I never mentioned the photograph to Miss Millet. It must have been two years later, as I was preparing for an examination, that she put on a vinyl recording of a Beethoven sonata. I sat mesmerised by the exquisite playing, knowing I would never achieve such excellence. She glanced up at the photograph and murmured, 'Who would think?' I stared at her. My father's hands belonged to Artur Schnabel, one of the greatest pianists of our time.

The 'terrible twins' Jim and George.

Music has accompanied my life from the first moment I can remember. My mother's soft contralto surrounded us with songs from the auld country. Folk music, in the form of song, dance, playing piano or bagpipes, was a natural part of our lives. Alongside the folk traditions came my growing love of the classical world, fed by Burilda Millet with her passion for the keyboard. In my teen years she gave me the opportunity to accompany singers at concerts and share that unforgettable feeling of artists working together. Much later, it was with great pride that I would invite her to the operas I directed, sit with her and receive more valuable criticism than any music critic ever gave me. The great library of music she bequeathed to me, and which I have since passed on to her nieces, extends through the entire history of Western music. But it is Schnabel's hands that remain fixed in the memory of this time in my childhood.

My father's shop was very busy. Young women sold bread and pies every morning and flirted with soldiers on leave. The war seemed to make every moment of life important. Shoppers listened to radios blaring from everywhere with news from the Mother Country, now in mortal danger. The Battle of Britain was on everyone's lips and I leant forward at the minister's instruction to pray for the people of London upon whose heads German bombs were falling. London! That magic word! I wondered how many theatres had been hit in these terrible raids. In that one thought lay my childhood obsession, the dream of one day making the pilgrimage to that great city and joining the fraternity of English actors.

What is it that triggers, in the heart of a small child, a fascination for something that would become a life's journey? From the moment I first became aware of other people I needed to amuse, entertain, dress up in others' clothes and find words to weave fantasies and create drama. I have a vivid memory of an eight-year-old triumph, standing on the stage of a community hall dressed in a home-made military uniform, making dramatic gestures and singing my boy soprano's heart out. Later performances at eisteddfods and on school stages gained me the reputation of being a show-off. But how could this be, when dry-retching preceded every entrance onto that magic platform? And yet, at every curtain call, I would long for the next time.

But I kept these ambitions to myself, for fear of being 'different'. I knew I was meant to spend my life doing this acting; my heart told me. Being different would haunt me through my youth. A genial uncle, complimenting my brother on his football prowess, had added in his broad Highland voice, 'Young George is a wee bit of a Jessie.'

The service ended and, as everyone began to move out, the dreamer awoke and dashed away on his bike to reach the swimming pool before lunch. There were competitions coming up and he was determined to be a finalist. Also on his timetable was the school musical, produced by his adored Miss Garden. To cap it all he had written a play about the Lyrebird that the class would present as part of Gould Bird Lovers' Week. Life was wonderful for this ten-year-old Jessie.

In 1930 my parents had emigrated from the north of Scotand to Goulburn where, on 5 March 1931, my brother Jim and I were born. We lived in rooms above the bakehouse and our day began at daybreak to the sounds of ovens being lit and dough being slapped and chopped. Later the smell of new bread would float up to the breakfast table.

Portrait of the author's father, Stewart Ogilvie.

Childhood, for me and my brother, encompassed two worlds. While my anxious parents spent their days in the bakehouse and shop, keeping a growing family alive through the Great Depression, we responded to the call of a nation of sportsmen, spending our energy in the sun, on playing fields and in swimming pools, and wasting impatient hours in the classroom. In the evenings we were drawn by romantic stories and ballads to that other world across the sea my mother called 'home'. Once a week our living-room would fill with other such refugees, recalling in lilting Highland accents life as it used to be. We would snuggle into bed to the sounds of songs from the auld country, dreaming of roaming through the heather and wielding the claymore at Culloden.

Stewart Duthie Ogilvie and Agnes (Cissie) Davidson Murray were born at the turn of the century, in Elgin, a small town in the northeast of Scotland, in that wild and heather-covered land between the Grampians and the sea. Their parents were traders in boots and bread, their parents before them having drifted into the towns from farms and fishing villages along the north coast after too many sons had been lost in the wild North Sea. The Protestant work ethic was the foundation of life among these hardy families. Work solved most things; it brought in money to keep alive spare but healthy bodies; it kept minds and souls busy and empty of idle thoughts; and the week climaxed every Sunday morning with a visit to the kirk, to thank God for it all.

Furnishing the world and their subsequent families with useful careers was required of all young men, and my father joined the honourable band of apprentice bakers. In time he became a journeyman and, as a last rite of passage, received his certificate as Master Pastry Cook and Baker. With his apprentice years over, he was ready to carve out his life, independent and useful to the community he loved. My mother's education was different. Emily Pankhurst had fought so that women like my mother could have opportunity. Cissie's parents sent their only daughter to university where she earned a Bachelor's degree in science from Aberdeen and a Master's from Edinburgh.

But during their growing-up years the world around them went crazy. Every family they knew sent their young men to fight the good fight against the hated *Boches*. The First World War shattered the lives of thousands of families, as old men in Berlin and Whitehall plotted the deaths of sons and grandsons. A decade later, the Depression took hold. The workers of my father's generation went on strike to seek justice in their penury, trying to maintain some dignity, some respect for the work they saw as the very foundation of life. But their demands fell on deaf ears.

My parents, having met, fallen in love and wanting to marry, were bewildered by the times. Everything they had been brought up to believe in no longer sustained them. Years later, they would talk of the fateful decision they made one late summer's day on their beloved Bow Brig. They joined the cavalcade of emigrants from their old green world and headed towards a new and uncertain one, not just across the water to Canada, as so many did, but to the far south, to Australia. Here, they prayed, they might carve out a future for the family they dreamed of having.

The new world of Australia welcomed them with unaccustomed sunshine and very little else. Like a dreadful epidemic, the Depression had spread everywhere. My parents settled into the New South Wales town of Goulburn, where they set up a shop and bakehouse. Jim and I, with the addition of a sister, Nancy, would spend the first four years of an active childhood here. In due course there would be seven of us, including another set of twin boys.

As children we were blissfully unaware of the poverty and suffering around us. Years later our father would regale us with tales of these anguished days. The sight of bread in the window of the shop was a magnet to the men, women and children who tramped the country roads seeking work. Dressed in their suits, marks of respectability to let the world know they were worth better things, these men would stand shame-faced with begging hands.

The sight of hungry young eyes staring at an iced cup-cake would be too much for my mother who would thrust the prize into dirty hands and watch them run off. At the end of the day, my father would fill the van with the unsold bread and drive down to the makeshift camps by the river. The comradeship of poverty was never more real than the sight he had, one day, of a circle of small children watching patiently as the eldest carefully peeled an orange and handed out a segment to each child.

Life for those 'terrible twins down the road', however, was full of adventure. Hand-in-hand, an identical pair with large sunhats on, we would run off, at age three, to the local cinema at the end of town. There we would sit on the steps, smiling sweetly at passers-by who would reward us with jelly beans and liquorice. Eventually, a familiar, good-natured policeman would gather us up and return us to our fretful mother. My brother swears I was the ringleader on these jaunts—an apprentice actor.

Our store was above the back door of a greengrocer, who, at the sight of us, would let off a stream of Italian in the vain hope of scaring us.

Two wriggling eels were too much for his vigilance, however, and booty was regularly consumed in the back shed accompanied by giggling plans for the next adventure. Our reputation climaxed with the incident of the bag of flour. On this fateful day, we managed to drag a bag of flour to an open trapdoor and called for the unfortunate greengrocer. The little man ran out at the sound of the dreaded voices and, looking up, received an avalanche of flour over his face and body. This proved too much for my parents. Immediate plans were set in motion to banish us out of harm's way, to the farm of my father's sister, Caroline, who, with her husband and growing family, had migrated to a dairy farm outside Canberra. On the day we were to leave, however, I discovered a huge lime pit next door and put my balance to the test by walking around the galvanised-iron perimeter.

This is the first, detailed childhood memory I have, and I can still conjure up the excitement I felt as I stepped carefully around the edge, slipped and fell in. Jim's raucous yelling brought my father from his bakehouse to fetch me out by the pants. Thankfully the pit had not been touched for some days so that the corrosive lime lay at the bottom of two feet of filthy water. My weeping mother cleaned me up and deposited us in the old car in which a family friend was to drive us to Canberra. My reputation as 'the brat who would eventually kill his mother' was now established and I left Goulburn feeling the thrill of having nearly died but being very much alive.

Throughout my childhood I hated Shirley Temple. This little saint's films proved that I was a totally corrupt child. By degrees, however, I began to suspect that the filmmakers were pulling my leg—or, at least, I came to believe this to assuage my guilt when I was at last able to see how difficult those years were for my parents. Bankruptcy forced them to close the bakery, pile everything into the van and leave their new home and friends. A chance for them came in Canberra and, with little Nancy, they followed their errant sons towards the new capital. In later years, when a certain comfort made life a little easier, the memory of this time would continue to haunt them like a scar. 'Never owe a penny to anyone,' was a phrase intoned throughout my youth. It has lived with me ever since.

While his sons continued their unthinking, happy, childhood games

George and his mother leave Australia 'forever' on the *Otranto*.

on field and in pool, Stewart Ogilvie built his new bakehouse with his own hands, fired up his old ovens and resolved that his family would not suffer as he had suffered during those terrible years of poverty and stress. We will never know his pain and humiliation. This stoic Scot kept such things to himself, wearing his quizzical smile under his trilby like a badge of identity, one of dignity and courage.

On an autumn evening in 1952 the SS *Otranto*, decked out in multi-coloured streamers, sat patiently waiting for whistles and horns to bellow farewell, for sailors to release her from the wharf and allow her, finally, to drift into the harbour. On the top deck, a group of frenzied children ran along the rail, hurling streamers down to the crowded wharf below, while adults stood quietly, leaning over the rail, holding clusters of them, tightly, as if they were lifelines, watching them snake down towards the waving crowd, to lose themselves in intertwining patterns. The shouted messages and antic holiday fun for the benefit of their loved ones below were long finished; the only communication left was mute gazing and a wish for it to be over. Occasionally, a shout of triumph erupted as some enterprising man separated his streamer from the rest and discovered it was still connected to his loved one on board.

Suddenly, a warning note boomed from one of the huge funnels and a quiet voice beside me said: 'It's time.'

I came out of my reverie and turned to my mother. We looked at each other and smiled a little, suddenly apprehensive. Turning away, we searched for the man below. The noise of gangways being pulled away from the ship made the search more urgent.

'There he is,' she said, pointing with a gloved hand still clutching her streamers.

I tried to follow her direction through the maze of coloured paper but could not find him. Tears welled up and my heart began beating fast as I called out over the shouts of others, 'Where? Where? I can't find him.' But my voice seemed weak and girlish. People were jostling for position on the rail to watch the final severance from Australia and wave a last goodbye.

The 20,000-ton P&O liner pulled away from the wharf, as the water between them began to boil and the ritual entered its last phase. Thousands of streamers grew taut and snapped, filling the air with fine strands of colour. I caught a glimpse of my father, staring up at us, his eternal trilby still firmly in place. My mother gulped noisily, holding back the tears she never showed in public. I drew a little nearer, the closest act of affection we allowed ourselves.

We were on our way, moving out of Sydney Harbour to make the six weeks' voyage to the other side of the world; to the moon; to the fabled places in the heart. My mother would see her mother and brothers for the first time in twenty years. And I? I would discover my roots. I would see for the first time the small town my parents called 'home' and which we children had come to know so intimately through tales told throughout our childhood. I would understand at last what it was to be a Scot, descended from men of the Clan Ogilvie who fought in the third line at Culloden.

I felt suddenly afraid and guilty. It was my entire fault, this trip; and it had very little to do with roots and the fabled Highlands of Scotland. How could I do this thing, knowing that my father could ill afford to finance my mother on this long journey? One answer lay in knowing my father's generous heart, his finding in my rebellion a wonderful opportunity for Cissie to see her people once again and bring them at least one of her children. The second answer lay in my need, since childhood, to become an actor.

I was thirteen when the Canberra Repertory Society gave me the chance that sealed my destiny. With these fine actors, many from the Department of External Affairs who filled my head with stories of European theatre, I had begun learning small roles in Shakespeare. Then in 1945 came *Tomorrow the World* by James Gow and Arnaud d'Usseau. This play gave me the major role, a member of the Hitler Youth who is then taken to America to live with a Jewish family. His re-education is the main story and under the direction of Ric Throssell, I lived and breathed for a few months the life of an actor. Following the opening night I made a promise to myself I would one day become a professional.

I needed to become an actor so badly that I had put down my pen in the middle of a final taxation exam and walked from the room, knowing that by so doing I had rejected forever the life of a chartered accountant. I needed to become an actor so badly that during my school years I would lie, cheat, flirt with anyone in order to be part of any performance. My only reality became those moments on stage, performing in front of an audience, becoming someone else. In those placidly conventional days of the Menzies Government any extra curricula activity, apart from sport, proved once and for all that the boy was not a man but a 'poof'. I preferred the title of Jessie. I wore it proudly in order to stand on the stage and sink into a character of myth, whether it was the Herald in *Othello*, Emil in *Tomorrow the World* or George in Thornton Wilder's *Our Town*.

Bells began to sound across the deck as lunch was announced. I was reluctant to leave the sight of Australia disappearing on the horizon. I wanted to stay and see this country disappear from view and from my life, this country that dismissed my ambitions as childish nonsense. But my stomach won over and we descended into the bowels of the ship to eat our first meal on board, served by British stewards whose exotic language and accents kept me reminded of my secret project. Over the following six weeks, by diligent study of their voices and manners, I would leave behind forever the casual and flat vowels of my youth and become an Englishman.

I clung to the rail as the spray darted at me, stinging my face. As I stood back to avoid the next fountain of water, the *Otranto* rolled and dipped into the huge sea. I lost my footing and fell back against the wall of cabins. I sat on the damp deck and looked up at the angry and threatening sky. A storm at sea! All my imagination was at work, as Captain Hornblower called all hands on deck. But this deck was deserted, as was the dining room. Almost all the passengers, including my poor mother, had remained in bed, too seasick to care about anything Captain Hornblower might do. It came to me that even the hero of my youth was seasick when he first put out to sea. I, on the other hand, revelled in the heaving, bucketing dance as the liner swung away from Australia and headed into the Indian Ocean.

With a surge of exaltation, I got to my feet and ran the full length of the deck, my overcoat flapping wide open, yelling an open-mouthed cry of triumph. For a moment I joined the dance. I was Ariel, obeying my master, Prospero, at the beginning of Shakespeare's *Tempest*, plunging the ship into a storm of my own making, all the while laughing at the terrified human beings below. At full tilt I rounded the corner—and crashed into a young officer. We both fell to the deck, entangled. I had a momentary glimpse of the young English face. Hornblower was still a lieutenant.

Embarrassed and excited, I scrambled to my feet, stammering apologies, and waited for the heroic scene that would take place on a stormy morning at sea. But the young officer, almost winded by my charge, could only gasp, 'Christ, I thought there was a fire. Sorry.' He grinned weakly and wandered off, clutching at the rail for support as the ship once more took a dive into the deep. I was left feeling very foolish, made suddenly aware that reality always seems to disappoint. The romantic world of my mind and heart belonged up there with Handel, Tchaikovsky, Great Acting, C.S. Forester, Schumann's *Dichterliebe* and my sacred, small collection of French cabaret singers on 78 rpm, wrapped carefully in my suitcase below.

The other side of the deck was more protected and a few brave souls sat huddled in deck chairs. I joined them, watching the drama of the sea as it rose to engulf us and as quickly disappeared below the rail. My mind wandered back to those waiting years and the first real decision I'd made to steer myself towards my goal. It had taken seven years to fulfil a promise made at fourteen. Seven years of despair, hope and obedience to my parents.

I had tried. In 1948, at 16, I had passed my leaving certificate with fairly good marks and Dad took me to the big city to begin life with a large firm of chartered accountants. Such a job would give me a lifetime's security and my father was pleased at my acquiescence. Canberra airport was a long hut attached to the RAAF airfield, known to everyone during the war as 'The Drome'. Forty years later my mother would still say to me, 'Isn't it time you set out for the Drome?' It was my first flight on a Douglas aircraft and, I do believe, my father's as well. He was as excited as I was. Our whole large family was there to see me off, twin brother Jim, sister Nancy, two more twin brothers Robert and Stewart and two little sisters Jean and Caroline. I would be the first to leave home.

We spent a few wonderful nights in a city hotel and my father allowed me to choose our entertainment. My film enthusiasm took us to *Rebecca*—mixed with my enjoyment of the film was the pride of seeing an Australian actress, Judith Anderson, making a triumph in an American film. The child in me took us to Luna Park and my dream to *Oklahoma!*. Oh, that musical! I could hardly contain myself. At the end the tears coursed down my face as we applauded madly. My father put his arm around me to comfort me, but knew he was helpless.

Finally, I was lodged in Mascot with an old Scots couple and in my new suit attended my first day at Allard and Harvie Ltd of O'Connell Street, a bastion of Australian commerce. It was the end of childhood. My father left Sydney with a strong shake of his baker's hands and I was alone.

My new job threatened to send me into chronic depression, but I refused to allow it. I became a junior to Reg and George, both warm and open as Australians can be. George came from money and the North Shore, while Reg was from the western suburbs, but they shared a lust for accountancy quite beyond me. Many of the staff were returned from the battlefields and lunchtime was always an occasion for stories about the War. Some would not talk of the horrors they had encountered and such reticence was respected. I applied myself to accountancy school at night but the figures and equations only encouraged my mind to wander.

As the first year progressed news of my family filtered through. Jim was already approaching his journeyman's ticket and my father sent him to Melbourne to continue his studies at a specialist baking school. For one winter he was able to follow his own dream. He was a promising Australian Rules footballer and had been chosen to play with Carlton as a junior. I spent my leisure hours at the Glaciarium skating rink. My little landlady and her husband soon found they could not cope with a teenager bashing around the house and suggested a shift to younger friends in Marrickville. This move changed my life and brought me into a society that welcomed and supported me for the following three years. They made these waiting years not just bearable but set me on a search for meaning that has sustained me to the present day.

The little Petersham Presbyterian Church with its fellowship of mostly young people became the centre of my life. Certain times can only be seen for their importance from a great distance; these years have meant more to me than I can hope to explain. It was the late 1940s the aftermath of Hiroshima, and the cinema had revealed the horrors of the Nazi prison camps. How could the human race face these events and hope for salvation? Nothing seemed to make sense of the evil in the world. Evenings and weekends were spent asking questions and seeking answers, until a gradual awareness of the importance of faith took root. Doubt remains an important element in my thinking even today, but it coexists with the certainty that goodness lies buried deep in every heart.

Despite the fever of this time, I was nearing my final exams and my need was becoming unendurable. One day the German soprano Erna Berger came to Sydney, to the Town Hall. Her singing of Constanza's great Mozart aria, 'Martern aller Arten', still rings in my head fifty years later. I have never heard Mozart so celestial. One day I would direct the opera, *Die Entführung aus dem Serail* and Joan Carden would bring back this precious memory. But it was Erna Berger who showed me that the time had come to prove once and for all that if there was an artist in me I should act. The final decision came during a concert by the Sydney Symphony Orchestra. My passion for classical music had been fed by the regular concert series for young people conducted by Eugene Goossens, and since then I have always associated Sydney with music. It was during Beethoven's Ninth Symphony that I knew it was time to exorcise the chartered accountant and to clear the way for action.

A few weeks later, I joined other juniors from the firm to sit for our final taxation examination, the passing of which would open doors to certificates and security. I sat down in the examination room at the appointed time. I could see I had an even chance of passing. But after thirty minutes I put down my pen, stood quickly and left the room under the astonished gaze of the monitors, one of whom ran after me, protesting that I had broken the law. It was over. I felt sick and rather foolish. My mother was in Sydney at the time. We sat opposite each other in the kitchen, both as white as ghosts.

'What will you do, son?' she asked.

'I'm going to take a boat to England and become an actor.'

The drama of the situation was brought down to earth days later when my father, after looking at me intently and silently for a long time, asked, 'Do you have the funds for such a venture?'

Every penny I could save had gone into a fund, which had slowly risen to the necessary £57 sterling that would take me to the other side of the world. Reckoning I would need a few pounds a week until I broke through into theatre, I set a target of £100. It had taken four years.

When Dad discovered that I had indeed saved the necessary fare, he called me home to Canberra to spend the summer with the family and earn a little more before sailing away. We did not know then of his secret plan to send my mother with me, nor of my twin brother's plans to marry his sweetheart, Rita. The wedding would come as a gift to us all after one of the worst summers in Canberra's history.

That summer of 1952 brought horrifying bushfires, endangering our whole district. On one day we all became firefighters. I found myself separated from Jim, who was fighting a fire alongside my best friend from school, David Begley. When driving down a road through suffocating smoke, their van swerved from falling branches and ran into a gully. Both suffered severe burns. The next morning we gathered at the phone to receive the news. Jim was stable but David's burns had been too severe and he had died in the night. That I could lose someone I knew to be a friend for life was impossible to believe. I rang David's parents without knowing what to say and dissolved into sobbing grief.

For weeks I sat around wrestling with what seemed to be totally inexplicable. Why? For what reason? There is hardly a human being alive who has not had to face these questions on the death of someone close. I had to bring to bear all the faith I had found in Sydney to help me accept this sudden and useless death of my friend. Beside it my adventure abroad became a silly fantasy. I considered cancelling; the whole family felt a guilty relief that Jim quickly recovered from his ordeal.

The mood continued, until one day Terry Moore, from the Canberra Repertory Society, asked me to come and talk. She was going to do a production of Thornton Wilder's *Our Town*, and wanted me to play the role of George. Theatre seemed to be so trivial after the tragic reality of the previous weeks. But Terry was a wise woman. 'True,' she said, 'but this play is also about loss. I think you'll find that Wilder will help you to understand it. Give it a go.' So I did.

As the character of George makes his way to the cemetery and prostrates himself in front of his young wife's grave, the grief he feels is tempered by the love they had together and which he will carry with him for the rest of his life. Rather than a requiem on death, the play becomes a celebration of life. At this time I also saw the film, *All Quiet on the Western Front*. Moved by the death of the young boy, I began to see, as in *Our Town*, that drama could elevate events into poetry and by so doing, celebrate a human life. David Begley remains in my memory as if he were still alive. I hear his laughter often, in cafés and in theatre. Here was a friend with an acute and funny slant on living, with whom I could discuss any secret, any hope, any ambition. To whom could I talk now?

'The King is dead, long live the Queen.' It was 1952 and Jim and I had just turned 21. Whatever wonders the future might hold for the young Elizabeth, the year hovered in front of me like the bucketing sea. This would be the first year of my new life since my dreaming began, as it would be for my brother Jim, who, only two weeks previously, had walked down the aisle with his new bride, flanked by Nancy and myself.

The cockney porter chattered as he wielded the large trolley bearing our suitcases. We were here, at Tilbury dock and walking alongside the liner, heading for the train to London. I was beside myself with excitement, bouncing up and down accompanied by my mother's shushing. I tried out my new English role on the porter. The little man looked at me with some surprise.

'How long have you been away then, sir?' I could have kissed him.

'Oh, not long, you know,' I said cockily. 'A trip to see distant relatives.'

My poor mother stumbled in shock at this downright lie. I maintained the façade, safe in the knowledge that my English accent was well learnt. Despite my innocence about most things, I was fully aware that an Australian accent would get me nowhere in the British theatre.

We arrived at the train and in lordly manner I handed over an enormous tip to my new friend. When we were alone my mother turned to me with angry eyes.

'God almechty, George, what will become of you?'

'It's only another performance, Mum, that's all.'

'But it's a lie, son.'

I had no answer to that. Was the nature of the actor simply one of evading the truth, reinventing oneself constantly, like a child running away from the bogeyman? I shivered a little.

My mother shook her head. 'Where does it all come from?' She sighed and murmured, 'A Scots accent might have been closer to the truth.'

'But, sweetheart, I'm not very good at a Scots accent. Besides, I'm looking for work in London, not Scotland.'

'Not yet, you're not, so just behave yourself.' With that, her last word on most things, she settled down as passengers surged into the carriage.

I realised that patience would indeed be necessary. A change in trains would take us to the north of Scotland to meet our family. London would be left behind. What to do? There was no way I could let my mother travel alone to Elgin. Besides, I must discover my roots myself before I plunged into a new life. The next step would take care of itself.

The train ride to London swept aside the personal as gaping bombsites silenced all chatter in the carriage. The journey through the East End revealed the suffering endured during the war years. Poverty seemed to hang over the city like a cloud. I could not help wondering if the spirit of the Battle of Britain was still alive. At Victoria Station we took a taxi across London to Kings Cross Station. It was like a dream come true. Theatres swept by and London double-decker buses wheeled and turned in our path. Even my mother became excited as the ride took in so much of the city. It was all there, waiting for me.

Kings Cross was crowded with a hubbub of British accents. Although summer was beginning, most people were wearing overcoats, scarves, hats and gloves, as if they knew that sooner or later this bright day would betray them. Despite my mother's warnings, I lifted my voice into the ship's officer's arrogant tone and elbowed our way onto the train. Even my mother was impressed. It was time I stopped thinking about my future and thought of her.

This journey to the North would take her home after twenty-five years' absence; twenty-five years away from the Highlands. In that time she had given seven children to the world and packed away her university notebooks, never to be seen again except by her teenage sons, curious to know what this other woman was like. As we settled opposite each other at window seats, she found me staring at her.

'What is it?' she murmured.

I did not know what to say, so I smiled and shrugged my shoulders. She knew what I meant.

'I know,' she said, searching for a handkerchief. 'I can't believe it, either.' Her lip trembled and tears formed, filling her eyes as she turned away. I suddenly thought of my father. He should be here, this man who loved Robert Burns and all the stories of his country. I felt a traitor who had taken his rightful place. How could I thank him?

Cissie Murray graduates from Aberdeen University.

Elgin would be the next stop; my parents' birthplace and in an important way, mine also. From the age of five I had recalled this town as the place my mother called home, the place to return to one day. For me it was a place in which to discover what it was that had made me what I had become. Two hours ago, as we slid into Aberdeen Station, Mum's shoulders had shaken and the tears had flowed. For the first time since childhood I wrapped my arms around her as she re-imagined the familiar places of her youth. Now at Aberdeen crowds of students would be descending for the next university term and her beloved King's College. With memory so strong, Agnes Murray was back in 1921 as she leant out the window expecting to see a young girl alight with all the others, clutching a satchel and suitcase. After this powerful recollection, she began to talk of her student days in the granite city of the north; and her eyes lit up as I had never seen them. She took from her handbag a photo of herself as a promising student with bicycle and stylish clothes. She smiled at the sight of it—then suddenly we were back in 1952.

She was better prepared for the sight of her eldest brother, Jim, waiting expectantly on Elgin station. He beamed at us through the window as we gathered up suitcases and stumbled towards the door. It opened and they were hugging each other. The tears flowed as he murmured, 'Cissie, my dear, dear Cissie.'

Then he broke the embrace as if to pull himself together and laughed at me. 'And this is George. Well, well, eh?' His large calloused hand grabbed mine and shook it mightily. 'I have the car.'

It was time to be busy and he grabbed suitcases, leading the way down the platform and out to his splendid English Rover. Jimmie, I knew, had done well for himself. We drove through town and my mother gasped at the memory of so much.

'You'll not find much changed,' Jimmie laughed. His strong Highland accent rang in the air and already Mum was settling back into the same intonations.

I sat in the back and thought of my grandmother, Agnes Davidson Murray. She'd be over seventy now and yet all these years I had thought of her as that lovely girl posing for that special photograph in the dying days of Victoria's reign.

We arrived at the cottage and my mother climbed the stairs alone to meet her while Jim and I waited below. Quiet sobbing, then laughter could be heard and Jim stood with tears in his eyes and a grin on his face.

'She's missed her, you know. Oh, mercy, yes.'

When I finally met her, I discovered the years had been kind. Her wonderful sense of humour had kept her sweet face alive, even though her body had failed her. We took one look at each other and burst out laughing. Of all things past, growing up without my grandmother has been my chief regret.

Later that afternoon, my delightful uncle Bob, the youngest of the family, arrived home from his work at the printing office and took smiling charge of me. We walked out into the early evening light and for the next hour he showed me through their childhood and youth. His passion for Scotland and for this corner of the Highlands made him a storyteller. Everything I saw I seemed to recognise; buildings known in a dream now became a reality. My mother's academy where she had flowered as a child still lived and breathed with students. We walked up out of town and sat on a heather-covered hill to gaze back at the place of my origins. There was no doubt that part of me belonged here. The romantic streak that my entire family had inherited, and which I suspected to be a chief component in whatever talent I might have, came from this land. In later years when I discovered the German Romantic movement with Schubert, Schumann, Beethoven and the landscapes of Caspar David Friedrich, I felt drawn in the same way to their poetry, music and mythology. That day I relaxed and stopped aching for London.

The weeks went by and new discoveries were made every day. I went shopping with my mother and watched as she met old friends and began those singing Highland conversations that seemed to come from a foreign opera. I would see faces that seemed familiar, as if I had known them in another life and was returning to renew acquaintance. Bus trips with Bob took us along the coast to the places of early family, from my mother's favourite, Lossiemouth, to the fishing villages in the far corner, to the old kirkyard where so many of our clan were buried and which still stood bravely against the winds as they swept in from the North Sea. Years later I recalled those excursions when watching the film *Local Hero*, filmed in the village of Penan, where, just along from the little hotel, my grandfather was born. In the other direction the bus took us to Inverness and beyond, to those places where great-grandfathers had fought in the glens. It was magic. Public monuments brought the stories alive. We could not know then how the North Sea oil discovery would ruin the romance of this town, so filled with the past. The Western Isles seemed to be waiting and I longed to go.

During tea and scones at a little café in the High Street an incident brought back a night nine years before. When I was twelve and about to enter high school, we left the two rooms behind the shop and took possession of a huge house with an orchard and garden. Its large living room allowed the weekly Scots get-together to grow until it held up to forty grown-ups. But we were still at war and nights of nostalgia became gatherings of refugees anxious for news of their friends and families enduring raids and death across the sea. Songs once joyful now brought tears and heartache. On this particular night I was woken up and asked to accompany a guest on the piano as she sang 'The Rowan Tree'. For one evening I joined in this never-to-be forgotten ritual. My mother, in her lovely contralto, sang 'The Herding Song', a lullaby she had sung to us as babies. I still recall the rapt look on my father's face as the song carried him back to the Isles.

One day my grandmother suggested that I should meet some of my father's people. A certain mystery surrounded my father's background and names other than Ogilvie often entered a quiet conversation. One of these was my middle name, Buchan. It would be the Buchan family I was now to meet in a neat cottage on the edge of town. A beautiful woman answered the door. She was dressed severely in black and her hair was swept back into a tight bun.

'You'll be George,' she said, and put out her hand.

She ushered me down a long hall to a room dominated by a round table, around which were nine adults who smiled and murmured, 'Good morning.' The welcome was slightly blunted by the fact that they were all dressed in black. In the centre of the table was a huge Bible. Was I to be a sacrifice in some family ritual? I took my seat and morning tea was immediately served, in a calm silence. Before the tea was poured one of the men suggested I might say grace, which I did, elaborating a little to include a happy meeting of long-lost relatives. From the Amens resounding around the table, I began to suspect that my family had a black sheep in the fold. Considering the lack of information we had received during childhood, it could be my father himself.

I was about to take my first sip of tea when the man opposite, whom I took to be a cousin once or twice removed, opened the conversation in his soft Highland lilt,

'And how is the state of Evangelism in Australia, George?'

The next hour passed in a sort of nightmare of improvisation. I tried to explain my liberal education and the fellowship of the young people in Sydney, but their responses were uncompromising. The moment one of them mentioned Calvin, I leapt at the cue and began asking when it was that our family had been converted.

'Converted from what, George?' someone asked.

'Why, from Catholicism,' I said. 'Our entire family was Catholic at the time of Culloden.'

'That was a time of ignorance,' came the sharp reply, 'and it doesn't do to dwell on such things.'

These people were fixed in their way of life, determined not to fail their God by falling for the temptations life offered. I wanted none of it. Such fierce, unquestioning adherence to such strict dogma causes great suffering; and its centre harbours a violence that can become a force for destruction. I left, thanking God for parents who had allowed the word 'doubt' to be part of family discussion.

When I arrived back, my grandmother burst out laughing at the sight of my face and, embracing me, promised never to put me through that again. 'They lack a sense of humour,' she said.

At that moment, my mother appeared from her bedroom with a telegram in her hand. My father was on board ship on his way to join us. 'He couldna bear it,' she laughed. 'He's on his way.'

This meant that I could take the train to London, meet him, put him on a train to Elgin and begin my career. Perfect!

Agnes Davidson Murray, George's loved maternal grandmother.

Mary Martin turned around and smiled straight at me. I was sitting in the dark and she was standing in a blaze of light, but I knew she was smiling at me. She stepped into a wooden shower cubicle, so that only her head and feet were visible, turned on the water and began to sing 'I'm Gonna Wash That Man Right Out of My Hair'.

The young colonial boy watched, hypnotised, from the packed upper gallery of the Theatre Royal, Drury Lane as Mary Martin performed, reducing that huge stage to the magic aura surrounding her smile. She was at home and teaching me a lesson I would never forget. She did not 'make' this performance happen, rather she 'allowed' it to happen. All the rehearsals and study that had brought the role into being had been long discarded, buried deep inside. Now she stepped onto the stage like someone newborn, responding to the dialogue and songs as if they were heard and sung for the first time, making every performance a new experience for her and the audience. Considering the number of performances Mary Martin had given of this, her most famous role, her immediacy on stage was a lesson for any young actor.

On that night in Drury Lane I was overwhelmed with anxiety. How was I to go about my mission? I had met my father from the ship and the following day seen him off on the train to the North. As it steamed out of the station I had a long moment of real fear. For the first time I was without any human being to turn to. It was entirely up to me now, to prove that promise to myself. As I walked back to my digs through the dark London streets after the glory of *South Pacific* I tried to stem the rising panic. That night I dreamed of being given a huge role and forgetting all the lines.

Early the following morning, shaking off bad feelings, I set off across Primrose Hill heading for the city. This, I decided, would be a day of walking and discovery. I was very grateful to my mother's friend Edith, who was providing me with a bed for a little while. I stopped on the highest point and looked across London. It was a cold, clear day and down below the city waited. The dome of St Paul's shone in the early light. For me London was a modern Troy, an impossibly brave city, with heroic citizens who had withstood huge odds and, unlike the city of legend, won through. I felt privileged to be here so soon after the War. I hurried down the hill towards Westminster. I knew, without admitting it to myself, that I was heading for RADA, the famous Royal Academy of Dramatic Art. Friends in Canberra had told me about it and I had harboured the knowledge for years. Here might be the key to a career in England. The morning seemed brighter.

The living legend of London captured me as I rounded by Regent's Park and the exquisite buildings bordering it; along the Baker Street of Sherlock Holmes and round into the entrance of Marylebone Station. This required a stop and a cup of tea in its busy café. How many English films had I seen with young film stars alighting from taxis to take trains into the country?

I moved onto Wigmore Street. A very special pilgrimage this one. I wanted to stand in front of Wigmore Hall and hear the echoes of Myra Hess giving a Mozart concert as bombs fell over London. People hurried past as I hesitated in the entrance. Perhaps they had been part of her audience? I envied them their exhilaration and terror. I thought suddenly of my own growing up, safe and warm—and then of my twenty-one-year-old face that looked fourteen. How could I become an actor with this? I hurried away, promising myself that I would learn and suffer. Blocks of elaborately embellished eighteenth- and nineteenth-century buildings finally brought me to Gower Street. Fifty yards down and I was standing opposite the art-deco entrance to the school.

The double doors were severely shut, so there was nothing to do but wait. Any sensible person might have sought a café, but I was rooted to the spot, my mind filled with sudden questions. What would I say? What would they ask me? Would I have to do something to show them I was talented, and if so, what? Perhaps I should have a list of performances? I could answer none of this to my satisfaction and over the next hour my resolve grew weak. Suddenly the doors opened. Here it was, the next step. With a sudden lurch I crossed the street and walked through the doors into a reception area.

A woman sat behind a desk at the back. She saw me hesitate and called, 'Can I help you?'

I hurried over and gazed at her, not knowing what to say. She smiled and said, 'Yes?'

'I want to be an actor,' I said in a high, cracked voice.

She smiled again. 'Does that mean you would like to come to this school?'

I smiled in great relief. It was so simple. 'Yes, thank you,' and waited.

She took a brochure from beside her, corrected a phone number and handed it to me. 'You will find the audition dates and fees inside.' She said nothing more as I stood, hesitating.

'You will find all the information you need there. You do know you have to be at least eighteen to enter?'

'Oh, yes, that's all right, I'm way past that.'

She laughed a little as I moved away. Her voice stopped me at the door. 'You don't have a grant, do you? We have several, but I'm afraid you have to apply in Australia before coming to England.'

I stood there, paralysed, with one hand on the door; not only by news of grants of which I knew nothing, but even more, her recognition of my accent. I thanked her hurriedly and exited in great need of a toilet.

At last, sitting at a table in a Lyons Corner House with a cup of tea in my hands I could sort out the shame of the last hour. To think I might have arrived here with a grant to study. The brochure informed me that auditions were months ahead and the fees beyond anything I could afford. Farewell, Drama School. I sat looking out at the busy London scene feeling hopeless. Things did not just happen; they required planning, thought and careful preparation. I had done none of these. Perhaps, as I sat there over my cold tea, I grew up a little—which I take to be that state of realisation that, despite friends and family, one must take responsibility for all that might or might not happen.

I remembered the day I had made the promise to become an actor. Along with this memory coursing through my head other thoughts mingled. I thought of all those prayers we sent to God for help and succour in times of need. However, I also believed we had a duty to Him to use our gifts. To blame God for my own lack of planning was a ludicrous idea and my heart began to pound with new courage.

Walking! I suddenly decided. Walking! I would walk London, throw off all negative feelings and begin again. There must be a way.

Somehow there was a way to enter this world I knew to be mine. So I walked and walked, gradually discovering and falling in love with London. In 1952, despite the war, much of old London was still standing, beautiful and welcoming. Charing Cross Road appeared, a curving street of knowledge filled with old bookshops and the smell of leather binding. For hours I wandered from one to another, filling my lungs with the aroma of history. I put temptation aside and crossed over to a tiny newsagency for my first newspaper. A rack stood outside and among them, poking out behind the stacked periodicals was the word *Stage*. I extricated the paper, offered the few coins and retreated to the same Lyons Corner House.

Thus I was introduced to what became weekly Holy Orders. It was a newspaper devoted to theatre throughout the United Kingdom, and with astonishment I discovered a vast number of small professional companies, alive and popular. Page after page gave news of not only London theatre but also the hundreds of small repertory theatres playing weekly or fortnightly repertory throughout England, Scotland, Wales and Ireland. I was beside myself with joy. With admirable control I sat there and read from cover to cover, then read it again. I treated myself to a pie and sauce and began to plan my life. I would write a passionate letter to every one of these theatres and beg for a job within their sacred walls.

So the weeks went by, writing, walking, buying *The Stage* every Thursday, receiving rejection after rejection but continuing undeterred. London was becoming my home. I grew thin with my imposed thrift, but I knew that someone out there was waiting for me. The only photograph I had was from the production of *Our Town*, which had done so much for my spirit. I had copies made from the negative and flooded the UK with them.

Despite their obvious poverty and the still-rationed food, the British were proud of themselves and their War. And they worshipped their new Queen. The Festival of Britain had been an enormous success and proclaimed to the world that Sterling would lead the world again. For me, with my narrow vision of the theatre world, life too was exciting. The great company at Stratford-upon-Avon shone like a beacon with young actors and actresses emerging from war service, led by John

Gielgud, Laurence Olivier, Michael Redgrave, Peggy Ashcroft and the young Paul Scofield. The West End was busy with revues; *The Mousetrap*, by Agatha Christie, had just opened. From the gallery of the Haymarket Theatre I saw N.C. Hunter's *Waters of the Moon*, with Sybil Thorndike, Edith Evans, Wendy Hiller and Kathleen Harrison. To sit and watch these great women of the theatre play out the well-made play, that foundation of modern theatre, was a memorable event. English poet-dramatists like Christopher Fry and T.S. Eliot were giving theatre a last surge of romance before mutterings from within its walls exploded with the new working-class naturalism of John Osborne. And walking through London on Sundays usually brought me across the Thames to Southwark Cathedral where English history, music and devotion meet.

Occasionally, in the back pages of *The Stage*, some small company would advertise for someone specialised, but the Positions Vacant column was never more than an inch or two of newsprint. On this particular day, like any other Stage day, I was seated at my favourite table reading rejection mail again and writing a card to my parents, on tour somewhere in Scotland, to reassure them that something would happen soon. A small advertisement stared at me, seeking a young male assistant stage manager to play and do stage management duties with the Midland Touring Company. My reply was in the post within the hour, including my last photo.

Three days later a reply arrived. I opened it with my usual beating heart, and there it was, an offer to join the company immediately, with instructions to take train and bus to a town in Wales. I sat down abruptly on the bed and almost stopped breathing. After all these years was it really happening? I kept looking at the letter to reassure myself that it was. A door was opening and my new life would begin. I trembled all day as I walked to favourite spots to say goodbye. Little sleep that night, goodbye to my mother's friend the following morning, my one case packed, an exorbitant taxi to the station and a deliriously happy lad took a train out of London, heading west.

Two

THE APPRENTICE

I looked around at the people on the bus, wanting to shout out, 'I'm going to be an actor,' but I remained silent, hugging my suitcase to me. It was light brown and had a curved top to it. I thought it was very smart. The seat beside me was vacant but I held the suitcase tightly, my only security as my heart pounded from excitement to terror. What was I heading into? What will they expect? Who would meet me? The letter did not say. Again and again I pulled it out of my pocket and read it over and over. It contained nothing more informative than directions for travel and the fact that my wage would be three pounds per week.

Having exhausted thought on the letter crumpled in my pocket, my mind began to work on the one that had got me the job. How many lies had I told? How long would it take them to discover what a fraud I was? Experience? I had suggested this, but what experience? School plays and a few roles with the Repertory Society. Apart from that? I kept hearing my mother's shocked voice, 'God almechty, George, what will become of you?' A form of panic set in and perspiration covered my pale face as I tried to control the urge to get off at the next stop and vanish. Other people boarding the bus jolted me out of my nightmare. They all seemed tired and bored. I mentally shook myself; I had no right to feel negative. These passengers were only going home. I was on my way to glory. I laughed out loud. People turned in surprise, but I smiled back, not caring.

The train trip from London to Shrewsbury had been uneventful, but I had thrilled at the stationmaster's lilting cadence as he called the towns on route and the train connections. Now a bus was taking me

The author at twenty-one. His first publicity shot.

to a village in Wales, the name of which I could not pronounce. The journey would end within half an hour. My feverish mind retained nothing of the crossing from England into Wales. The beauty of this country would have to wait for a calmer day.

We seemed suddenly to be in a sizeable town and a number of passengers alighted. The door closed and the bus began to move off when a shout was heard. The bus braked, the door opened and two young people tumbled in, laughing and apologising to the driver. They were out of breath and beautiful. She was small, blonde, with a pretty, oval face and a smile that lit up the gloomy bus. He was well built, with dark hair and the haunted face of a young cavalier. I could not take my eyes off them as they wove their way down the aisle. They were actors. They had to be—they carried magic.

I sat, not daring to look, as they talked together in whispers. I took out the letter once more and busied myself with it. When next I stole a look I found the young man watching me. He grinned and I smiled nervously. I felt hot and uncomfortable. I stared out of the window as the bus came to a halt. Oh, God, this was it, the village in the letter. I had to get out here. I stood with my suitcase and stumbled into the aisle. At the same time the couple scrambled up and we all collided mid-corridor.

'Are you George?' the girl asked.

'Yes,' I said, and we all laughed as if it was very funny, and suitcase and bodies bundled themselves out into the street. Back on firm ground the girl turned to me.

'You're coming to us, aren't you? The Jimmie James Company?'

'Yes, yes,' I stammered. 'I have a letter.' Which they found hilarious. The bus moved off and we were standing in an empty village square.

'I'm Pat,' she said, putting out her hand, 'and this is Harry.'

'And I'm George,' I said. This proved too much for them and more laughter ensued.

'Come on, it's not far,' said Pat and all three of us began walking down the hill.

Was this it? The road to Glory? This grey Welsh village straight out of *How Green Was My Valley*? It seemed deserted on this late afternoon. My suitcase became heavier as we hurried on and I began to wish that I were back in Lyons Corner House.

'You've come up from London, then?'

'Yes, yes.'

'And Australia before that?'

'Yes, Australia, yes.' I felt Harry look at me sideways.

'You don't seem to have an accent?' Pat said.

'No, no, I don't.'

'Why not?' Harry asked.

I paused at the terrible question, then the truth. 'Because I got rid of it.'

'Why?' he asked.

I stopped, if only to give myself the chance to put my suitcase down. I looked at them for a moment. There was a genuine question in their faces and I had to deliver a truthful answer. 'How many roles would be available in your Company's repertoire for an Australian accent? Don't you find, Harry, your American accent a little restricting?'

'Yeah, I suppose I do. Probably why I'm going back.'

'Well, I'm not going back. I'm staying here.'

Pat listened to us, then asked, winningly: 'Do it for me... just a little.'

'I'm from Orstralia, where are yous from?' Gales of laughter greeted this. I laughed along with them and picked up the suitcase, wondering for what roles Pat's North Country accent qualified her. We continued down the hill a little more relaxed with each other.

'I hope you don't mind sharing with Harry,' said Pat. 'Digs aren't easy to find here.'

'No, not at all... By the look of things the audience might be difficult to find, as well.'

'Oh, Lord no, they're coming from miles away.'

Suddenly I was nervous again. How could they know that I knew nothing of what might be expected of me? My case was heavy and I hoped the journey would end soon. Pat became conscious of my state and put her arm through mine.

'Don't worry, you'll get used to things quickly. You only have a few lines tonight.'

A few lines! What did she mean? Surely I wasn't going on stage tonight. My mind was a riot. Should I say something? Or was this usual? I stumbled over the suitcase and nearly fell. I recovered and in a sick, tight voice, asked: 'What's the play tonight?'

'*Deep Are the Roots*,' said Pat, as if it was a play I would know. 'We're doing it for Harry as it's his last night.' She put her arm around him and they kissed, holding onto each other as we continued down this interminable hill.

My mind was in chaos. Not only was I to play in this presumably American play, but it would appear that I might be replacing this dark Adonis in the repertoire. What a laugh! I was already planning not to unpack and, as soon as I had made a complete fool of myself on this Welsh stage tonight, I would run, or rather stumble up this hill again and leave Wales forever.

'How's your American?' Pat's voice cut through the nightmare.

'American? Oh, not bad. I've just done *Our Town*.

'Oh, Harry's done that, haven't you, darling?'

He looked at me with some amusement. 'I played the Stage Manager. I suppose you played George. You look young enough for it.'

'A bit of makeup might help tonight,' said Pat. 'You're playing the Sheriff. It's only one scene. I'll bring the script over to your digs. You can look at it before coming over to the hall.'

Harry grinned. 'It might be better to call him Deputy.'

'If you come over early,' said Pat, 'you can meet Dad, and see what we've got for you to wear.' (So she was Pat James.) Then she added wickedly, 'And I suppose we'd better go over the scene.'

All this was making me feel very ill. What make-up creates a sheriff? Or a deputy, come to that? The few sticks I had in my bag merely pointed out my inadequacy in that department. Oh, God help me, what had I done? What deep and abiding shame awaited me? At this moment we turned the curve of the hill and an ugly squat building revealed itself in the middle of the square. It was a miserable looking hall, almost black with ingrained coal dust.

'There it is,' said Pat with delight in her voice, as if she was showing me Shangri La. 'We've only been here a few days but business is marvellous.'

I gazed upon this horror, this temple of my dreams. It would be here in this village hall that my debut as a professional actor in the role of Sheriff/Deputy would take place. A role learnt over tea and rehearsed as the audience was filing in. Nothing could have been further from my imagination. Perhaps it's true what they say about the fantasies of a Piscean-born human being: that nothing can come up to their fevered hopes and dreams. Self-pity brought tears to my eyes and for a long moment I felt real desolation.

What madness had brought me here? Why put myself through such agony and fright? Here I was, heading for public humiliation and disgrace with only myself to blame. If I had known these feelings would continue throughout my professional career would I have continued? Perhaps I would. Buck up and get on with it.

'What's the matter?' said Pat, with a little laugh. 'You look as if you'd just seen a ghost,'

'No… not a ghost,' I murmured, 'my future.'

Pat smiled and put her arm around me. 'Oh, I've got such a good feeling about you.'

Harry grinned and, picking up my suitcase, said, 'I'd take notice of that, if I were you. She's a bit of a gypsy.' I looked at her smiling, warm face, and felt better.

'Okay,' said Harry, 'come on. A cup of tea at the digs, then come down to the hall and arrest me.'

My apprenticeship was about to begin.

I opened the little exercise book and gazed at it in stupefaction.

'Can you read it?' asked Harry, from the other side of the table. 'Michael played it last time, but he's long gone back to Ireland.' The page was covered in scribbles. I could make out the word Sheriff, but very little else. 'Here, let's have a look.'

Harry took the book from me and looked down the page with his mouth full of scone. 'You enter here.' He indicated a place. 'It's only three speeches; you'll be fine. Eat up your tea. Supper's after the show; you'll be hungry.'

'But when is the scene?' I bleated. 'In the play, I mean. Is there a full text somewhere?'

'Oh, don't worry, the Old Man'll show you. It's about halfway through.'

I shut up and spent the next ten minutes trying to work out each word. Gradually it made sense and I longed to go somewhere and try out an idea forming in my head. I gobbled down tea and scone and leapt upstairs, locking myself in the toilet. I sat muttering words to myself, gradually taking courage to speak louder.

'That sounds good,' a voice called. 'We'd better get going; the Old Man can't stand being kept waiting.'

On the way to the hall Harry kept referring to a fat exercise book, muttering lines. I had already decided that my Deputy should be a whining Southern boy with a high voice and a vicious attitude. I would make sure the audience hated this nasty human being. Harry stopped suddenly and turned to me. 'Let's go over the scene, what do you say?'

'Fine, that would be great.' In the middle of this quiet Welsh street Harry opened the scene in full voice. I followed suit, giving vent to all the hatred this white man had for the black intelligence. Only then did I realise that, in this grim drama of American racism by the authors of *Tomorrow the World*, Arnaud d'Usseau and James Gow, Harry, a white Canadian, would be playing a black man. That was the way of things in those days.

Harry gave me a new look at the end of it. 'That was just great. You give me real motivation for my beliefs.' He laughed suddenly, looking beyond me. A man stood in his garden clutching a garden fork, as if wondering if he should run or defend himself. I was full of gratitude for the praise, feeling easier as we continued on our way.

'Don't you have a full script?' I asked.

'Oh my, no. The Old Man doesn't believe in them; too expensive. He says by writing out your role it helps you to learn it; which in fact is true. You're going to be a busy boy over the next few weeks.'

'How many performances do we do of *Deep Are The Roots*?' Harry stopped abruptly and looked at me. 'You know nothing about this company, do you? About how it works?'

I could only shake my head, knowing that something terrible was about to be disclosed. There was a low brick wall nearby; Harry took my arm and led me to it. 'The Old Man can wait ten minutes.' He grinned at me, lit a cigarette and began to talk. I can only say that I am forever grateful to this young Canadian for preparing me, over the following ten minutes, for the most extraordinary beginning of any acting career.

'At the hall, you will find an old actor, Jimmie James, his wife Bessie, with their two daughters Celia and Pat. These three women are among the best actresses I've ever worked with. There is a son, Albert, who only acts when necessary. He is their stage manager, driver and organiser. The leading man is John Farley, who is married to Celia James. He is also a very fine actor. There, you have it, the Company. Born to do what they do. Apart from Sundays they perform a play every night of their lives. Add a few people like us and they can play every modern play you can think of, up and down the country.' He paused for a moment, reflecting on his words. 'I have to move on, you know, but I'll sure miss them and the life.

'This is a fit-up company, probably the last of its kind. This means we do a different play every night. We pull down one set every night and put up a new one every morning. There must be approximately thirty plays in the repertoire and every now and then the Old Man adds a new one and discards others. We never stay in one place long enough to exhaust the repertoire, so that we travel constantly, sometimes staying only one week and returning months later with a batch of new ones.' He grinned at me again. 'So, as you can see, you're going to be busy—unless of course, like most of the actors from London, you run away after a few days. Think on it, it's up to you.' Without another word he stood up, threw his cigarette away and strode towards the hall. I hurried after him in a torrent of emotion.

We walked around to the back of the hall, passing an old truck with an open, empty back. A man was beating the dust out of a couple of rugs, hung between truck and door. He was slim and dark-haired, with a lined, hard face. He acknowledged Harry with a nod, but ignored me. Harry muttered, 'Albert, you'll meet him later,' and ushered me into the dark, back room of the hall.

A string of lights had been set up along one wall with a long bench holding a chaos of make-up tins, creams, towels and small mirrors. Arranged along the other wall were a number of huge theatrical skips, all open with various pieces of clothing hanging nearby. In the corner an immensely fat woman of about sixty sat at an ironing board pressing clothes, a cigarette dangling from her mouth. She wore a light overcoat and had a pretty straw hat perched on her head, as if she had just popped in for a moment to help out. She looked up and grinned at us. It was a smile that warmed the room just as her daughter Pat's had done. Her dark, gypsy eyes looked me over intently.

'This is George, is it? How are you, Harry? Ready for your last night?'

'I'm not sure, Bessie, I feel I'm going to be a bit lost.'

'So will we, my darlin'. Those trousers you have on will do for the Sheriff, George. I'll find you a shirt and badge.'

A loud and peremptory voice sounded from within the hall. 'Albert, where are those rugs?'

An equally harsh northern accent answered from outside. Albert entered, muttering to himself, with the rugs under his arm. Bessie spoke to him quietly as he passed.

'Don't take on, Albert. You know what he's like with Harry leaving.'

At that moment, a small whirlwind of a man swept in. He was an extraordinary sight in this dismal room. Wrapped up in a beautifully tailored camel overcoat, with a smart trilby, a warm scarf, a expertly-tied tie and an immaculate shirt, he glared at me through thick lenses set in huge frames that overwhelmed the little face of an old elf.

'Where's new feller?'

'Here, Mr James,' I said, moving forward with my hand outstretched. He was taken aback by my forthright manner but took my hand. 'How do, young feller. Come up on stage and I'll take you through it.'

I followed him up the stairs onto the stage and walked into a small gathering of people. Pat was there, grinning broadly at me. Harry had followed quickly behind and without any further ado Jimmie James showed me where to enter and exit for my scene, leaving the rest entirely up to me.

The evening passed in a sort of dream. I found a gentle guide in John, the leading man. He led me to a place for my make-up, understanding instantly my inadequacy and terror. He sat with me and asked if I saw the Sheriff in my mind. I told him my idea and in a few words he suggested what little make-up was necessary. He planted me in the wings and told me he would come by later. Alone, I watched the Company as they acted out this story of the American South with passion and relish.

Suddenly John was behind me, whispering: 'Your scene is next. Deep breath, walk on and take over.' Which is what I did—to everyone's satisfaction it seems. Certainly everyone in the hall must have heard my loud, poisonous high register.

Finally it was over. The packed audience clapped heartily and everyone was toasting Harry in the back room. Pat was awash with tears but Jimmie was not there. Harry was not to be forgiven for leaving. In the midst of the celebrations, an exercise book and a full script were thrust into my hands by a smiling John.

'Tomorrow night's a farce, *See How They Run*, and you, my young lad, will play the Reverend Humphries. You have the privilege of a *full* script because you must write down your role. It's some time since we've done it. If you're here about ten you can give Albert and me a hand with the set. We'll run through the entrances about 11 o'clock. And don't forget to bring the full script; it's the only one. Think you can manage that?'

The young apprentice had been given a great task. I excused myself and headed, running, for the digs, where, over a supper of potato soup, I began writing down my quite sizeable role in Philip King's popular play. Supper was long over and the landlady in bed before I put the pen down. My first script in my first exercise book! The Holy Grail was never more sacred. Harry was right. The task had already made me familiar with the play.

By 3 am I could do no more. Harry had returned and was now asleep, but I lay, still wakeful. Images of the evening swam in front of me. These actors were truly at home in their theatre. Would I achieve so much?

Harry and I shook hands and the gesture turned into a hug. 'Have a great time,' he said. 'I've a feeling you'll do fine.'

'Thank you,' I said and he was gone. I walked to the hall in the Welsh morning. Passing through streets of council houses made it all seem ordinary, as if I was off to work for the day.

A woman at her gate said, 'Lovely play, last night. What do you have for us tonight?' 'It's a comedy tonight,' I said, 'It's very funny.' 'Oh, that's good, bach, you need a laugh on a Saturday night, don't you?'

The Welsh lilt coloured the morning for me as I turned a corner and stopped. The hall lay ahead of me, no longer looking dingy and depressed; last night had transformed it into a place of drama filled with applause. I knew already what Pat's affectionate smile had meant. I hurried on, muttering lines to myself, and arrived at the hall ready for whatever the day might bring.

The dressing room was empty but noises were coming from the stage. I found Albert and John dismantling the set; and so began a job I came to love—helping to sweep away last night's world and build a new world for tonight. Albert was in his element; he smiled at me as he expertly took apart the canvas-covered frames. One flat was painted to resemble dark, panelled wood; John posed in front of it and turned towards me. 'Drama,' he said, and reversed the flat to reveal a bright wallpapered wall on the other side. 'Comedy. It's that simple.' And indeed, it was. Two sets, one for drama, the other for comedy, shifted around to create French windows, doors and casements, all roped together according to the plans Albert kept in his satchel. He dropped a pile of bright material in my arms. 'A bit of an iron, George.'

I raced to the back and began ironing curtains for windows and French doors. Other covers were a mystery to me until I returned to find they covered cane furniture, armchairs, chairs and sofa, everything light and easy to move and recreate. Within a short time the stage was transformed into the living room of the Reverend Toop. Albert presented me with a list of properties.

'These are for the set,' he instructed, 'and the others are personal. You'll find that some of the cast have them in their own kit. The stuff we don't have, try the shop down in village; they're very obliging.' This village was obviously a regular date for the Company. The applause last night was not only for the play, but a welcome to old friends.

A dark-haired woman came on stage with mugs of tea. 'I'm Celia, welcome to the Company, George.' She turned to her husband. 'What are we playing tonight?'

John shook his head in mock despair. '*See How They Run*, darling, and you're hopefully playing my wife.'

Celia laughed and pointed a finger at me. 'Oh, goody, that means you're playing your first scene with me. Oh, God, that means Dad will play his comic German.' She laughed again. 'He has the worst German accent you've ever heard—but he is funny.'

Gradually the rest of the family wandered in. Two more actors were introduced who completed the cast. I was soon to discover that the 'other' actors were a highly moveable feast.

From start to finish, the rehearsal took twenty minutes. Twenty minutes more typical of the Crazy Gang. Cast members kept reminding each other which entrance was which and when they happened; where people sprang from and when they had a special moment on stage. John took pains, during this mayhem, to show me my various comings and goings. Jimmie James himself was not to be seen this morning—busy arranging the next dates—so constant shouts substituted: 'This is where Dad enters' and, 'Oh. God, Albert, don't forget the gunshot tonight, you remember what happened last time.'

The moment the rehearsal was over, I dashed around the various members of the cast with my props list. Julie, the third actress, gave me a hand dressing the set for the performance. I raced down to the village shop to entreat some glasses, cups and saucers. A little girl handed me a bunch of flowers, 'for the stage, you know'. I was astonished by their kindness and willingness to help. Lunch was forgotten; in fact, lunch played no part in this next period of my life; I learnt to rely on a good breakfast to get me through the day. By mid-afternoon I had completed the props table and the stage dressing, mumbling my lines to myself as I went about my tasks. Celia arrived and took my measurements. 'For later,' she said.

Albert arrived to check the stage. He gave me a nod of approval. 'Nice work there, lad.'

I felt I had been given an award. I finally got back to the digs in time to wolf down bread, butter and scone before returning to make up for *See How They Run*. I gazed at my image in the mirror, pleased with the meek little clergyman who stood there. But my thoughts were interrupted by a voice from the doorway.

'John, where do I hide myself in the second act?' Jimmie, dressed for his role as an escaped German prisoner, demanded immediate attention. Patiently, John put his make-up stick down and followed his father-in-law onto the stage.

'You should have been at the rehearsal, Dad,' came Pat's angry voice from behind her screen. 'He'll probably end up having tea with the Toops.' Everyone laughed, eager to have a good time, as the audience poured into the hall. For me, this was to prove a momentous Saturday night.

John had also suggested I wear my glasses, to 'peer a little' in my role. No one had thought to question me as to the interpretation of the part, taking it for granted I would know what to do. John had merely patted me on the back, saying, 'Don't overdo it; just let his niceness and innocent nature shine through.' Only a few words, but all that was necessary to bring the Reverend Humphries to life. All was ready and Albert arrived backstage from the front of house with his takings and took over the 'corner', to pull curtains and make sure his father got all his entrances right. The curtain rose and the play began.

I had spent the previous five minutes dry-retching out the back, but now I was there, at my first entrance, waiting to knock on the door of my destiny. The moment came and I knocked so hard the French windows shook as if a storm was approaching. A gravel voice from the corner muttered, 'Not so hard!' For a moment I thought I would faint, but the door opened and the lovely and reassuring figure of Celia greeted me.

'Reverend Humphries, how lovely. Do come in.'

'Good morning, Mrs Toop. So nice.' I passed Celia and walked onto the stage to greet the Saturday night audience.

'I've dried!' Celia's voice whispered urgently in my ear.

Never before, or since, has my world come to a stop as it did at that moment. I knew every word of my role but not one of anyone else's, except for a short cue. I continued walking into the middle of the stage, spread my arms wide and circled on the spot emitting a long 'Ahhhhhhhhhhhhh'. Then I brought them together with a long 'Mmmmmmmmmm' and finished with, 'What a lovely day.'

The audience exploded with mirth. 'At last,' they thought, 'a comedian.' My terror pursued me as the blank look continued on Celia's face, so I curled my leg around another and in a voice of agony went on: 'I pricked me finger with a rose this morning ... Ooooooooooh, it did hurt.' More laughter from the audience and round-eyed astonishment from Celia. Nothing could have stopped me now in my pursuit of madness. Contorting my body again I continued. 'My wife insists on growing roses with thorns that prick so. Every morning when I pick some for her, my neighbour looks in and says, "Getting yourself pricked again, Reverend?"'

The bawdy Welsh audience found this too much and laughed themselves silly, which gave me a moment to recover and look around to Celia who herself was incapable of speech. I stood there without any idea of where it had all come from and slowly the kindly clergyman returned.

'I'm so sorry, Mrs Toop, you were saying? About the bazaar?' I had suddenly recalled the content of her first speech. 'Perhaps you'd like some pricked, I mean picked roses, for the stall.'

After another choking fit, Celia recovered enough to carry on with the script. As she did so, I became conscious of the entire cast standing in the wings clapping silently and laughing. I had passed the test. This had been an initiation, a testing of my ingenuity and nerves. I was soon to discover that improvised recovery on stage was essential to survival in the Midland Touring Company.

The play was nearing its finish and I had one scene to play. I was standing in the wings waiting and, as I stood there, it came to me that I was at home; that all the years had led to this night in a remote Welsh village.

John nudged me as I prepared to go on. 'Wait, watch.'

Jimmie, as the escaped soldier, was on stage trying to hide but encumbered by a huge rifle and getting caught up with legs and curtains. The audience roared their delight. This was what they referred to as a 'special moment', a tradition that went back to the Middle Ages. After a roar of applause, John pushed me on to complete the scene.

As we took our final bow to the delighted audience, Jimmie took me by the arm and pushed me forward to receive a solo bow, a gesture I have never forgotten. Later on in the dressing room, he glared at me.

'Well, young feller, I'll write to London tonight and get you a wardrobe. Feel like staying with us?' I could only nod.

That night, as I climbed into bed, I burst into tears and lay weeping; a young vow had at last been kept.

For the fiftieth time, I opened my gift and stood looking down at the contents. It had arrived yesterday, by train from London and was presented to me by Jimmie James, whom everyone called the Old Man.

'There y'are, young feller, make most of it.'

I was being given my wings. I was no longer just a member of the Company, I was part of the Family, a young Arlecchino tasting life on countless small stages throughout Wales, proudly seated on the back of the truck among skips and flats as we wheeled into the next village, passing out posters announcing the coming of the actors. Two weeks of improvising clothes, learning roles far into the night and wandering Wales.

The skip was made of cheap but strong basketware. It was three feet long, two feet wide, twenty inches deep and full of clothes and props for the stage. Gently I began to unpack the wonders it held. Time was on my hands for the first time in days. I was in the back room of a hall, half listening to the second act of a thriller being performed on stage. My role of the gardener, Stanley, was finished and I could indulge in trying on my new wardrobe, which a group of charitable ladies had packed for an aspiring young actor in the provinces.

Taking pride of place was the dinner suit, to be kept immaculate and ready for those many nights when rich folk gathered with cocktail glasses to celebrate a wedding, or stood noble and melancholy as shocking news interrupted drinks before dinner. Two fine, grey suits followed for all the lawyers, clerks and businessmen who peopled modern drama. A blazer with greys and white flannels would dress all those university wags in smart comedies; and folded importantly below all this was a splendid frock coat.

At the bottom of the skip were scattered small but important treasures; dress shirts, collarless shirts and collars to starch and make perfect. A fancy waistcoat accompanied the frock coat and—joy of joys—a grey top hat that sprang to life at a mere touch. A box in one corner revealed cuff links, shirt studs and bow ties and in another, held securely by elastic bands, lay two well-made moustaches and, wonder of wonders, a bald wig.

To allow the lower classes an occasional appearance, a working-man's singlet and trousers were tucked in at the side. Along the length of the skip lay a walking stick of fine wood and, wrapped up in a flannel shirt was a good pair of all-purpose black shoes. A warm old cardigan completed the treasure trove, protecting a fine old pair of leather gloves. My letter to the ladies to thank them for their gift was the most heartfelt I have ever written. I stood in the brightly-lit dressing room surrounded by my booty, trying on pieces and wondering who might have worn them before me and in what roles.

The play continued through the second act and I listened to an encounter between John and Celia as they pumped life into the mundane dialogue. The thriller was an important item in each week's program. From forgettable authors to Agatha Christie, the audience lapped up a good murder. That night, I learnt another lesson I would never forget. Talent and technique brings to life a character on stage, but something more is needed, a passion for the encounter between two people. An encounter that not only brings the characters and text alive but which heightens the passion of being there; the tremble in the body caused by listening to every word that others say and the feeling of coming alive from toe to crown as words spill from you.

I was suddenly torn from my reverie by angry voices calling my character's name. 'Where could Stanley be? In the garden perhaps? Probably in the kitchen… with cook!' This last was given with rising venom and 'cook' exploded into a shriek. I stood, paralyzed, not knowing what was going on. Then Albert's furious face appeared round the door and gestured towards the stage. I peeled off my new dinner jacket and ran to the wings. Before I knew what was happening, Albert had thrust me on stage, but not before grasping the back of my head and tearing off my new grey wig. I was met by the baleful, dark eyes of Celia and a shriek of laughter from Pat.

'Oh, there you are, Stanley, what was it you wanted to say?'

As I had no idea I started in about some trees that needed cutting down. They soon realised my predicament and began bringing the subject around to the fact that I had the vital evidence that would later prove Celia had conspired to murder her husband. How this was achieved is beyond my memory, but after an eternal play of words, John, turning his back on the audience, grinned and gestured me to exit. I ambled off, murmuring something about getting back to the trees and collapsed in the wings.

In the corner Albert muttered out of the corner of his mouth. 'When you write out your bloody part, write out every bloody scene.'

Days turned into weeks as plays began to pile up in my skip and in my memory. Every evening was spent writing out parts, learning parts; writing lists for the following day and swigging down large doses of a tonic called Metatone. I had no idea what it contained, but it became a nightly companion. I had taken to the life as if born to it. The stage was becoming my new home as surely as the swimming pool down the road from my childhood home, where overarm, backstroke and breast stroke had been practised and performed until the pool belonged to me. Now this Family had taken me to their gypsy hearts and Jimmie's call for 'young feller' became a daily ritual as he passed on the skills of his 'special moments'.

Young actors came, as I had done, only to run away in terror at the consuming workload. One of the young actresses who attempted it was a willowy girl called Felicity, just out of RADA. There seemed no way she could last, but Felicity had courage and determination. Day after day, performance after performance, her face pale with stress and lack of sleep, she soldiered on—until the night of *Harvey*. This gentle American comedy about a man with an invisible rabbit was a favourite; and the audience loved Jimmie in the role, even though he was far too old. That night he announced to the Family that this would be his last performance in the role. Felicity played the nurse in the Doctor's surgery and was called to leave the stage hurriedly, with tears in her eyes. By this time she was reaching the end of her patient tether and the build-up of tension burst. Tears became sobs as she ran full tilt for the door. She pushed instead of pulled the door wildly and in an instant the entire three walls of the set were flattened, disclosing the large empty stage behind.

In the terrible silence that followed, broken only by the sobbing of Felicity, Jimmie turned to his invisible friend and said gently, 'She was a bit upset, Harvey.'

The audience went wild with applause and Albert slowly brought the curtain down. We put the set together again and Albert was heard to mutter, 'The Old Man'll want that to happen again next time.'

Felicity left us soon afterwards, despite our entreaties to stay. She was fortunate, perhaps, not to witness the performance a week later of *Wuthering Heights*, during which some local lads catcalled a scene of Bronte magic. John and Albert leapt over the footlights, ran down the aisle and booted the offenders out of the theatre. Applause brought them back to the stage, Albert to his corner and John to continue his savage and romantic performance as Heathcliff. The incident became legend in the county as we travelled on towards autumn.

Carlyle: Farewell, my own Isabel.

Isabel: Till time has given place to eternity.

Her hand touched his cheek for a moment, then fell lifeless beside her, striking the floor sharply with the ring on her finger. The curtain slowly fell in silence except for the audible sobbing of the audience. In a sort of daze, and dressed in my splendid frock coat, I joined the cast to take a bow amid applause I had seldom heard before. This experience of nineteenth-century drama left me trembling and breathless. Many years later, taking a bow beside Joan Sutherland, I would feel again the overwhelming emotion that a truly great performance can provoke.

That night, in a small hall in the town of Cardigan, the performance of Mrs Henry Wood's *East Lynne* aroused in me very mixed emotions; principally anger, that I should be so affected by a play for which I had little respect. Yet for days my eyes would fill with tears at the memory of it. Only much later would I begin to unravel this paradox.

Isabel was performed by Celia, a role that had been played years before by Bessie, and her mother before her. And what a role! A woman with a passionate love for her husband and children, but who suffers, like Othello, from a jealous nature, is maliciously persuaded to see her husband in a false light and leaves him and their children. For years she endures separation; the truth is not revealed until she is close to death and reunited with her husband. Such women have been the subject of drama from the tragic heroines of Lorca's plays to Hollywood vehicles for Bette Davis. Celia's performance shone like a trembling light in Victorian darkness. It would remain in my memory as one of the unforgettable theatre experiences of my life, as would her later performance as Blanche in *A Streetcar Named Desire*—the same heightened quality of performance in a very different play.

Jimmie's choice of plays was practical and canny. They had to fit the small company of actors and be familiar to the audience. Noel Coward was popular, and a number of West End successes, but Tennessee Williams was the closest he ever ventured into poetic drama. Every London success was read and considered, but it was not in Jimmie James' Company that I first learned about the canon of English drama before 1850.

As we approached winter in South Wales the exercise books began to fill the corner of my skip and my memory became photographic.

New plays were added and others discarded. For one role I learnt forty-five pages of dialogue in one night. My parents had long left these shores and I wondered if I would ever see them again. They were happy with their return to Scotland, but not for a single moment were they persuaded to stay. Australia had penetrated their souls and that was where life and family belonged. As with so many emigrants who had dreamed of returning, they had found their original home to be something retained only in their memories.

They had given me a legacy, though. Their tales of earlier days were more real to me than anything Australia could offer; and my dreaming life as an actor was being fulfilled. Perhaps I could be accused of being a child who had never grown up or perhaps an adult who refused to face today's reality, but nothing could be more real to me now than my life with the James Family.

Life was hard, being constantly on the move, in digs wherever we could find them. My friend Ray Cooney, who will enter the story shortly, reminded me of the week we had to sleep on a billiard table for lack of accommodation. Money was always short, we lived on the poverty line and the lack of sleep was a constant accompaniment to the work; and yet I was content.

The entire Family breathed excitement as we arrived in the small town of Cardigan. Here was a favourite place to perform, a country centre that appreciated the travelling actors and fêted them with love and applause. In all weathers they came from the surrounding districts to fill the little hall; some came several nights a week, at two shillings a seat, to bathe in the comedy and drama we gave them. I had wonderful digs with a young family and every Saturday morning I was invited to hear the astonishing male choir of which the town was justly proud.

To assist in the good times, Jimmie sent to Ireland for Michael Ryan. This tall Irish actor had worked often with the Family and now arrived to play leading roles in his fine rolling baritone. Ireland had a strong history of the fit-up company and several still travelled and performed. Full houses continued for every performance. For the whole Company it was a time of smiling, a time when we felt needed and important to the community.

One unforgettable night, as we took our bow, Jimmie stepped forward and in a moving speech announced the death of Gertrude

Lawrence. To the Welsh country audience this great lady of the theatre might not have meant much, but, as Jimmie told them, she was one of us, one of those artists who serve the community with their talent to entertain. For him, she was a great artist who called for our respect and love. The audience understood this and Gertrude Lawrence received a most moving acclamation in the depths of Wales that night.

It was evident within a couple of weeks that our stay here could be extended for quite some time if we had the repertoire. This and the arrival of Michael from Ireland persuaded the Old Man to include some of the plays with which he and Bessie had grown up, dramas from the last decades of the nineteenth century. During the coming weeks, as he brought out these plays, I began to realise that the source of the Family's passion and technique was derived from the theatre we know today as melodrama.

The first of these was *Maria Martin; or Murder in the Red Barn*. Writing out my role as Maria's young brother was a distressful affair. This was no play—just a series of scenes hardly connected, finishing with the hanging of the murderer, William Corder. My role of George had only two scenes and he seemed to be a simple, pleasant young farmer who loved his sister Maria. So during the performance I spent most of my time watching from the wings. The effect was extraordinary. Michael's performance as Corder was enthralling in its passion and need. Here was a man obsessed with life and with Maria. The highly-coloured language lent itself to his vibrant voice and sweeping gestures. And the whole Family, I noticed, had moved into heightened presentation, so much so that my first scene followed suit and I found myself expressing my love for my sister with a generosity of voice and presence that freed me from formal constraint.

The stage grew larger as emotions grew stronger, so that, by the time it came to the hanging scene, Corder's confession seemed accompanied by a choir of voices soaring to heaven. In later years, whenever I heard the heightened poetry of Shakespeare reduced to naturalistic dialogue, I would long for Michael to appear as Macbeth and bring back the great cry to heaven as Man confesses his weakness.

Here lay the source of the Family's art. From the Victorian drama and beyond came its traditions. This was theatre that displayed itself with a generous heart; which was proud of being a theatre of actors, a theatre that could trace its roots back to Henry Irving and the great moral melodramas of the nineteenth century.

East Lynne followed soon after. Here was a much better play. Not to be compared with the greatness of an *Othello*, but one that gave opportunities to the actors to take the audience beyond domestic drama into the poetic expression of emotion. After *East Lynne* came *Mother of Men*. This play was notable for the appearance of Bessie in the major role. Poor health now prevented Bessie from giving many performances, but here she gave full measure and poured out her heart for the Welsh audience that night. As her youngest son, whose last scene was one of bitter weeping at his mother's grave, I had the opportunity to participate in this storm of emotion. I felt like part of a majestic symphony, like the Beethoven Seventh.

Melodrama is a word that has been devalued. From my description of this extraordinary experience, it could be taken as overacting. But overacting is bad acting; performances given without the passionate conviction and enlarged expression required to take the audience on a journey of heightened awareness. For many actors today who believe in realism it smacks of sensational and crude sentiment, a style of drama long out-of-date.

But this was 1952. Hollywood was coming to the end of its own great period of film melodrama, the bell was tolling for this working-class form of theatre and actors and directors would lose the knowledge and experience to revive it. The new realism would penetrate classical companies and Aunt Sally in the back row would no longer be able to hear the actors without amplification. I still ache for those thrilling moments in both film and theatre when actors and audience are transported by passion. But today they are very rare.

Weeks passed in this most delightful place. The weather was closing in and fires were lit in the hall every day so that, by evening, it was warm and ready for the audience. One morning found me helping Albert and John set up the special effects required for *Smilin' Through*, a sentimental favourite from Jane Cowl and a perfect play for the Family.

'Dad'll be opening the trunk any minute, you'll see,' said Pat, who was giving a hand.

John hooted with laughter and looked across to me. 'And there's an Uncle Tom, wouldn't you say?'

Pat laughed with him and nodded. 'It's a wonderful role, George, perfect for you. The Old Man'll probably give you the day off to learn it.'

During the following days I forgot about the ribbing until one morning, arriving to do my daily sweep, I found a small, tin trunk on stage. Jimmie was kneeling at it as if it was an altar, gently taking out some small paperbacks of which there seemed to be hundreds, packed tightly in an orderly way, like the exercise books in my skip. Pat stood beside him and grinned as I approached. Jimmie looked up, glaring as usual, and handed me one.

'There y'are, young feller. Have a read and we'll do it on Tuesday. You can take Monday off and get the children organised; Michael to play Simon Legree, you Tom.'

It was a well-worn, falling-apart copy of Harriet Beecher Stow's novel, *Uncle Tom's Cabin*. On closer inspection, I found it to be a highly-abridged version, the story told in many short scenes. I looked up from my reading in bewilderment. Jimmie had wandered off, but John and Pat remained, waiting for my inevitable questions.

'We pin each scene up in the wings, read it, go on and improvise. You're playing Uncle Tom and the Old Man expects you to gather together some village children to whom you tell your stories in an early scene. It'll also give you a chance of using that splendid grey wig of yours.' With that, they hurried away, leaving me to contemplate this latest strange challenge from the Family.

I looked into the trunk and discovered many more old stories and famous books converted into what were known as 'penny dreadfuls', thin paperback editions printed cheaply for poor people's reading. During successful seasons, when Jimmie extended a stay, these curiosities were brought to life as the actors improvised dialogue and followed the storyline.

The following weekend was frantic with activity. On Friday I whisked up to the local school to entreat help of the teachers. They were delighted and together we chose twelve likely children prepared to go on stage with 'the actors'. News that they would be allowed time off on Monday to rehearse with me at the hall brought many more volunteers.

The weekend was spent in learning the role, or rather, thinking about what might be said within the context of the story. It was unusually long because of the stories he told to the children. I also spent hours with my wig and make-up trying, hopelessly, to recreate the old black man from the South. The rehearsals went well on Monday and I spent some hours with the children on stage, making sure they wouldn't feel shy or fearful. A quick get together with Michael and the rest of the cast, the ritual of posting up the scenes in the wings and we were ready for an evening of *Uncle Tom's Cabin*.

Behind the curtain I arranged the children seated around me, the hall lights went out and the curtain rose. I opened my mouth and began to speak. Every child turned their back on me. Dazzled by the sight of their public, they took over the stage, waving and calling to their friends in the front row. I called their attention to my story but it was useless. My Southern timbre was quickly losing its music and I began to sound like a Methodist preacher.

Then, a miracle happened. A little girl ran off the stage, down the steps, up the aisle to hug her mother—and then ran back again. The audience was enraptured. I knew what I must do. I abandoned the stories and played a game of animal hunting in the swamps, which took us all over the auditorium and back on stage again. The applause was deafening. Finally, the children were content to let me get on with the scene and the play progressed to its fearful climax when the wicked Legree stands over the body of the dying Uncle Tom, to the accompaniment of a sobbing audience.

I took a bow with the children who were now stars of the town. Jimmie was so delighted he broke his rule and announced a second performance the following weekend. The hall was packed to the rafters for the event and *Uncle Tom* was the talk of Cardigan for a long time afterwards.

Despite all the new work, Cardigan gave me time to contemplate my position. Later times would have their rewards, but in the small world of this touring company, unknown outside the perimeter of the towns in which we played, we were an essential part of the community, not because we 'did' acting, but because we 'were' actors, providing a meeting place for the town and celebrating life as participants in ritual. I think I have never felt as content with myself as I did in those days with the Family.

The truck rumbled, skidded and ploughed its way through the sleeting rain towards Aberdare. I sat, squeezed into the cabin, huddled in my greatcoat, occasionally nodding off to sleep. The months of late-night learning were taking their toll and I longed for the rest that was coming.

We were to open in Aberdare that night and would play there for the week leading to Christmas. For the week following, Jimmie and family were heading north to Manchester and relatives, leaving everything locked up for the opening on New Year's Day. I had assured them that I was also heading up north to relatives; but the truth was I had no money to journey anywhere. I decided to keep my mouth shut and let each day look after itself.

The beautiful countryside of Cardiganshire was far behind us and the landscape began turning into mountains of coal waste as we drove through the outskirts of Aberdare. Weaving through streets of miners' homes blackened by coal dust and dismal winter weather gave no welcome to a company of tired actors. The theatre was larger than I had experienced. It stood, sturdy and brick-built, on a hill surrounded by industrial warehouses. As wearily I climbed down to start unpacking, my eye caught sight of the town lying below, washed by the grey rain. I wondered if this had been the young curate's first view in A.J. Cronin's *The Citadel*, and a surge of young adoration swept over me for Robert Donat.

'Come on, lad, you'll get soaked.' Albert backed the truck against huge back doors to prevent the sets from being drenched. Here was a real theatre, with flies and top gantries to run along. This theatre was built for the Family. I hoped that Jimmie would include one of the grand melodramas in our season here. However, tonight it was to be *See How They Run*, a play now more than familiar to me. I spent the few hours we had before opening helping Albert bring in black wings and cloths, to create a background for our small sets on this cavernous stage.

Aberdare was no village. Here we stayed in professional bed-and-breakfast houses, very expensive for my pocket. Here we had no community ready to help the players get ready and any props needed would come from a department store in return for the promise of a mention in the program—which, as usual, I would belt out on Albert's old typewriter. By 7.25 pm the theatre was full and I was suddenly nervous. Something else was needed tonight. I felt sick and raced out the back to dry retch.

The Family took the stage. There was the answer. It was if their bodies, their personalities, their every gesture had expanded just that much so that every word and nuance could be enjoyed in the back row of the gallery. The small lift of the head, enabling everyone to catch the smile and the movement of the eyes, seemed perfectly in keeping with the slightly larger-than-life character to whom the audience was introduced. It was only later that I realised this heightened awareness was instinctual, born of long experience. This is what it was to be an actor. In the years to come, when I heard the phrase 'heightened expression' used for the classics, the term would bring back flooding memories of the Family at work.

The Aberdare audience responded to *See How They Run*. The Reverend Humphries was a comic triumph. They laughed long and loud as if escaping from the grey world outside, and gave a warm welcome to the week's program. The face of things seldom reveals the truth about people. Years later I heard the conductor Sir John Barbirolli being asked why he chose Manchester as the home for the reconstituted Hallé Orchestra. 'I looked,' he said, 'for the coldest, industrial city. There, the people would make great music.'

I was still none the wiser about my Christmas break and continued to weave the lies that so shocked my mother. On the day of their departure I vacated my bed-and-breakfast digs, which I could no longer afford, and accompanied the Family to the station, bundled up like them with baggage and winter gear. I waved them a cheery goodbye and sat in the railway cafe drinking tea after tea, trying to think of a way out of the situation. If only, I thought, I had a free bed at night, I could spend the few pounds I had on a crack-up Christmas dinner and toast my own family so many thousands of miles away. There seemed no answer and I sat there helpless.

At that moment an idea came to me and with beating heart I set about it. It was already almost dark as I walked up to the deserted theatre. The back toilet, I knew, had a faulty window. I pulled an old box up to it, and squeezed my thin body through it onto the toilet seat inside. One by one I pulled my things after me. The suitcase was too big, so I opened it carefully and pulled the contents in, one piece at a time, leaving the bag by the wall. I could only hope no one would see it in the night. I then stumbled in search of Albert's torch, made a comfortable bed for myself with cushions and blankets from a theatre skip, and went to bed hungry, but warm and content.

The following week was the loneliest of my life; but it was also a week of introspection. I felt rudderless without the Family. Without the audience I felt like a non-person. I had not read a newspaper in months, nor listened to the radio. I had no opinion to offer about anything or anyone. I began to see myself as no more than a filter through which to reproduce other people's ideas. Give me a small lit platform and an audience and I would take on their lilting accent and enthral them as Emlyn Williams' murderous boy in *Night Must Fall*. That was it. To be someone else. To fill the body and mind with the persona of another and through them to communicate what it is to be human. To be an actor. The other thought knocking at my mind was to do with the company I kept. The company of actors. Being with those who truly understood me. I waited impatiently for the Family to return. I walked the wet streets of this large Welsh town, feeling the grimness of its life. I would snuggle into a pub to keep warm and try valiantly to swallow their terrible beer. Occasionally, I would hear the unmistakable voices of a Welsh male choir issuing from a hall and I would steal into the back to listen. Perhaps I am wrong to call it the loneliest week of my life. A better phrase might be the most solitary. My imagination was certainly fed by what I saw.

On Christmas Day I kept my promise. Dressing up spic and span I had a slap-up dinner in a grand hotel. As each day approached for the Family's return my spirits rose and when New Year's day finally arrived and I was once more standing on stage with my company of actors, I felt again that heart-stopping moment of being exactly where I was meant to be.

The spring of 1953, by contrast, brought about the happiest days of my young life. By this time I had played the Company's entire repertoire and every few weeks a new one was tested on our hungry Welsh audiences. Among them was the family drama by Wynyard Browne, *The Holly and the Ivy*.

'First thing to remember, young feller, is that when you're drunk, you try to convince everyone that you're not. In fact, you try to convince the world that your knowledge and wisdom are unassailable.'

With these wise words from Jimmie came also the suggestion that the final scene with my father that I was to play as Mick, should be rehearsed as if I were sober. Good advice. By doing this the full import of the boy's daring, and its consequent revelation of family problems, were exposed. I was able to see that the boy could never have made his stand without support of some kind. Drink was that support. The scene became one of pain and clarity, with alcohol as the underlying agent that brings about the resolution.

As we wandered towards North Wales, we drove one day into the yard of a small hall. Pat approached with a young man and work stopped while she introduced Ray Cooney as the newest member of the Company. There was something immediately appealing about Ray. This tall young man had an excited gleam in his eyes as if at last he had found what he had been seeking. I recognised the delighted appraisal he gave of everything he saw. We had had quite a turnaround of actors hired as juvenile leads, and, as Ray also revealed a talent for comedy, the Old Man soon began to bring out his repertoire of comedies and farces and to introduce new ones. Here was someone to whom everyone responded; the whole Family fell in love with him. He soon became a close friend and one with whom I came to share digs.

The following months introduced me to the complexities of making laughter in the theatre and I began to study terms such as 'light comedy', 'high comedy', 'knock-about comedy' and 'farce'. In the meantime, as a still unthinking, intuitive young Arlecchino, I just had a good time with Ray, who could transform himself from one comic character to the next in an instant. And always the audience were our masters. Their reaction taught us timing and the style of playing demanded by each play.

John Farley and Celia James of the Midland Touring Company.

Ray's later worldwide success as a writer and director of boulevard farce came therefore as no surprise. Soon after leaving the Family he began writing, by the mid-1960s he had his own production company and today is known as co-author of such classics as *Charlie Girl*, *Not Now Darling*, *Move Over Mrs Markham* and *Run For Your Wife*. Ray Cooney had decided early in his youth that comedy would be his life and he pursued it with grace and generosity. He is, to this day, as actor and author, still making London laugh.

The Family was a close-knit group and very few others were permitted into the circle. Very few people stayed long enough to become a part of their world. Family arguments and quarrels peppered their lives as their volatile natures clashed, but the play was paramount and nothing could prevent it from going on every night. One night Jimmie arrived at the theatre, muttering dire threats under his breath.

'Oh, no, not again,' Pat murmured helplessly and hurried away, leaving the rest of us in the dark.

That night we were playing *The Happiest Days of Your Life*, a popular farce by John Dighton about schooldays. During a scene in which the young teachers were gathered, Jimmie, playing the janitor, suddenly burst across the stage followed by an irate Bessie dressed as headmistress. They disappeared into the wings and we stood paralysed for a long moment, then cast and audience exploded in laughter. Later in the evening a distressed Pat spoke quietly to Ray and me. Jealousy was a disease with this great old man of the theatre. Any man who dared pay attention to his wife became a target. Age had nothing to do with it; it was a part of his nature. A gentle inoffensive character actor called Derek Coleman, who was with us at the time, had become Jimmie's target.

The climax came the following weekend with the performance of *Murder in the House*. Jimmie was playing the detective, searching for the murderer among guests at a country home. During the second act he made an unscripted entrance to announce that Mrs Farlowe, (Bessie), had fallen ill and taken to her bed. He then stomped off. In great alarm, Pat followed, leaving the rest of us to improvise. A few minutes later, she returned and passed the word round that Bessie had locked herself in the toilet and was determined not to reappear until Jimmie had recovered his senses. The second act somehow came to a finish and during the interval Pat and Celia tried to persuade the furious Bessie to release herself, while Jimmie stomped and swore out the back—but to no avail. We gazed at each other in consternation. It was serious, but it also had the elements of farce. Bessie was playing the character that turns out to be the murderer. What should we do?

As usual, John took over and within ten minutes had rearranged the third act to provide another murderer. We got through but the audience might well have had a few questions about the logic of the outcome. During the following week, Derek left us with much regret; for us, it was with great relief. Life had penetrated my worship of this old actor and never again would I imagine another human being to be infallible. The incident was a lesson about life as important as my growing knowledge of acting and it made me pause a little in this hectic program of daily work. It was my first experience of being close to behaviour that appeared irrational. This was a deeply-felt, uncontrollable, part of Jimmie's nature.

The Old Man had discovered that I could bash out a tune on the piano, and a revue was now added to our program. Pat taught me my first routine, singing and tap dancing, between racing from piano to stage. Just being, every night of my life, in front of an audience, brought with it new skills. Because my memory bank held every play firmly in place, I could now give each role more thought and begin to develop character. With Ray I began to play many comedies and Jimmie's advice was always on hand. Later, when failing audiences and the arrival of television put fit-up companies out of business, I would look back and feel great sympathy for young actors who would never experience the kind of apprenticeship that had been my privilege.

One day, I was sorting out some props and softly rehearsing one of our revue songs when I became aware of Bessie, sitting in her corner, cigarette dangling from her mouth and a sweet smile on her face. I laughed, going on working.

'You're happy, young George, eh?'

I stopped suddenly and looked at her, puzzled a little by this.

'Yes, Bessie, yes, I am. You must enjoy the spring days?'

'Yes, yes, it makes me want to sit in the sun ... and stop.'

Just for a moment the world stopped and I gazed at this lovely old friend, not wanting to understand exactly what she was saying. Bessie was aware of what she had said and looked at me as if wanting me to understand the import of it.

'I'm tired, darlin', very tired.' She gave a deep sigh and returned to her ironing without another word.

I returned to my sorting with my mind on fire. I should have pressed her for her thoughts but I was fearful of the answer. That this life might stop, come to an end. It's not possible! I thought of the death of my school friend David Begley. Ominous thoughts arose of life coming to an end. And felt ashamed the moment after. My life was not coming to an end, only this part of it, but I wanted it to go on forever.

I tried to forget all this and dived back into life, leaving my feelings unresolved. The countryside burst into blossom; green vistas went on forever; and for the first time since arriving, I began to explore the country. With Ray and Pat, we made excursions on Sundays to old castles and churches that filled our imagination. But, despite these distractions, we were conscious of change occurring. Jimmie spent less and less time on stage. He and Bessie went for walks and sat together in the sun, leaving the work to us. When Jimmie did appear there was an irritation about him, as if he could no longer be bothered with the day-to-day business.

Then, as early summer days began to raise the temperature, John suggested tea in a little café and Celia joined us. We chattered for a while, enjoying the warm weather and the quiet little town.

'What sort of teacher do you think I might make, George?'

A long pause as I looked at John. I finally swallowed and answered.

'A good one, John. You've taught me so much. Any young actor would get a lot from your experience and knowledge. Besides, you love actors.'

I was conscious of Celia listening quietly. John just nodded and went on with his tea. I remained silent, my look demanding something more. Celia put her hand out and held mine.

'There has to be a time, dear, when all things come to an end.'

The actor who had replaced Derek Coleman was an old friend of the Family, who had played with them on and off for many years. Paul Stanton was a darkly handsome character actor and it gave me a lot of pleasure watching him work. That night, after the performance, I was clearing the stage when he suddenly appeared.

'Nice performance, tonight, George. You have quite a future ahead of you.'

I was astonished.

'You certainly do. Isn't it time you thought about it?'

With that he disappeared, leaving me stunned. Was there a conspiracy, somewhere, that on this day I would be assailed with notions of ending? I thought of Bessie, of all the extra work that Albert was doing and of quiet conversations between members of the family. It was not difficult to guess what was in the air: this last fit-up company in England was in its last phase of life.

Albert called me to lock up the theatre and I walked down to my digs in the early summer night. I could no longer push it aside. At supper that night I asked Ray about London, a city he knew well, and what he thought were the chances of work there.

'You have to be there,' he said. 'Give yourself a bit of time and I'm sure you'd do well. Why?' he added, startled. 'Are you thinking of leaving?'

'No, of course not. But one day… you know?'

'Oh, yes, I suppose you're right. The Old Man isn't getting any younger; and Bessie's not playing at all, now. I should think of what's next, myself.'

When faced with it, there was no next for me. I had enough money to get on a train to go somewhere, but no more. Perhaps I should sit down and write again to all those companies I wrote to so long ago. A sort of desolation set in over the next weeks as summer gained strength and our playing continued as if nothing had happened. It was so easy to believe that this life I had fallen in love with would never end.

As if to prove this, a local play was added to the repertoire that required a young man to speak his role in Welsh. John took over the rehearsal of it and I spent many nights learning the Welsh and enjoying hugely the rhythms of this beautiful language. The night we presented it the hall was packed and as I began to speak there was a murmur throughout the theatre. I thought for a terrible moment it was the beginning of a protest, but as I finished the first scene and made my exit, the audience roared their applause for the young Welsh actor. The play was repeated each week for a month. I began to deceive myself that no decision would be required of me.

Then, one night, after the show, Paul took me aside and handed me a letter. 'Read that,' he said, 'and think about it.'

He left me staring at a fateful piece of paper. It catapulted me, like an unsuspecting Hobbit, out of a warm and familiar world, and set me on a journey that has never ended.

I raced around the dressing rooms to announce the fifteen-minute call and hurried back to my table to finish my make-up. A bland, middle-aged face stared at me as I carefully fitted on my balding wig to become Mr Twine in *Rookery Nook*, my first role from the series of Ben Travers comedies known as the Aldwych farces. They had made their name through the 1920s at London's Aldwych Theatre starring the comedians Tom Walls and Ralph Lynn.

'The young Welsh actor', c. 1953.

Satisfied that everything was ready, I went up on stage looking for something with which to keep busy. The stage was huge, as was the auditorium of this seaside theatre in Aberystwyth and the set, especially built for this play, matched the size. Summer was well advanced and audiences were large enough to make this seaside summer season worthwhile to the management of the Little Theatre.

Five minutes to curtain rise and, as I once more made the rounds, I experienced again a wave of guilt and betrayal. I had left the Family and still felt shocked and dazed by my actions. Finally I stood on the stage behind the red front curtain waiting for it to rise and for a moment, imagined them there with me; but they were up North playing somewhere, in some small hall.

As I had done every night since my defection, I wished them well and hoped that Jimmie would one day forgive me. Only weeks separated us in time, but it seemed forever. A year later I learnt that the Company had indeed disbanded; Jimmie and Bessie had retired to Manchester, John and Celia were teaching down south, Ray was back in London and Pat was making up her mind to give up the business altogether. I still felt a real sense of betrayal and wished that I had remained with them until the end; but now I was playing leading comic roles in a summer season at this popular town. For this I had to thank Paul Stanton.

His letter had been an offer for the summer season at the Little Theatre, in Aberystwyth, only fifty miles away by train and offering more than double the money. I looked at him, bewildered by it.

'I'm sorry,' he said, 'it was my doing. I know the director and I also knew he needed a good young comic actor. I wrote and recommended you.'

'But I can't leave the Family.'

'That's up to you, George, but they'll be leaving the business before long and you have your whole life ahead.'

A sleepless night brought about a decision and in the morning I had to find the courage to face the Old Man. It was one of the worst ten minutes of my life and for the next month he refused to speak to me. John, Pat and Celia supported me with sympathy and encouragement, but I needed to keep tight control of my emotional nature. The day I left was one of enormous relief. Bessie gave me a hug and Ray shook me by the hand, but Jimmie wasn't to be seen. This Family had nurtured me and taught me things I've never forgotten. What had I done? And why?

'I have to move on, you know?' Harry's words, spoken, it seems, so long ago, kept coming back to me. Is that what I was doing? Moving on? Is this the way ambition works? I was so certain that ambition was not part of my nature, but the thought of not being an actor was unthinkable. The arguments whirled around in my mind.

In the meantime I went on with the life of an actor, but in very different circumstances. One whole week! Here in Aberystwyth I had one whole week in which to learn a role. This was a weekly repertory company of which there were hundreds scattered throughout the United Kingdom. They housed thousands of actors, all doing summer seasons and hoping some London producer, agent or critic would catch their performance and catapult them towards that Mecca of theatre. Aberystwyth was far too far away from London for that to happen.

The Cambrian Players were led by an enterprising man of the theatre, Jack Bradley. I was employed as assistant stage manager as well as actor, and among the Company made two wonderful friends. June Lockhart was a leading lady of many years' experience in the repertory system and I came to value her advice and friendship. My other friend was the stage director, Alec Foote, a young Scotsman from Glasgow with a wonderful sense of comedy.

Jack recognised my potential as a comic actor and introduced into the season a series of Aldwych farces, which gave me the chance to display what I had learnt with the Family. This experience of Ben Travers' craft would remain with me and be put to good use later in Australia.

I was also given other roles that extended my range and encouraged me to think that I might go far in the profession. Unlike the Family, the actors spoke of nothing else. I was becoming part of my profession and began wondering if London might be possible, now I was able to save a pound or two each week. Meanwhile I had become part of a long-established employment network that would support me.

Every company used the repertory system. Actors could move from one theatre to another, swapping the good digs and fitting in wherever a role was available. Most actors spent their entire lives within this system until it was killed by television. Some few companies, better endowed than others, became fortnightly. These were much sought after, mainly because reviewers were more likely to see their work. With two-week seasons even Shakespeare and other classics were possible for these companies, but such plays were as yet unknown to me. The modern play was the weekly food for most companies. *Little Women* was the closest the Cambrian Players came to doing a classic in the way Jimmie had fed his audiences on versions of the Bronte sisters' stories.

As autumn approached Alec and I began a plan to play knockabout comics in Christmas pantomime in Glasgow. Almost every actor alive wanted a Christmas date; it meant work during the off-season and the pay was lucrative, as twice-daily performances were usual in those days. We spent many hours pouring over old pantomime scripts and working out routines and gags that I had used with the Family. We even had a photograph taken and called ourselves 'Lachlan and Lee'.

By now it was 1953 and, beyond the walls of my small life, world events were passing me by—or so I thought. During the summer I did become conscious of the excitement in London over the Queen's Coronation and the fact that the Korean War had come to an end. All that seemed so distant when the present was so exciting. However, something else had escaped my notice during the last two years, despite my determination to become an Englishman: that Australia was part of the Commonwealth and that, as a British resident, responsibilities that affected all young Englishmen also applied to me.

Towards the end of the season a letter arrived which turned my life upside down. I came down to my dressing room to find a long brown envelope on my make-up table, bearing the stamp of the British Army. My heart stood still. Jack Bradley appeared in the doorway and looked at me with understanding.

'Perhaps you won't pass the medical. I've noticed your feet are fairly flat.'

A small hope in the gloom. I shoved the letter away until after the show.

At supper that night I sat in my landlady's dining room and knew I must open and read it. At that moment Mrs Lewis appeared with a plate of food.

'Oh, my goodness, one of those! My son is away, you know. My goodness, yes; in Malaya would you believe.'

'In Malaya?' I said, startled and uncomprehending. 'Why Malaya?'

'He's in the jungles. I wonder if I'll ever see him again.' Her eyes filled with tears at the thought.

The letter was a call-up notice for two years in the British Army. I must present myself for medical examination in a few weeks. I began to eat, ferociously, not willing to even think about it. At that moment my fellow lodger, a young policeman called Stan, came in for his supper and saw the envelope.

'Ay, ay,' he chuckled. 'A spot in the army, is it? That'll do you some good. Get you away from that silly acting of yours.'

I glared at him.

'George, bach,' said Mrs Lewis, 'you're Australian; why don't you go home?'

I sat stunned.

'You couldn't do that, boyo, the army'd find you. They always do.'

Home! Go home? Go back to that country I had vowed never to see again? No, I could not. Better to try the army. But Malaya! Hot jungles and killing people!

Bed that night was a tossing nightmare. Perhaps fortunately, I had no role in the following week's play and instead was stage manager. As I sat in the corner trying to concentrate on cues, I tried to reason the whole mess out. This was more than just a question of whether to go home or not. Going back meant abandoning my career. Could I find the courage to be a conscientious objector? I could spend two years in prison.

My interest in newspapers and the radio was now thoroughly aroused; and I found that the army prepared their recruits with six weeks' training before shipping them over to Malaya and other foreign hot spots. The prospect was dismal in the extreme. Finally, I recognised the choice was entirely up to me. Only then did I remember that I did not have the money to return to Australia. I felt very stupid. Resignedly I took myself off to the army doctor for the dreaded medical. I have worn glasses since the age of eight and hoped he might find this a disability. I did my best to fail the test by misreading the chart; but the canny doctor examined my glasses and warned me of the consequences of lying. As I had feared I was declared in A1 condition and promised a wonderful time when my call up came towards the end of the year.

Now my fate was settled I thought it necessary to inform my parents and wrote a difficult letter to my father making light of the situation. His reply came immediately: 'Passage booked on *Orontes* leaving January 10 love Dad.' A mixture of relief, gratitude and frustration assailed me.

The season finished in November, without a word from the army. I sped up to Glasgow with Alec to meet his family; said goodbye to him, pantomime and Lachlan and Lee; journeyed up to see my grandmother, knowing I would never see her again; spent New Year with my Uncle Bob and took a train to London for a few dismal final days, before boarding the *Orontes* for Australia and a bleak, angry, future.

The author as Laurie in *Little Women* with the Cambrian Players, 1953.

I stood on deck with a newspaper under my arm, watching the activity as the ship docked at Melbourne. My destination was Sydney in two days' time, where the family would meet me, so I was in no hurry. I wandered along the deck and into the lounge, looking for a quiet corner. There was general pandemonium as families gathered to disembark. Most of them were returning from the mandatory trip to the motherland, and most of them were glad to be back. The P&O holiday which had begun with streamers and shining faces, was now ending; faces were quieter, a little tired and for many, resolved. The trip had been accomplished, never to be taken again but retaining many hilarious travel tales to tell.

Above all, they were now Australian. The romance of the British Empire, with the glittering memory of the young Queen's coronation, was over and they had found themselves to be as good as, if not better than, 'them over there'. For some the jokes about chains dropping from convict ancestors had provoked many an incident in the pubs around

Earls Court. There were others who had fallen in love with Britain and would remain Anglophiles all their lives. Some had also timed their return in these early weeks of 1954 to coincide with the first visit of the Queen to our shores. My young brother Stewart had written the words to a 'Song of Greeting', to be sung for her by schoolchildren.

I was, of course, to those Australian patriots, in a much more shameful category. For two years I had tried to eradicate Australia from my being. My determination to become English had been so successful that this retreat to the past was now unendurable. For most of the trip I had been angrily convinced that I should have joined the British Army and accepted the consequences.

With a hopeless sigh, I opened the newspaper and idly scanned the pages. 'The Heroes Return', headlined a long, triumphant article, filled with adulation for the tennis stars, Ken Rosewall and Lew Hoad. Their shining faces stared from the pages. I sat there, hating them. This was what my country was all about. To be a sporting hero or heroine was the ambition of every right-thinking youngster. Only in this direction lay fame and fortune. Looking back over the years, as I write this, little has changed.

I closed the paper and sat back. Angry tears once more filled my eyes and self-pity sickened my thoughts. I rose, determined to throw off this mood, when the entertainment page caught my eye. There, in a quiet corner, was a small advertisement for the Union Theatre Repertory Company, within the University of Melbourne.

I have no memory of the play being advertised. I only know that I sped down the deck to obtain an exit pass and, within two hours, stood outside the entrance to Melbourne University. Hundreds of students, many with baggage, were arriving at the gates; the 1954 academic year was about to begin. I wandered down the road and sought direction.

I found the Union building with its huge, crowded café. Desks were placed down the corridors and students were signing up for their favourite activities. More directions took me around the building to a staircase, which led to a small office and a pleasant young woman behind a desk. She listened to my story with wide eyes, said 'Just a moment,' and disappeared through a door behind her. The walls were crowded with posters of plays. It all seemed as familiar as if I had walked into a repertory theatre in England.

After a few minutes, she returned and beckoned me into the inner office. A man was sitting behind the desk, writing in a block notebook. He looked up as I entered and I met a severe, penetrating stare. As he stood to shake hands, he revealed how tall he was. I launched into my story. When I came to the fact that the British Army had chased me out of England, he laughed, long and loud. I had finished and he was silent for a long moment.

'Ever worked at Dundee Rep?'

'No, that was a fortnightly, too grand for me.'

He nodded, understanding what I meant.

'It's where I began, really. It's very different here, but exciting. This is our very first season and we are playing the last play of the year.'

I must have looked puzzled, considering it was February; nothing finished in February.

'This is a student theatre,' he explained. 'During the student year they take over the theatre with their drama clubs. We begin again in September.' My instant disappointment vanished as he continued. 'However, if you care to write to me in a few months' time, I'll see what can happen.'

I stood with hope in face and voice, shook him by the hand and left. In the outer office I asked the young woman for an address and, in an embarrassed whisper, who it was I had been talking to. It was John Sumner. I fled, little knowing that I had met the man who would become the major influence in my professional life and would remain a close friend.

As I crossed the concourse I went over every word I had said. Oh, Lord, poor actors! How often must they tell their story? My career was just beginning and already I was questioning my story. Was it the right story? Did I show that I was just the actor he was looking for? In the years to come I would feel increasing sympathy for actors as they reinvented themselves in front of me.

Waiting for a tram, the panic of the last hour subsided and I seriously began to assess the previous two years. Where was I now? What had I achieved in the profession I had chosen? With no training whatsoever and relying simply on an instinct for it, an actor had been born—or rather been thrust in front of an audience to sink or swim. Without more direction than a few astute words from my peers, I had been given the chance to grow without being judged, obeying the feel of an audience and the connection on stage of fellow actors. In the years ahead I would see these two years as an apprenticeship unparalleled for an aspiring young actor.

I had performed in front of many hundreds in more than fifty plays. I knew that my skills had improved and I had become highly self-reliant, but was also aware that the expertise of the company I played with had been essential to this success. Arlecchino had earned his journeyman's ticket, but this had only been possible among people who loved the game as he had done. If John Sumner were to offer me a season with his company, would I find the same passion and commitment among his actors as I had experienced in the last two years?

As the liner ploughed slowly through Bass Strait towards Sydney and the summer sun shone down on brown bodies, deck games and swimming larks, I thought about this man Sumner, and about Australia. Could this lotus land of ours reinvent itself and find theatre to be as important as the game of tennis? The girl who had won the Mobil Quest only a few years ago was now singing at Covent Garden. Had Joan Sutherland's voice gained the headlines that our Davis Cup players received? There was a long way to go. Would I, or could I, be part of it?

Three

THE ACTOR

Meeting the Classics

'Two people are waiting for you in the lounge!' My mother's whisper was urgent with anxiety as I stepped into the kitchen. I looked at her blankly.

'Who are they?'

'I don't know! For heaven's sake, go and find out.'

I put down my Bible and walked into the living room, leaving my mother with her hand to her mouth and fear in her eyes. Ever since my return, she had nursed the conviction that I had escaped from the United Kingdom rather furtively and was now a refugee from the British Army. This being Sunday morning in Canberra, I had slipped back into old habits and returned to the church fellowship I had left behind in some other world. It was very pleasant, but in my desolate heart somewhat meaningless.

Two people stood up with smiles on their faces.

'George? My name is Anne Godfrey-Smith and this is Ralph Wilson.' Two people less likely to be emissaries from the military could hardly be imagined. She was warm and giggly. He was tall and benign. They proved to be messengers from the Canberra Repertory Society.

The amateur group that had fostered my career had expanded during the last two years. Now it had a professional director and administrator in Anne, who was recently arrived from Tasmania and university drama. Ralph Wilson, a teacher of languages from my old high school, was about to direct his first play with the society and they had a proposition for me. The leading actor in Ralph's production of

Ben Jonson's *The Alchemist* had fallen ill and the opening night was a short week away. Could I possibly help out?

Of course I said, 'Yes, how exciting.' Anne and Ralph beamed and handed me a fat script marked 'Subtle' to read before rehearsals that night. I waved them goodbye, marvelling at the way Ralph slid his immensely tall frame into Anne's Austin A40, and as they disappeared down the drive, my mother murmured, 'How did they know you were home?'

'Probably the army told them,' I grinned.

'Och, behave yourself,' she laughed, and went to prepare lunch.

I sat on the veranda and opened the text, confident in my ability to learn lines super fast. I sat there, aghast. From the first word to the last, I could not understand a single syllable. Every word of every play I had ever performed had been fully grasped, not only by me, the actor, but also by every member of the audience. Not to be understood was anathema. As I sat there, I thought of Jimmie James and knew why he would never do a play like this. We, the actors, were there to communicate clearly—ideas, situations and feelings that the audience had had or might experience. How could I play this character, Subtle, unless I understood every word? And if, finally, with a great deal of help, I did come to understand, how could I make the audience understand me?

These questions would haunt me for the following four decades, every time a classic text was put into my hands; but on this day, only one question occupied me. I turned back to page one again, searching for some understanding. With a glimmer of hope, I recognised the first sentence, spoken by Subtle. 'I fart at thee.'

Slowly and painfully, I gathered that two lowlife figures were having a barney, and that a woman was trying to intervene. Exhaustion set in after that and I retreated to lunch, informing my family that my homecoming debut in the theatre would commence with the words, 'I fart at thee.'

The rest of the afternoon was spent underlining every word I did not understand, and penciling questions in the margin. The script began to look like that of the Sheriff in *Deep are the Roots*. I then paced up and down, shouting the argument, until my mother banished me to the orchard, where, 'You can scream your obscenities out of sight.' I was beginning to discover an exciting rhythm in the lines. Even if I did not understand the meaning of so many of the words, they propelled me into the kind of screaming match that one might overhear coming from a drunken household. This heady exercise persuaded me to leave meaning behind and concentrate on the sound of the words. Years later, when young actors did the same thing, they earned my sympathy even while I corrected them.

That day in the orchard I discovered for the first time the beauty of Elizabethan language. The sound became music and I found myself singing the lines; learning and conveying the meaning would come later. I was reminded of earlier times when my music teacher, Burilda Millet, introduced me to Schumann's *Dichterliebe*. Like this play, the first hearing produced a seductive sound, but without sense. Gradually, with proper study of the words, the depth and meaning of the songs revealed their greatness. I waited impatiently for the evening and my first rehearsal with Ralph Wilson. It would be the beginning of an association that today I value more than I can easily express.

Dinner that evening was full of local news and problems in which I had no part. How strange it was to return home to a house and family after two years of a career which had begun to change the way I thought and lived, and to find as many changes here. Jim and Rita had their own home and two children, my sister Nancy was planning her marriage, my young brother Robbie was now an apprentice to my father and already escorting a young girl called Jan; while his twin, Stewart, was about to begin a career in Sydney as a commercial artist. Two little sisters, Jean and Caroline, remained at home and school. Every evening had seemed interminable as my thoughts flew abroad, wondering what role old friends were playing that night.

Tonight, however, I would be back among actors. This was where I had begun a dozen years ago.

In the summer evening I rode my old bike down to Riverside, where a long army hut, so familiar during the war, stood among trees. Lights were already on, even though as usual I was early and, also as usual, nervous about this new venture. I stepped into what turned out to be a long dressing room on the side of the building, to find Ralph already there. Ralph was at a record player and, as he saw me, smiled and said:

'Do you think this expresses Subtle's character?'

With that, the hut filled with music both swift and full of bravura. A trumpet sang above the orchestra, seeming to mock the world, laughing at all the fools who take themselves too seriously. I stood with my mouth open, seeing Subtle running and twisting around the corners of life. It was my first experience of music being used to express drama and it began a lifetime's practice of finding music which might express the play on which I was working. Music has an immediate communication with an audience and, if the right sound is heard, an ambience of understanding is created. Decades later, directing the battle scenes of *King Lear*, I was reminded of this moment when I chose a collage piece by Arvo Pärt that seemed to represent all the mindless horrors of war that the sightless Gloucester was forced to suffer. This moment also began an association with Ralph Wilson, which kept me in Canberra for two years, learning how to direct my unthinking instinct as an actor towards a disciplined research practice.

Margaret Topham and Terry Jullif, two keen amateur actors holding good jobs within the public service, arrived to meet their new Subtle and Ralph took the three of us through the first scene. It suddenly felt like being with the Family again as the two actors began helping me find the role with which they were now familiar. The difference lay with the director—and what a difference. After confessing to an almost total ignorance of the meaning of the dialogue (to which Margaret and Terry were gratefully sympathetic) Ralph ensured we understood the text before attempting to communicate it. Another lifetime practice began, of sitting with actor and text until the meaning was clear and agreed upon by both of us, before taking it on stage.

The night then became a leaping, swirling dance. Gesture joined word to relate clearly the manner in which these three tricksters conned the world. Ralph Wilson knew every word of the play; not only the meaning of every word but the rhythm of every sentence and, by so knowing, could reveal to me the intention of the character, very like a conductor who knows every note of a symphony and the value of each instrument.

The music inherent in Jonson's writing points to where the emphasis should be and thus onto the road the character will take. In discovering this I began to realise that sense can be communicated, even though some words remain obscure. In later years, with Shakespeare, a study of the iambic pentameter, in which so much of his work is written, became paramount. Jonson's dialogue was less easy to uncover, but Ralph moved among us like a great swooping bird, ready at any moment to clarify. He laughed generously at our antics, encouraging us to illustrate meaning with action. Once the meaning was clear to me, the learning became easy and by the time the evening rehearsal was reluctantly brought to a close, I knew much of the early scenes of the play and had gained a wild hope that opening night might after all be achieved.

The following week opened up a new world. After two years of pursuing theatre through everyday language, I was now introduced to seventeenth-century poetry in drama. From meaning to intention to direction and finally to performance, this fantastic black comedy took shape. For the first time I became aware of the role the director plays in the theatre. Hitherto in my experience it had seemed to need only actors.

Now I needed to plan the journey my character would take. From being aware of only myself and the audience, the task now became that of finding a way to fuse actor, audience and text together to create a whole. I suddenly thought back to that evening in Drury Lane when Mary Martin demonstrated her courage in letting go of all the study and rehearsal to enter a world in which the audience and performer become one. I became proud of my newfound knowledge and wanted to display it, but all the audience wanted to see was a lowlife, dirty rotten trickster, conning the world with word and gesture.

Opening night in the little Riverside Theatre was a happy affair. Ralph seemed pleased and the audience responded to our antics with much laughter. I was back with a family of actors. For Ralph, and the friends I made over the following months, theatre was the love of their life and they brought to it a scholarship and enthusiasm from which the professional theatre could benefit. This was not simply social activity, it was based in genuine regard for what theatre could teach and reveal.

The Family had taught me that a true ensemble could be achieved by a group of actors selflessly playing together with the audience as master. Ralph Wilson taught me to use this instinct to deepen the performance and to love great drama. When I finally began to direct, the countless things he taught me would sustain and urge me on. As I write today Ralph is no longer with us, but I remember his generosity of spirit, his knowledge freely given, his intense love for the theatre and for actors, and his research into the world behind the play. These things became the model for my future work.

A few weeks after my arrival home and after the heady experience of *The Alchemist*, my father waved his hand in front of my face—'to get my attention,' he said.

'Isn't it time you earned some money?'

I was shocked. I had slipped back into family life, like a school child expecting board and keep. I still remember, vividly, the crimson blush that suffused my face that day. With a grateful heart I put on a white coat and took over the expanding small goods section of the shop. The shop and bakehouse had been part of my life for nearly twenty years and now it was like joining the cast of a well-known play that I had seen them perform.

I would ride my old bike down, early enough to clean the shop and get it ready for 9 o'clock customers. I would make lists of small goods required from wholesale vans arriving each day, and soon settled into a long run. What else could it be? Australia had not changed its habits in the slightest since my departure. I began to believe that those two years had been a strange dream. So I tried to live in the present, attending to my daily life and the pleasure my parents felt in having their wandering son working in the family business. It soon became evident that they hoped England had cured me of my odd ambition. So I put on a smile and played the role as best I could. My new association with the Repertory Society made it easier. In time it proved so fruitful I found thoughts of John Sumner and the Union Theatre fading. So much could be learnt right here in Canberra.

On a quite different level I was happy to be re-associated with my twin brother, who by now was a master baker and pastry-cook and virtually head of the business. We found ourselves grinning at each other with unexpected pleasure as I descended each morning to greet him

The author at his delicatessen counter.

and the other bakers who had been working since the early hours. Our friendship strengthened during the next years and now, as we creep into old age, I am infinitely grateful for our love and care for each other.

My younger brother Robbie was well into his apprenticeship and already indispensable to the running of the business. Every morning excitement rang through the shop as the first batch of bread came up from below and tray upon tray was pulled up on the bread lift to fill the cases. The smell of newly-baked bread has accompanied me throughout my life.

In the quiet afternoons I remember my father sitting in his small office working over the accounts as the smoke from his cigarette curled up over the partition. His handsome face with its aquiline nose would reveal very little of the financial worries that beset him. He had chosen one of the most stressful trades, one that rewarded him with little profit. He dreamed of a factory in the new industrial area and his quiet determination would finally make it a reality—but too late for him. It would be carried through by his sons.

Occasionally my sister Nancy, home from her nursing career in Sydney, would look at me with raised eyebrows and demand to know when I intended resuming my career. Always ambitious for me, she was determined to keep me from settling into the safe corner I had begun to occupy. Her own life would take a right hand turn shortly when she married a young graduate from military college, Graham Stewart, and moved into army life, so different from anything she had so far experienced. The house would gradually empty as Stewart, Robbie's twin, a tenor and artist, followed his own star to Sydney. My young sisters kept the family tradition with Highland dancing and Jim, too, was pipe major in the Highland band. My mother remained the centre of our lives. She gradually became bowed with age but for many years the growing family would continue to assemble in her home for Christmas. I was always grateful for the sense of humour we had inherited from our parents; that and a stoicism that has helped us all to survive.

But there were still moments in those quiet afternoons when I would stand lost in the memory of nights in the theatre with my English Family, and find my father staring at me, understanding where my thoughts had taken me but incapable of sharing them. In the early evenings, I longed, foolishly but desperately, to be back there.

Portrait by Enid Drayton of the author as Argan in *The Imaginary Invalid*.

Soon after *The Alchemist*, Anne cast me as Archer in George Farquhar's *The Beaux' Stratagem*, and the learning process continued. This production and others to follow helped to reconcile me to my life in Canberra. By uncovering an amazing historical world I became a student again, sharing in the knowledge and love that Anne and Ralph had of the classic theatre.

In Canberra my intuitive approach to my work was gradually fed by the research my mentors found natural and which I found new, exciting and, eventually, imperative. Anne would speak about Farquhar and his world of early eighteenth-century London as if it were her own world, intimate and present. This period comedy in her hands became as modern as the manners of our own time. Playing the role of Archer became as familiar to me as playing any modern young spark, albeit in the costume and manners of another era.

From the delights of Farquhar, Ralph introduced me to Molière and his play *The Imaginary Invalid*. As a French scholar, Ralph knew the play intimately and the translation received meticulous attention to ensure the play remained French in its style, attitude and manners. For the first time I learnt how important the *commedia dell'arte* tradition was to Molière's history, and began to learn what a world of research was available for the realisation of a great work.

Looking back on that early experience and the classics I came to direct in later years, I have often questioned the value of taking a play out of its period into a modern setting, in order to bring it nearer to an audience. I venture to say none, if the director and cast really understand the period from which the play derives. It is that knowledge that will communicate the greatness of the work and show how modern it was when first performed.

But my excitement at this new learning process also needed balance. Both Anne and Ralph would encourage me to use my instincts and not let study and rehearsals curb a natural outlet. I remembered Mary Martin and made a real effort to let go of the study and perform in the present.

This amalgam of study and instinct has become, for me, essential to the craft of the actor. In the years ahead, as a director in the theatre, the more I could assist the actor, not in the way they perform, which is an intimate, private affair, but in the world that surrounds them within the play, the better the performance. During the run of *The Imaginary Invalid* the artist Enid Drayton came by and drew a portrait of Argan of which I am inordinately proud. Life became full at Riverside.

As the work progressed with the Repertory and I became more at ease in the shop, the time came to write to John Sumner. I let it pass. Here was a chance to return to the professional life that had meant so much to me and I was turning it down. The world I had discovered meant more. As more and more roles were offered in plays of great stature, I knew I would learn more by remaining longer in this atmosphere of scholarship. Somehow I knew that I would take up my professional life again, but not yet.

The months moved into 1955 and my friendship with the members of the Society strengthened. I loved to hear them talk, as I had ten years before, and a fascination with European theatre and its traditions grew, which would have its effect in the years to come. Old music hall was among the entertainment that Anne produced, in-between Molnar and Shakespeare, and it gave me great joy to become part of that world again.

A self-centred thirteen-year-old boy had been set on a lifetime's path by a tall, gentle director called Ric Throssell. Now, some ten years later we would meet again as he joined the cast to play Macbeth. I had no idea he was also a charismatic actor who from the first rehearsal displayed a rare talent. It was my first experience of a man of the theatre who combined both, and later I learnt that he also wrote for the theatre. His compassionate play *The Day Before Tomorrow* about the aftermath of an atomic explosion, would be directed by Anne a few years later.

At the first opportunity I asked him why he had not thought about a professional life in the theatre.

He grinned at me. 'I dreamt like you of such a thing, but, unlike you, couldn't make it happen.'

Ric had chosen a diplomatic career and had been posted to the Soviet Union. His parents were the eminent novelist and playwright Katharine Susannah Prichard and Captain Hugo Throssell, a distinguished soldier who had won the Victoria Cross at Gallipoli.

Katharine was an avowed Communist and, sadly, Ric's diplomatic career stalled after his name was (unfairly) mentioned in the 1955 Petrov Royal Commission, which in an emotionally-charged electoral climate, attempted unsuccessfully to divide the country by uncovering a Soviet spy ring in Australia.

Occasionally, even with my preoccupation with Riverside, I was made aware of things happening outside. The horrendous event of the Maitland flood brought me down to earth. A natural disaster had robbed me of my best friend. Floods and bushfires remain a seasonal challenge in our country.

During the months of 1954, here in the national capital rumours began to circulate that something was happening in government circles that appeared, unbelievably, to do with theatre. A consortium of citizens had persuaded the Government to celebrate the young Queen's visit to Australia by establishing an Australian Elizabethan Theatre Trust to support opera, ballet and drama. The old Majestic Theatre in the inner Sydney suburb of Newtown, refurbished and renamed the Elizabethan, would furnish the Trust with a home. The first production to play there in 1955 was Terence Rattigan's comedy *The Sleeping Prince*, with a cast of English notables including Dame Sybil Thorndike and Sir Ralph Richardson. Good perhaps for the box office, but hardly a hopeful beginning of what Prime Minister R.G. Menzies called a propitious start to a truly national theatre of Australia. However, it's only in hindsight that I can say this. At the time it represented the first move made towards the performing arts by a governing body, and who was I to criticise? In 1955 we were all part of the British Commonwealth.

Finally, towards the end of the year, a company of actors was formed, to play *Medea*, a rendition of Euripides' tragedy by the American poet Robinson Jeffers and starring the expatriate actress and film star, Judith Anderson. The rest of the cast would be Australian including the young Zoe Caldwell. Nearly thirty years later she would make the role her own on Broadway and later, in Melbourne play the role to open the State Theatre of the Victoria Arts Centre.

To cap off the excitement, the play would begin its tour in Canberra. A plea from Anne to the management got me a job as assistant stage manager for the Canberra season and I found myself standing once more in the wings among a professional company of players, this time in my own country and at a truly historic event.

My excitement was so powerful I could hardly breathe. There were no rehearsals to attend, only a lighting session during the day, so I was utterly unaware of the play and its progress. I recall standing in the darkened corner as the play began, half aware of a shadowy figure approaching and standing beside me. Suddenly it gave an almighty shriek, which so shocked me I joined in until the stage manager's hand was smartly clapped over my mouth. As the apparition proceeded on stage, intoning her opening lines, she gave me a glare right out of *Rebecca*. Mrs Danvers had turned Greek.

Towards the end of the year, the exciting news came of a company of actors to be formed to tour Australia the following year. Anne encouraged me to write for an audition. By this time I had been with my father for almost two years and knew I would hurt him by leaving, but the time was coming when I needed to go and this audition gave me the opportunity. He was, of course, expecting it.

'There's no way of stopping you, is there?' he grinned.

I shook my head and he sighed.

'Away you go, then.'

Anne offered to help me prepare an audition for the English director, Hugh Hunt, and was amazed to discover I had never done one. The audition was a nightmare process that seemed to be a matter of simply 'doing something' on stage for a darkened figure in the stalls, who then said 'thank you' without another word. No kind words, no encouragement—just silence and a curt 'thank you'. Several auditions later, I was asked to join the new company, and I swore that one day I would find some way of lessening the horror and cruelty of that process for the actor.

I was delighted, of course, that the job was mine; that I could once again call myself a professional actor. And yet I found myself reluctant to leave behind these two years, perhaps because I was about to re-enter a world of ambition and struggle. Those days in Canberra have continued to mean a great deal to me and have influenced my thinking, both as actor and director.

I have one last memory of that time that affected my life profoundly. There must be, in the life of every actor, one role that leaves an indelible impression. This was so for me, with Anne's production of Christopher Fry's *A Sleep of Prisoners*. Fry was one of the poet dramatists that England fostered during the 1940s and 50s. This play was not one of his West End successes, despite a cast that included Denholm Elliot and Stanley Baker. It was written to be played in a church.

Four British prisoners-of-war, placed in the temporary prison of a church somewhere in Europe, sleep, dream and act out the eternal struggles of man against man, from Cain and Abel to Abraham's sacrifice of Isaac. Although I was far too young for the role, Anne persuaded me to play the oldest soldier, Meadows. I can never thank her enough. It gave my life an impetus which I still feel today. This was my first experience of performing a play in which something more was required of the actor: an examination of personal belief. With this play, I was obliged to face the fact that seeking a meaning for existence was important to my nature. I recalled in every detail how *Our Town* had reconciled me to the death of my friend David. *A Sleep of Prisoners* helped me to understand faith. Fry, with the words he gave Meadows, gave me a mantra by which to live.

> Good has no fear.
> Good is itself, whatever comes.
> It grows, and makes, and bravely
> Persuades beyond all tilt of wrong;
> Stronger than anger, wider than strategy,
> Enough to subdue cities and men,
> If we believe it with a long courage of truth.

'In-between my time with Canberra Rep and the Union Theatre Company, I was in the Elizabethan Theatre Trust Drama Company,' I used to tell people.

'In-between' implies killing time, and this is how I remember the years 1956 and 1957. We toured two plays each year all over Australia.

The Australian Drama Company: James Bailey, Madge Ryan, Clement McCallin and Dinah Shearing in *The Rivals*.

Four plays? I used to do that in a week. Admittedly, these were classics: *Twelfth Night* and Sheridan's *The Rivals* the first year, and *Hamlet* and Vanbrugh's *The Relapse* the second. I was cast in the smallest roles of serving men and attendants, which left me bored out of my mind; but other factors contributed to the boredom and resentment of that period. Canberra continued to draw me. Ralph Wilson remained my mentor and at every opportunity I would take a plane to Canberra and seek out his company over a bottle of scotch. My time with the Trust could offer nothing to compare with this continuous, warm dialogue with my teacher.

When the day arrived for the first rehearsal, the company gathered in the rehearsal room behind the Elizabethan Theatre. What an unhappy experience it was. Actors who were strangers to the group prowled around the edges trying hard not to feel outcasts, while those who knew each other fell into each other's arms like long-lost lovers. I was both a stranger and one playing the smallest roles. I was grateful to be left alone to observe a rehearsal, the like of which I later swore would never be repeated under my direction. I was to meet the experience again when I later directed in the commercial world. There a cast of actors, strangers to each other, meet the director in an uneasy truce and spend many days trying to find ways to work with each other. A good director will always find a way to achieve a level of trust, so that the play can move forward; but we remained uneasy and suspicious.

This first rehearsal of this brief, pioneering Australian Drama Company remains a vague, shadowy affair, with what seemed to be a ghost of a man directing us. Hugh Hunt was a shy, nervous Englishman and I remember hardly a single word he said, either to me or anyone else. Anything he did say was whispered into the actor's ear, so that by the end of the first day I had no idea what he thought of Shakespeare, *Twelfth Night*, the actors, the production or life itself. And it remained a mystery, locked away in some personal vault in his breast. Weeks later, there was one moment, when I was rehearsing Feste the clown, which I was to play in certain cities. Mr Hunt wandered over to me with a shy smile and whispered, 'No, not like that'—and immediately retreated, as if he had said too much already. That is all the direction I ever received.

The following year in the rehearsals for *Hamlet*, he dared to suggest that Osric should be played like a butterfly. Considering my entire costume was sky blue, including blue stockings and a blue hat with a huge white feather, this instruction was superfluous. Our down-to-earth Hamlet, Paul Rogers, muddied the issue further by suggesting I should play him as a wasp.

An atmosphere of quiet and refined courtesy prevailed over rehearsals, created in part by Hunt, so as not to offend the sensibilities of the ladies and gentlemen from the world of radio. These were big stars in Australia. The whole country listened to Sunday night radio, our family amongst them. My mother was particularly enthralled with the beautiful voice of Dinah Shearing, our Viola. She was thrilled to think I was playing with her on stage. My only slight concern was with Orsino, played with direct and immediate gusto by Leonard Teale, another star of the airwaves. His identity as Superman was so entrenched I found it difficult not to feel that he might levitate at any moment in pursuit of evil.

There was one actor to whom I felt immediately drawn. This was Clement McCallin, an English classical actor of many years' experience and a warm and willing nature. In 1960 he became the National

Institute of Dramatic Art's first teacher of acting. He would become a special friend. Other actors became friends in time, but on that first day we were refugees gathered at a strange tea party. I waited for the Mad Hatter to appear and allow everyone to laugh and relax.

Instead, it was Elsie Beyer. This extraordinary, dynamic woman in perpetual dark glasses and overcoat, even in the hottest weather, and who might have been Margaret Thatcher's auntie, came directly from London West End management. Like Hugh Hunt, she spoke in gentle, low tones and was often heard murmuring about the 'lovely dream' this venture was. She remained for the actors a pale, stern figure on the sidelines of rehearsals, until an intrepid actor had a request to make of management. The eyes would turn to gimlets and the actor would be reminded 'how lucky we are, dear'. These were the people the Trust had put in charge of the birth of an Australian drama company. The sense of patronage from our English masters was at times unendurable.

In the years following the War, when we began seriously to seek our own identity, a genuine Australian theatre culture was virtually non-existent. Theatre had flourished in the last century and the early Federation period, but the coming of film, followed by the Great Depression, had put paid to it. Now we were in need of proper leadership. To be willing to learn is the first step towards building an ensemble, but this is impossible if the management simply follows old ways and misuses the artists' talents. The performances we gave evolved from our preservation instinct rather than any organic process. The future of Australian theatre had been sold, we quickly realised, to the masters across the sea.

The Rivals was much more like the real thing. It was in the hands of the young Sydney director and stage designer, Robin Lovejoy, who managed to draw this unhappy and disparate group of actors together. His beautiful designs set off this eighteenth-century comedy perfectly and the cast had a good time, relaxing and getting to know each other. The fact that the rehearsal room was filled with Australians certainly helped this play. Sheridan's Irish wit matched the dry Australian humour and without the authoritative English visitors present we began to be more ourselves than we had so far dared.

One of my most enduring memories is of the rehearsals between James Bailey and Clem McCallin, two actors experienced in classical work who were playing father and son. McCallin had come to Australia for J.C. Williamson's and Bailey had settled in Australia after touring with the Old Vic Company in 1948 with Laurence Olivier and Vivien Leigh. Their knowledge and love for this era reminded me of my experience in Canberra with Anne and Ralph and the important discovery that if the actor is at home in his world, then the play becomes as modern as today's news.

There were many delights in the plays themselves for our audiences as we toured from city to city. But somehow it felt out of joint as we travelled through the summer months. We never doubted that Australian actors were fully capable of establishing our own professional theatre, but the atmosphere imposed reminded me of one of those family companies that toured India with Shakespeare, bringing imperial culture to the masses. We were being similarly patronising; a company led by English theatre practitioners with English values bringing culture to deprived Australia. I remember one woman, after seeing a performance of *The Rivals*, sighing that it was 'just like being back in dear old England'.

Like a beacon of things to come, one play that toured with us that year gave us hope for the future. Ray Lawler's *Summer of the Seventeenth Doll* had won a competition run by the Trust and had opened in 1955 at the Union Theatre, directed by John Sumner, who was now manager of the Trust. By now it was bringing a new awareness to the Australian psyche. Here was a working-class play about barmaids and seasonal workers that in every way opposed the polite English standards Hugh Hunt had been imposing. Its impact was not to be denied.

The power of *The Doll* and its effect on the community were immediate. To sit in a theatre and feel great drama created out of our Australian character, our unique accent and ironic sense of humour, was a sudden, proud moment of true recognition that brought tears to our eyes. It was a further lesson to me to discover that when, to Australia's excitement, Hollywood bought the film rights, the result was a ludicrous failure. They had absorbed nothing of the play's real meaning or way of life. They were something only we understood.

To be close to this new miracle was very exciting and gave hope to other young writers, one of whom became a great friend during our two years of touring.

Peter Kenna, a young actor in the Australian Drama Company, came from a large Irish Catholic family very different from my Scottish Presbyterian background, and grew up in Lewisham, an inner suburb of Sydney. With his wicked sense of humour, his fearless approach to people and fiendish enjoyment of life, he personified, for me, the brash Sydneysider. He was a great storyteller and I came to know his parents, brothers and aunts through his colourful stories of their exploits and catastrophes. These stories supplied Peter with the basis for his future writing for the theatre; comedies and dramas about the country's battlers, revealing their essential Irish-Australian poetry and humour.

In 1959 the Trust would present his first play, *The Slaughter of St Teresa's Day*, at the Elizabethan. It was set in the house of a starting-price bookmaker, Oola Maguire, in Sydney's Paddington and was inspired by stories of the famous madams of the day, Tilly Devine and Kate Leigh. But the characters that gathered at Oola's party and sang around the piano were really the vibrant personalities with whom he had grown up. His best-known play, *A Hard God*, written twenty years later when he returned to Australia to join the new wave of playwriting, was a darker, more autobiographical work, which recalled the death of his father and his teenage torment in coming to terms with homosexuality. It was this play that earned him a place among our finest playwrights and for itself the title of an Australian classic.

Late nights were spent arguing over the future of our theatre world. We had both had the experience of good amateur companies, Peter's with the Genesians in Sydney. He argued for an Australian renaissance, while I was still in the grip of my English experience. Peter's Irish heritage might affect his writing, but he would remain defiantly Australian. Even when he left Australia to enjoy life in London for several years, the experience never changed his Australian identity and he would return home unchanged. I, on the other hand, like a chameleon, changed colour in order to become part of the English theatre. These beginnings down under were so fragile and the British influence so pervasive it was difficult to feel highly optimistic. For an actor the Mecca was still London, containing, like the Moscow of *The Three Sisters*, all our dreams of romance and fame. Even as I write so many years later, our young ambitions are now centred in Hollywood, and the hope of being branded with that fateful title of star.

I recall summer days in the Adelaide of 1957, when the heat seemed African and the afternoons were spent boating up the river and picnicking on the banks. The *Hamlet* we toured was a dark and thickly-clad—and rather energetic—production; perfect for a winter in Scandinavia, but playing a matinee in a nineteenth-century theatre without air conditioning on such a day was the closest physical experience I have had to hell on earth. No wonder the Trust lost heart and warned that the second year would be our last.

Never did anything seem so misjudged as those weeks spent performing in a city which suffered every summer from the winds sweeping down from the desert, reminding us that an ancient world lay just beyond. One such matinee is to be remembered simply for the laughter that relieved the heavy dread in the heart of the company as the heat suffocated both audience and actors during the Players' scene. Clem McCallin entered as the Player King and in his sonorous voice intoned the dialogue as Hamlet sat close by. Claudius, Lloyd Berrell, wrapped in his Renaissance grandeur, dozed off and when bumped awake for his cue, rose in fright with a loud, 'Shit! Give me light.' Not since the days with the Family had I heard such laughter on stage, as the entire company fought to exit with the King, leaving the poor Queen to improvise. A line of laughing soldiers, running on stage, tripped on the stairs and tumbled down to land at the feet of a now helpless Gertrude. Maree Tomasetti, playing Gertrude, was an actress who, like me, was always in danger of breaking up on stage. Her shriek of laughter completed the fate of everyone around her and an unprecedented curtain was lowered in order to restore sanity.

Lying idle on the banks of the beautiful Torrens, I had no premonition that seventeen years later, on that very spot, I would lead a company of actors into a new theatre, built by government especially to house our work. In 1957 such an idea was preposterous. We talked endlessly about what could happen, but few believed it. Most quietly planned their exit.

Perth was the end of the tour and the end of Elsie Beyer's lovely dream. The exquisite Zoe Caldwell would head for America. Even Peter Kenna, encouraged by the proceeds of the General Motors Holden competition that The Slaughter of St Teresa's Day had won him, would spend years in London, an expatriate quietly writing about the country he loved. The talent drain from Australia would go on for a long time yet. In the meantime, amateur societies continued to foster talent in cities and towns; and one in particular has my undying gratitude.

My last memory of this time was a day in sunny Perth towards the end of 1957, during the interval of a *Hamlet* matinee, when the cry went up that it was overhead. A flurry of costumed actors rushed out to gaze at the sky. Sputnik, the first earth-orbiting satellite, slowly floated its way across the blue expanse. The entire company remained silent, watching this Soviet icon herald a new epoch in the affairs of mankind. As we returned to the wisdom of Shakespeare, I did wonder if Sputnik and its future children could possibly produce anything as fine.

Within a year Robin Lovejoy would rescue the remnants of our troupe as the Trust Players, and begin real efforts to find an Australian dramatic identity. Within two years the National Institute of Dramatic Art would open in Sydney to fill the professional ranks of brave drama companies. One such was the Union Theatre Repertory Company. John Sumner, its founding director, had left it in the hands of his assistant Ray Lawler, who then chose to act in his own play. It took him and the cast first around Australia and then to London and Broadway. It was twenty years before he settled back in Australia. Lawler was succeeded at the Union by its manager, Wal Cherry, a recent university graduate, who was making his name as a director. Despite my continued longing to return to England, I decided to write to him and, just as the season finished, I received a letter offering me work. I took a plane out of Perth heading east to Melbourne and the Union Theatre. My life as an actor would now charge forward.

Two young actresses peered down at me from a flight of stairs.

'Oh! You're quite funny,' one exclaimed, and the other laughed, their faces open in friendly grins mixed with surprise that someone could be amusing so early in rehearsal. I grinned up at them and continued my scene, script in hand, rehearsing the role of the evil companion to Wyn Robert's madman, in Joseph Kesselring's farce, *Arsenic and Old Lace*. The voice in question belonged to Patricia Conolly and the laughter to Kay Ecklund. They were playing the two old ladies who murder their lodgers. I had arrived that morning and found myself thrust immediately into rehearsal.

Wal Cherry had dared to take on a company of actors; a typical gesture from a young man who would, in 1962, open his own theatre at Emerald Hill in South Melbourne, and later become a professor of theatre studies first in Adelaide and then in Philadelphia. Wal had a flair for the unusual, taking chances with both plays and actors. These years of 1957 and 1958 gave me a chance to develop in further ways. The actors' lack of experience never deterred him as he presented an ambitious program of plays. I entered the company as a 26-year-old senior and life took off.

Four weeks to rehearse a play was madness. Not perhaps in the commercial world when such rehearsals are expected to be offset by a long run, but rehearsing a play for four weeks at the Union meant a four-week run of each play. Here was the madness. We did not have the audience numbers to fill the Union Theatre for four weeks. However, Wal wanted time to rehearse and took no notice of small houses. This certainly had an effect on his future with the Union but for us actors it was bliss. Rehearsals would begin at 10 am and finish at 5 pm, leaving us time for dinner and preparation for the evening performance. Such time for thinking, research and for experiment was an amazing experience for me. In England only such companies as the Bristol Old Vic and Birmingham Repertory could afford such luxury.

Where the Family, under the careful management of Jimmie, played a successful and crowd-pleasing repertoire, Wal introduced his young company and audience to the new American repertoire with the poetry of Tennessee Williams and to the Berliner Ensemble's Bertolt Brecht; to the Parisian farces of Feydeau and the Elizabethan knockabout comedy of Beaumont and Fletcher's *Knight of the Burning Pestle*. Two talented designers, Wendy Dickson and Quentin Hole, created ingenious sets and costumes. We played for two full seasons, during which Wal overspent mountainously, but audiences saw work never before seen in Melbourne. The talents of Roslyn de Winter, Monica Maughan, Maree Tomasetti, Dorothy Bradley and Robin Ramsay blossomed. Nothing was beyond Wal's fearless ambition.

Wal was always available to talk and listen. His fervour for American theatre was unexpected: England had always been my benchmark, but Wal redirected our enthusiasm towards the United States and its new drama. His production of Tennessee Williams' *A Streetcar Named Desire*, starring Patricia Conolly, also revealed his radical method of rehearsing. After the first reading and a talk from him, giving us the world in which the play was set, Wal would take the actors through the play achingly slowly, furnishing us with fine detail from the first rehearsal. This meant that by the time of dress rehearsal we had only been through the play once. It was an engrossing but nerve-wracking process. Opening night was magnificent but flawed. He had allowed no time to distance himself from detail, to see how the whole hung together and adjust the rhythm. The performances were strong and dramatic but the music needed more variety. It was like hearing a New Orleans blues number played over and over with no change of key.

Wal gave the same treatment to Williams' *Orpheus Descending*, in which he cast me opposite Monica Maughan in my only romantic role. When it came to farce, however, I put my foot down. Farce demands endless repetition in order to master the timing required, so that it can be forgotten in the playing.

Most of us lived in old cottages in Carlton, an inner suburb that had already taken on a strong Italian flavour. The Genevieve coffee shop was a favourite haunt and other, illegal, back rooms provided nights of cheap claret and bibulous discussion. We began to feel like real pioneers in a new world. Big successes, mixed with disasters, simply made life more exciting. Being unafraid of the unusual became the pride of the company. I was reminded constantly of the urgent life I had led with the James family and felt fulfilled in this pioneering atmosphere. Other artists joined the company; I have a particular memory of Barbara Wyndon with whom, in a rare revue, I danced a tango that, I'm proud to say, brought the house down. Audine Leith joined us, to be followed later by actor and writer, Barry Pree, both of whom had been leading members of amateur groups in Adelaide.

Here was a company of actors that somehow combined my experience of both the Family in Wales and the Society in Canberra. For Wal, research was essential in the preparation of any play. His rehearsals always left time for the actor to consider every move or thought the character might have. We were also performing while rehearsing and the work became all-consuming.

Wal's production of *The Threepenny Opera* was, for all of us, our first experience of Brecht. It was also my first taste of great musical drama. This was, without any doubt, Wal's most ambitious venture; a cast of 22 actors with an orchestra of six and a musical director in William Fitzwater. Rehearsals were divided between music and drama, and it was a busy four weeks for everyone. We had all heard about the famous 'alienation effect' that meant distancing emotion from the audience. This, however, was quite beyond me. I had spent my whole career seeking communion with the audience. To alienate them seemed madness. With rebellion in my heart I nodded a great deal as Wal tried to explain—and then got on with it. Years later, I attended a lecture given in London by Helene Weigel, Brecht's leading actress and wife. A member of the audience asked her to explain the theory.

She smiled, paused and then murmured, 'It means you need very, very good actors.'

Despite our ambition to deliver the best and the latest, audience attendance was vital, if the company was to continue. A satisfied audience is the only gauge by which actors can convince themselves that they are of use to a community.

Wal's association with his audience was a constant mix of ups and downs. The tumultuous applause given to *Streetcar* was balanced by the silent fury pervading the theatre during an ill-chosen production of the Greek comedy, *Lysistrata*, in a new American translation. I recall with shuddering horror my entrance through the audience as the Judge, dressed in wig and gown. This entrance was halfway through the play, by which time the audience had had enough and I felt their anger like a freezing wind as I swept down the aisle. A more demonstrative audience would have booed us off the stage. Jimmie James would have buried the play by the final curtain—but then, the Family always had another play ready to take its place. When a subscription season dictates the number of performances the choosing becomes all too important.

Such responsibilities, however, were not yet mine but a hint of what was to come was on its way: my first effort as a director.

One day Wal stopped me outside the Union, and challenged me to direct a play with the company.

'I'm not a director,' I laughed, 'and besides, what play?'

'Anything you like,' the appalling, smiling man said.

I wandered Carlton, trying to decide. Such an extraordinary idea had never entered my head. I was perfectly happy being an actor. I knew nothing about directing. I thought of Ralph Wilson and the extraordinary sweep of knowledge he brought to bear as he conducted rehearsals. I could not do that. I did not have the education of either Ralph or Wal, nor the capability to take the long view required in directing a play. My life was centred on the character I was to play.

However, the fact that I did not immediately refuse Wal's offer suggested, even to me in my reluctant mood, that the idea was worth considering. In hindsight I think it had much to do with what my future might be as an actor. I would never be given Hamlet to play or a Henry IV or, in my old age, a King Lear. I was talented as a character actor in comedy and to a great extent I was content with this. However, as a director I might get close to these iconic characters in a much more intimate way than playing Osric or the Fool.

By the end of the weekend I had made the rash decision: to say 'yes'; and to choose a play that I loved, but which I knew would also prove myself better as an actor. I had been reading the plays of the Spanish writer Federico Garcia Lorca.

'*Blood Wedding*,' I said to Wal.

'Fantastic,' he replied.

How to begin! I had no idea how a director thought. All my thinking, reflexes and instinctive action were focused on a single character. I thought of a violinist in an orchestra who only thinks of his role in the

The author's first attempt at direction: a Union Theatre Repertory Company
production. Patricia Conolly, Georgina Batterham, Rilla Stephens and Monica
Maughan in *Blood Wedding*.

symphony, leaving it to the conductor to place him in the whole. This
suggested that the director should know the play in such detail that
he knew the characters intimately, where they fitted into the play and
how they communicated its rhythm and meaning. But what was the
meaning of the play? All those words in three acts and they amounted
to what? I suddenly saw before me a mountain to climb. I set off for
the nearest equipment store—the University Library.

By the first day of rehearsal my mind was crammed with Spain.
I had all but learnt the language as I talked and talked. What I put
those actors through! Here was I, an actor like those in front of me,
behaving like a history teacher, determined to fill their minds with
Spanish mythology, with Lorca's views on life and all the meanings
that might lie behind the sparse dialogue. It's a wonder they survived.
But, Oh! I did have a good time.

A splendid New Zealand actor, Rilla Stephens, played the Mother,
Monica Maughan the bride, Patricia Conolly the lover and Audine

Leith the old woman. Other actors filled Lorca's female world and, I believe, did great justice to this play. The men, led by Robin Ramsay, were equally important, but it is the women I remember.

Of all the sins in which this first-time director indulged, demonstrating must be one of the worst. I was an actor, I could not help it. The conductor does not tell the violinist how to play the violin. He talks about the music and leaves the playing to those who play. This I have learned over the years, but it took a long time to let go of the instrument, remain outside the rehearsal space, observe, comment and supply the performer with the world that surrounds them, firing their imaginations with ideas they can use.

I knew it was wrong but I knew no other way. Instead of one character I now had many to bring to life. I even took to composing music for the play. Consultation with designers for the set, costumes and lighting were daily commitments and I began to see how busy the life of a theatre director could be. My excitement knew no bounds.

One day, arriving for rehearsal, Wal introduced me to an old man whose name was Jubal. He was a Russian teacher and director who had managed his own company in Vienna before the war. He was now retired, living in Melbourne with his sister. On my invitation Jubal watched a run-through of *Blood Wedding*, now just a week from opening night. At the end I gave a mountain of notes to the actors and programmed another run the following morning. Jubal offered nothing other than a quiet 'thank you' and a request that he might talk to the actors tomorrow.

The following day I sat back to watch and listen to the wisdom of this European director. But to my horror he simply asked the actors to run through the early scenes that set the tragic events in progress, and send the whole thing up. The actors leapt at the game and turned the play into a romp, accompanied by shrieks of laughter from both the actors and Jubal. I watched in growing consternation. At the end of this travesty, Jubal, who had avoided me all this time, then asked them to repeat it, but with the serious intention their director required, and reminded them they were playing ordinary people. This they did and I sat watching the fruits of my first lesson as a director. The actors were playing human beings instead of archetypes. The tragedy became one about real people.

I went for a walk around the University grounds with Jubal and he talked about Lorca and the problem of reconciling the abstract and symbolic nature of the story with that of ordinary human beings caught up in jealousy and revenge. He made me think of Jimmie and his family and how such passion can rip people apart. A very quiet director spent the next few days with his actors, trying hard to see what all this implied.

Finally, opening night arrived. After all that work and preparation, I suddenly felt useless, wandering around with nothing to do and having to let go of something that had been very precious. Then, suffering the fires of hell, I had to watch the actors' fine work receive no more than polite applause from a lack-lustre audience. I went into a tailspin. It was my fault. A failure, before I had time to begin. No more! No more! Wal was comforting and complimentary, but I remained firm. No more! A criticism of appalling rudeness was printed in the daily newspaper and every word seared itself into my heart. Ever since, after years of being ambushed by both informed and ill-informed critics who remain faceless, I have made the effort to avoid their judgments. The audience is my master.

Days later, when the performance had became too painful to watch, I was sitting in the Union café over a cup of tea.

A voice said: 'Well, you got him all wrong.'

I looked up to find a tall, graceful student standing over me.

'Prove it.' I said.

Germaine Greer proceeded to do so. She sat down with her coffee and talked about what it might be like to be a woman in Lorca's world.

Ideas poured from her and I listened with every pore open. Her eyes sparkled as she talked. Gazing at her, I guessed even then that one day she would take the world by the throat. I took the afternoon conversation to the actors and her words opened other gates. For the rest of the season we continued to work as much as we could, given that the poor actors were rehearsing another play.

A further walk with Jubal brought wisdom and sense to my bleak mind. Although misdirected in many ways, the play and Lorca's world of poetic tragedy had also been difficult for an Australian audience to comprehend, when not even his poetry was familiar. One important discovery I made was the extraordinary stillness these Spanish characters had about them. Their passion would rise like a whirlwind out of this stillness, transforming the scene, as Spanish dancing does. It was a palliative time for me and my heart stopped hammering.

The break brought us all down to earth. The students began their new year in February and the theatre would not be ours again until September. What to do? With six months to fill in, my life was precarious. Wal had offered me a contract for the following season—as an actor, thankfully, and I had *Blood Wedding* memories to occupy me. The thing would be to get an ordinary job for the months intervening, as there was still nothing offering in our theatre-less country, apart from the occasional J.C. Williamson musical. News had come from Sydney of the proposed formation of Robin Lovejoy's Trust Players, but that would take another year.

As I was about to take a casual job in a Government filing office, offers began to come my way from the student drama clubs, with perhaps just enough money to keep me alive, doing this scary thing called directing. At first I refused, tempting as it was to earn money in the only business I knew. To direct again and come another cropper? No way! Then a young playwright by the name of Alan Hopgood introduced himself and we talked. He had written an epic play called *Marcus*, an everyman tale set in a world of fantasy, and he had the opportunity to present it at the Union. Would I direct it? I told him I had decided not to direct again—but, perhaps, just once more, just to prove a point. I could not believe I had said 'yes'. He seemed to think I was right for the job.

It became an exciting adventure to direct this, his first play. It was my first experience of working with students, and they gave all their enthusiasm and young talent to the making of it. Prepared as I was for another flop, I was surprised by the response and began to feel more confident. The writing had a certain romantic naïveté but

Alan's talent was obvious. *And the Big Men Fly*, his popular comedy about Australian Rules football, would bear me out a few years later when it took Melbourne by storm. It would take another decade for the young Turks Jack Hibberd and David Williamson to emerge from Melbourne's universities, but the scene was already being set for a new wave of Australian writing.

The Marlowe Society then asked me to direct them in a production of Labiche's *An Italian Straw Hat*. Wal had given me a taste of French farce when I played in Feydeau's *Hotel Paradiso* and suddenly the idea of directing a comedy seemed absolutely right. So, from tragedy and epic theatre I turned to what I knew best. The play had a cast of twenty-five and the audition period was fascinating. Here was my opportunity to find some way of auditioning which would be less of a nightmare for the actors: by not being discovered behind a desk, going to meet them as they entered, sitting with them on a bench, reading through a scene with them in a relaxed manner and moving gradually into performance. These small things made a big difference, but it meant that instead of a ten-minute call, twenty-five minutes passed. The day went slowly, but productively, and I discovered some excellent student actors.

In the middle of this process, a young law student with an obvious flair for comedy presented himself. This young man, Leon Lissek, would soon join the profession to become a successful actor on the Union stage and then in England with Peter Brook's Theatre of Cruelty project and in film. He also became a lifelong friend. Other future professionals included an Englishman, John Joyce, immediately cast in a central role as the Father of the Bride; and Paul Eddy, a sharp young actor who would also achieve great success. John Ellis became an influential acting teacher and with his wife Lois would later establish the theatre company, the Church, in Hawthorn. Along with the playwrights, so much of the healthy new wave was beginning to emerge from these University walls.

Germaine Greer walked in on the day of auditions, informing me that I needed her around just to make sure I did less damage to French sensibilities than I had done to Spanish; so I cast her as the Countess. (Without an audition—I didn't dare!) It gave me much malicious pleasure to later advise her, unsolicited, that although her presence on stage was spectacular, it would be unwise of her to make acting her future profession.

Labiche was well served by a hilarious opening night, accompanied by the music Jacques Ibert had composed for the play. Once more I was aware of the magic music can infuse into a play as the wedding party, led by the Bride and her Father, lost in the labyrinth of mistaken moments, struggled to find the Groom.

My first attempt at directing comedy had been, for me, a sort of success and I began to wonder then whether I could pursue directing. In the meantime, as my second season with Wal began, I gratefully slipped back into the familiar role of actor.

In Shakespeare's comedy *Love's Labour's Lost* there is an entrance that has haunted me ever since I directed a student production. It is that final moment when love has triumphed and the world seems to be filled with laughter. Then a dark figure is seen approaching. Mercade is here to announce the death of the Princess's father, dissolving the rosy glow of romance and forcing the young lovers to face reality.

In February 1958 I was playing at the Union in *Lola Montez*, the first musical comedy I'd ever been cast in. It was a new musical with libretto by Alan Burke, who also directed us, music by Peter Stannard and lyrics by Peter Benjamin. To have the chance to sing and dance was a thrill every night. With friends like Patricia Conolly, Alan Hopgood, Frank Gatliff and Neil Fitzpatrick in the cast, my life could not have been more complete.

Mercade's entrance came in the shape of a telegram, which our stage director Ron Field had withheld until the final curtain. It was from my brother Jim, and told me of our father's collapse and sudden death. Ron and Patricia bundled me into the car and took me to their apartment. I could not cry or feel anything that night. It was like some distant dream.

Next day I flew home. Only when I met Jim outside our house did a dam of tension burst and we stood, clinging to each other, sobbing out our grief and bewilderment. For me it was for a father I hardly knew, I had spent too many years away from home. Now it was too late and my only tangible memento was the one letter he wrote me, expressing his love and hope for my future. It was harder for my young sisters who were barely teenagers; and for Nancy, his eldest daughter, whose coming baby he would never see.

Our mother bore up bravely over the next days, but that dreaded event of the funeral had to be endured. The church was filled with the Scottish community and many people witnessed their affection and respect for a man who had battled and endured through all the bad times, without complaint and with a smile and a wry humour everyone loved. I remembered as a young boy peeking down the hall to see him arrive home late one night with a group of businessmen, all the worse for wear. He sat them around our huge kitchen table and presented each one with a bottle of milk as a nightcap. Often, over the years, I would open his letter and memories would flood back of this quiet man with his quizzical smile under his trilby hat.

My brothers shouldered the problems of the immediate future and security of my mother and sisters, while I flew back to Melbourne, to resume performing. How easily one page from a book of memories disposes of a person's life. My father, having become an artist in the world of bread and confectionery, had battled for nearly forty years to keep his family and maintain his self-respect. I loved him for his courage, for his mistakes and for his enduring love of his family.

The year 1958 will remain in my memory principally for my father's death, but the later months held a further wrenching sadness in the life I was leading in the theatre. Jubal, that wonderful, funny Stanislavski student from Russia, had become more and more attached to my career and me. He had come to feel that he had within him a last possibility to create a company of actors dedicated to his beloved Russian playwrights. Other actors within the company also fell under the old master's spell. In a shock decision, six of us resigned from the UTRC and began work, without pay, on the birth of a new company. Wal was devastated. It was the end of the season and his contract for September was not renewed.

No forward planning was done for our new project. We would meet Jubal in the evenings at his home and begin a long study and rehearsal of Gorky's *Lower Depths*. I managed to find a job in the filing department of the Treasury and set myself a new timetable. The evenings were spent developing the intense concentration needed to become a character from Gorky. Jubal was convinced that I should continue to be an actor and cast me as the Actor in the play. At times even a workaholic like me found the going exhausting. But I never regretted a moment of the effort required for that journey into the Russian soul, filled with despair and passion. After months of such work with us, Jubal became ill and rehearsals came to a halt. Having left one company so emotionally, we were unprepared for this new crisis and prayed for his recovery, but our hope was sadly unfulfilled. He died soon after, unable to complete his last venture, and we who had become so attached to old master shared his tragedy. He had taught us much and his legacy remains with us.

I continued working at the Treasury, unsure of where to go next. I rented a small flat and with my salary as a filing clerk managed quite nicely. For some weeks I contented myself with dreaming and eating well. Out of work! The season was finished and Wal Cherry was already making plans to begin his own company in South Melbourne. As I was not a member of the company when he left I heard only rumours about his departure from the University. It had been obvious, although he never spoke about it, that the company had been losing money. Wal chose to ignore the consequences. None of us were really aware at the time of our departure that his contract would not be renewed. I remain grateful to this man who gave so many artists the opportunity to grow and learn to be proud of the title 'actor'.

As my exit from the Union had been fraught with tension I could not bring myself to ring him. Better to seek work elsewhere, but where that might be was anybody's guess. The year began with my mother and young sisters established in a new home. The family was growing, with new children for Jim and my young brother Robbie.

The Union Theatre Repertory Company, 1959. Joan Harris, Janne Coghlin and
Frederick Parslow in *A Taste of Honey*.

One morning in 1959 the phone rang and a voice said, 'Hello, George,
John Sumner here. What are you doing with yourself?'

'Oh, hello, John. Well, I'm working at the Treasury, as a matter of
fact.'

'Oh, yes? I was thinking, it's time you came back to the Union, isn't
it?'

'Well, yes, that would be nice. Are you back there?'

'Well, someone had to fix it all up.'

'Oh.'

'Wondering if you'd like to come back and do some directing as well?'

'Oh, but that would be... wonderful.'

'Good. Could you pop in today and talk about it? A lot to do—has to be quick.'

'Oh, yes, yes, I'll come in this morning.'

So began an association that claimed the greater part of my career in the theatre. Back at the Union! Back to the old stamping ground, to a theatre I knew well. Back to meet old friends, find new ones and begin directing alongside John. A few of us found a tenement house to rent in Gratton Street, Carlton, called Stella Di Roma, not far from the Union and established a place for sleeping, eating, drinking and talking late into the night. Among the actors who shared the house were Barry Pree and Graeme Hughes, an actor and German scholar. Many nights were spent talking about heading for Europe—a plan that gradually fused into reality, but not yet. John gave me the opportunity to take on directing as well as acting, and I began to understand what being a director could mean.

A memorable play for me was Shelagh Delaney's *A Taste of Honey*. Along with a great cast and a superb set from Anne Fraser, John gave me the chance to direct my first modern play. The hard, passionate world of the English working class required total commitment which the cast, Janne Coghlan, Joan Harris, Charles Haggith and Fred Parslow gave unstintingly. I consider it to be the first good production of my career. My heart was at last telling me that perhaps the right choice had been made.

A production of *The Ghost Train* brought back the days with the Family, as Arnold Ridley's classic thriller took shape with Freddie, Joan and Charlie giving it all its melodramatic power. A very young Lyndel Rowe was also in the cast. This pretty little girl, usually cowering in the corner doing ASM duties, came to trembling life on stage. I knew immediately that a major talent was here in the making. She would become important in my life as actor and friend.

Man and Superman proved complex and difficult; Bernard Shaw's rhetoric needs voices of great strength and colour, which was hard for a young cast. This play called out for the experienced talents of James

Bailey and Clem McCallin, but Goldsmith's *She Stoops to Conquer* was a play I loved and would attempt again in future years; a later play than *The Beaux' Stratagem*, and full of joys.

A tour of Victoria was also a strong reminder of early days, as we played *Sweeney Todd*. It gave me a chance, in the title role, to revive all the passionate seriousness which the Family had taught me to bring to melodrama. Although the play is one which an audience is bound to enjoy as a horror show, it is all the more important that we, the actors, should use our talents to make that horror as effective as it must have been to its original audiences. One engaging young actor making his comedy debut in this play was Bob Hornery.

Research was now becoming a serious preoccupation and my reading list and library began to grow. I began reading, for the first time, the history of the *commedia dell'arte* and the way the artists worked with mask. I knew that if I wanted to learn more on any practical level about the history of my profession, I would need to go elsewhere. About this time I began reading of the Genoa Stabile company in Italy, who still trained their actors in the traditional style and presented some of their scripts using the ancient masks. Though life at the Union continued to be stimulating, my thoughts and plans for Europe began to take shape as my bank balance slowly grew.

One memory remains as a highlight of this time and became, for me, the first truly innovative way of doing theatre that I had yet experienced. John Sumner presented the company with a play, *Moby Dick Rehearsed*, adapted by Orson Welles from Herman Melville's novel, *Moby Dick*. John proposed to present it at the Union, casting Frank Thring in the main role; the role that Welles had played in London. This play gave Frank the chance to shine, and shine he did. *Moby Dick Rehearsed* was my first experience as an actor of a production that discovered its life and setting in rehearsal; and it was almost unbearably exciting. The stage was stripped so as to appear like the stage of an old theatre where a production of *King Lear* is about to be rehearsed. Instead, the space is slowly transformed into the deck of Herman Melville's *Pequod* as an old actor creates a drama of the sea with the company, taking the role of the obsessed Captain Ahab. As the play proceeds, parallels with the character of King Lear become apparent.

Only objects and material used on any stage were employed to create the ship and the terrible seas that surrounded it, so that a furled sail was simply a rolled stage-cloth, partly hanging from its curtain line. Ladders were propped up for sailors to climb, and old boxes from the corner became the poop deck. A small thrust stage built over the audience became the small boat used to chase and harpoon the whale in the final dramatic scenes.

For the first time in my career, lighting became important and John revealed his knowledge of the art form. Although I was in the cast, I made sure I watched this process of something totally new to me. These days, the lighting design is as important as that of both the set and costumes, but the radical innovations of the 1960s in theatre design were then still in their infancy.

Moby Dick Rehearsed took us to Sydney, where it further established our reputation as a theatre of true worth, in a country just beginning to realise what its artists could offer. It was while touring that I began to think, for the first time, a career as a director in Australia might just be possible.

However, work was still scarce and the Trust Players' Company had a sadly short life. In 1960 actors were still looking towards London; the drain continued without a murmur from those in authority. On the contrary, it was taken for granted that an artist needed to go overseas to further their craft and reputation; Australia was like that. I became more and more interested in Europe and what I could learn there both as performer and director.

One day, John drove me downtown to a tiny theatre in Russell Street, close to Flinders Street. From the moment we walked into it I fell in love with it. Though I did not know it at the time I would do what I still consider to be my best work in this magical space. I call them the Golden Years—but that was to come. The Russell Street Theatre was to give John the chance to establish a permanent company of actors, away from the student atmosphere of the University and by so doing begin a real revival of theatre-going in Melbourne.

With my bank balance now sufficient to take me to Europe and study for a while, I took my plan to him, afraid I would distress him by abandoning the company at this crucial moment. Memories of leaving the Family still haunted me, but the idea was too exciting to ignore and my intention was an absence of no more than a year. John was immediately encouraging and offered a generous grant to help me on my way. I planned my exit to follow a last production for the company. *The Mystery of a Hansom Cab* was a late nineteenth-century thriller by Fergus Hume, set in Melbourne, which Barry Pree successfully adapted for the stage. The huge cast enjoyed themselves, as did the audience. This production would see more seasons.

When I study the photograph of the cast and those within this chapter of work, I see a group of pioneers: actors with talent and determination, who caused the theatre to grow and become important in our lives. Australia should be proud of them. Their love for their own country would keep them hammering at the door of indifference until they came through. For five years I had lived and worked with them; all with hope in their hearts that their creativity would earn them a respected place in the culture of their country; and put an end to the old prejudice that being an actor was not a profession.

The Union Theatre Repertory Company, 1960. Frank Thring leads the cast of
Moby Dick Rehearsed. (Photo: Harry Jay)

It felt strange boarding a huge liner again. Now it was 1960 and eight years had passed since my last exit from Australia; but now I was without the bitterness I had felt then. Effort was being made by some people to recognise the artist. They were still very few but this time I made no vow never to return.

I intended leaving the ship at Naples, taking the train for Genoa. An actress friend from the company, Dorothy Bradley, was on board and we spent many hours tackling the Italian language and avoiding the continuous music pouring out of two orchestras. Poor Dorothy was very seasick during the voyage and I felt guilty that once again I felt nothing but exhilaration as each day brought us closer to the Suez Canal and that extraordinary shipboard experience passing thrugh the locks as if the ship were carving out a passage over land. Over the years I have regretted so much the decline of sea travel, with its leisure and adventure. The few hours air travel takes allows no time for reflection.

Fate stepped in, in the form of a letter awaiting me at Naples from Roslyn de Winter, another Union company friend, who was living and working in Paris. Roslyn entreated me, before making a decision on Genoa, to come to Paris and meet an extraordinary teacher called Jacques Lecoq who taught not only the theatre of the *commedia* but the study of space on stage. This sounded too exciting to ignore. I packed my bags and prepared to leave the ship. Then doubts began to invade. Having set my mind on the Genoa Stabile, why change it at this last moment? And what about the language? I thought about my school French. What the hell! Lecoq sounded appealing and I was here to experience Europe. A quick trip overnight on a European train and then, if I did not like it, a return to Italy.

I bought a sleeping car berth, but found my compartment already occupied by a beautiful French woman. In embarrassment I gathered up my belongings, stammered apologies and left in confusion to seek my correct booking. The steward brought me back to my original berth where the woman was sitting, quietly smoking a cigarette. I froze in the doorway and began stammering apologies. '*Allez-y*,' she said, '*N'inquietez-pas*', and ushered me, baggage and all, to the seat opposite her. I sat uneasily, wondering what the protocol was for sleeping in this tiny, Marx Brothers cabin. This was all very well for sophisticated Europeans, but I suffered all the Puritan scruples my Presbyterian upbringing could foster in me. However, her charm soon relaxed me, and I began to enjoy the journey, telling my story in my pitiful French, with many prompts from Michelle. I wondered whether a sexual encounter might be part of the trip, but recalled the handsome Italian I had seen her with on the Naples platform. I soon vanished into the top bunk, much to her amusement.

As the night wore on, the rocking train lulled me to sleep, but soon woke, almost feverish, asking myself that question again. Why? Why this move to Paris, to Europe, with a career opening up for me back in Melbourne? After all, I was now twenty-eight and a new life as a director had been offered to me. I thought back to the bus ride which began my career, without any training or planning—just the need to act and the instincts I knew were within me. Then came Canberra and a world of research opened up.

To know more! That was it. To understand and be able to convey that understanding in performance.

Europe beckoned me with its glorious past. Words played around in my mind; words that offered an invitation to explore—*commedia dell'arte*, the Renaissance, the Sun King, Lully and Molière, the Enlightenment and the operas of Mozart—and then the Romantic movement of great music and painting. So many ideas, so much creativity, so much to learn and understand.

I listened to this voice inside me that kept encouraging me. I needed the experience of Europe to understand the canon of great plays. Also, as a performer still, I wanted more. Having toyed with the idea of studying dance, I knew my talent still fed on the clown. To study with people who understood the art of silence and gesture and what space meant on stage was irresistible. I suddenly felt good about this move. I woke up next morning with an excited heart.

As the train slid into the huge Gare de Lyon my new friend wished me luck and I watched her step onto the platform. An austere, distinguished middle-aged man was waiting for her. Her husband! He kissed her gently and, as he swept her away, she looked back and smiled goodbye with a gentle, raised eyebrow; my first taste of European mores. Then Roslyn de Winter was there, hurrying along the platform towards me. I picked up my bag and leapt onto the platform. We embraced and she took my arm.

'Come on, come and see Paris.'

The author (left) as Arlecchino on French television.

Four

THE MIME

Enfin Paris

I had been here before! I was installed temporarily in an old hotel in Montparnasse and Roslyn took me to meet Jacques Lecoq at his Studio of Mime in the rue du Bac in the sixth *arrondissement*. Upon meeting this vibrant young man I astonished myself by paying a year's fees and was accepted as a pupil to start the following day. Why did I do this? Roslyn returned to her duties as an *au pair* and now I was wandering alone through the streets of Paris. I had been here before. Or was it only a fancy? I was breathless with awe. This ancient city had, within hours, captured me, heart and soul. I would never escape. As each day followed the next it still felt familiar, as if I had an arcane right to be here.

Some weeks later I was walking alone through the Marais. In 1960 much of this old district still stood, exuding the past like a vibrating heart. I turned a corner and stopped suddenly, catching my breath in horror. I was no longer in modern clothes but in the garb of the seventeenth century. They were well-worn garments with a patched jacket, wrinkled stockings and old shoes, and my hair was hanging over my face. I knew at once that I was an actor, hurrying on my way to rehearse a play for the King. This moment seemed to last forever and then dissolved, leaving me panting and sick from the experience. It would be years before I could talk about that day, even to close friends.

This moment remains one of my most vivid memories. It tied me to the city. Over the following forty years I would return again and again to fill my soul with the past until finally, with the purchase of a small studio in the eleventh *arrondissement*, I would call it my home. I find myself absurdly proud of living in the quarter which is known as the Quartier Rouge, the birthplace of socialist unrest and the home of Léon Blum, the first Jewish president of France and leader of the *Front Populaire* in the years leading up to World War II.

A pair of black tights, a T-shirt, bare feet, a fast-beating heart, and I was ready for my first class with Jacques Lecoq in his studio. In rapid French, not one word of which I understood, Lecoq welcomed the students and began the day with exercises. Standing well back behind twenty students, I followed them and soon found myself relaxing a little and enjoying the hard physical work. And hard it was. For half an hour we focused on *équilibre*, achieved without tension. It had to be done with knowledge and ease. To stand on one foot with slightly bent knee and to know how to keep that balance while focusing on another action became the foundation of our work in those first few months. Lecoq would repeat this question until we understood:

'What happens to the body when it acts, or is acted upon, by the movement of pulling, pushing, straining, lifting, climbing, gesturing, carrying, throwing, catching, hitting, walking, running and even riding a bicycle?'

And once we understood this, 'How do we simulate it to make the action look perfect?'

How many years of work lay ahead of this task? And this was only the beginning. In the weeks that followed, I became fascinated by Lecoq's intensity. His ability to bring alive the movements and objects used in each action brought gasps from the students; but there was something else. From time to time a student would make a movement more dance-like than real and Lecoq would go ballistic. '*La vie n'est pas une danse,*' he would say. '*Cherchez la vérité.*'

In searching for the truth I discovered his aim—to find poetry in real, even commonplace movement. Just as a painter like L.S. Lowry found poetry in the mundane and sometimes ugly life of his industrial North, so Lecoq looked for poetry in the movement of climbing a wall, opening a window, rowing a boat, pushing the movement into an emotional and abstract world, but always keeping in touch with the reality. To see someone climb through a window is just that, an action to be taken for granted. But in bringing the window alive before one's eyes in the action of climbing through it, something else is created. The climber and the window become one and the result, if done with skill and grace, becomes a poetic expression of living and doing.

The following months were ones of exploration. Lecoq would prowl among the students, watching their progress, seeing his instructions were followed; but what was even more stimulating was his search for more; to encourage the student to go further. It was this concept of open exploration that would so affect my own future. Unafraid to say, 'I don't know,' he would urge the student on, to show him the way—and then, with passionate intensity, take up what he saw and push it further.

Roslyn and I practised together whenever her *au pair* duties released her, down on the banks of the Seine. On one occasion, while practising the illusion of physical fighting, a too-enthusiastic swing from Roslyn landed one on my jaw, splitting my lip. It won great applause from an audience of workers watching nearby.

I was intrigued to discover how few French pupils there were in class. We were Japanese, English, Polish, Swiss, American, and French Canadian but very few Parisians. They were all studying voice in studios down the road, I was told. To the classically-trained actor in France the voice meant everything.

'In each one lies the heart of a character, a window into a human being, created by a fine artist. Treat them with the respect they deserve.'

With these words Lecoq introduced us to the world of mask. Laid out carefully on a long table was a selection of half-masks, waiting to come alive. As we gazed at them, a pupil lifted one and was about to put it on when the angry voice of Lecoq demanded he put it down.

'This is not playtime. You must be ready to receive a mask.'

Later I would understand what he meant and the reason for his almost ritual awe of this art form. It was like looking at the score of a Mozart sonata, a lifeless object until the musician picks up his instrument and plays the composition. The mask needed to be worn by an artist who would subject his or her whole being to the image in the mirror and respond with body and heart to the creation of a character. We were not permitted to choose a mask for ourselves but were handed one by another pupil, so that thoughts already formed by glimpsing a mask on the table would not inform what confronted us in the long mirror. The effect must be immediate, spontaneous; within moments we would bring what we discovered out into the world. Many attempts failed; but when a true concordance of mask, body and spirit occurred, the result was magical. It never lasted longer than some seconds, but after many experiments with the same mask, a character started to emerge, with attitude, voice and a reason for living. Over many hours of experiment and study we managed to achieve living, breathing characters. Clothes were donned, some even acquired names and dialogue with other masked characters.

The world of mask continued with the Neutral Mask. Without leaving the world of reality, these superbly-moulded full male/female masks gave the pupil an opportunity to take the body through imagination into the abstract. The student's face was completely hidden behind the mask and the body language became all-important. By the use of pure mime the man/woman now struggled against the elements of wind and fire, becoming in turn like a fish in the sea, or a mythic figure experiencing the passion of grief or the glory of nobility. Here the hero/heroine told their story in broad sweeping strokes, allowing the student to push their body into unexpected grace.

As if to bring the student back to a human perspective, the joys of *commedia dell'arte* followed. A collection of half-masks, which a great caricaturist might draw, moulded into shape by the hands of the great Italian mask-maker Satori, were offered to us, and the rangy students began to act out the avaricious Pantalone and the cowardly capers of Il Capitano. The more portly students explored the self-important Il Dottore and the smaller active students like myself Arlecchino, the rascally clown of the *commedia* world. Alas for the poor girls, to whom only a derivative Arlecchinetto was available. These glorious masks, retaining their history and their eternal qualities, led us into the past as nothing else could. I treasure the one photograph I have of my appearance on French television performing Arlecchino.

The study of pure mime, character mask, neutral mask and the *commedia*, became intense; to these was added, in later months, the exploration of the Greek chorus. At first I regarded this study as distant from my immediate preoccupation. It was not until later that I understood that within this work lay the reason for my being at the school in the first place; and how, through its application, I would find ways of choreographing the movement of actors on stage.

On stage, as in life, there are those who listen and those who speak, those who move and those who remain still. There are leaders and there are followers. And these attributes are given not only by the words they utter but by the way others move and focus their attention. By exploring two antagonists and their followers, first with words and then without, a thousand possibilities opened up in that little studio. This exploration would become the foundation of all the teaching I was to do in later years, when study of a scene uncovered the power struggle at the heart of the text.

The prevailing memory of these years in Paris, however, is that of being hungry. I had already decided to stay another year in Paris and, after paying the fees, my savings and generous grant came to a very thin bag of francs. My mother, anxious for my health in foreign parts and convinced I would end up as a *clochard* (one who lives by their wits in the streets of Paris) sent me regular sums of money and, thanks to her generosity, I kept going. It became necessary to leave my lovely old hotel, my room was needed. I discovered to my embarrassment that it was a high-class brothel. Instead I found a tiny *chambre de bonne* or maid's room on the fifth floor of an apartment building in the sixth *arrondissement*. It was unfurnished, filthy, without electric light or heat and the lavatory was at the end of the corridor; but I had it in exchange for cleaning two sets of staircases on five floors each morning before class. In the flea market I bought a few necessities, a mattress, a kerosene heater, a kerosene lamp—the smell of kerosene will always be mixed up with memories of Paris—and a long mirror for my daily practice. I made it livable. My strength and resilience gained through class made life an adventure, even if the succulent smell of French food wafting from a restaurant as I strolled by with my bag of chips was at times hard to bear. Some evenings were topped off with *soupe à l'oignon* at Les Halles, watching the fruit and vegetable trucks arriving into Paris for the morning markets. Here I was like Chekhov's eternal student, happy to continue learning for the rest of my life.

The hypnotic and ancient beauty of Paris remained a constant as I wandered through old passages and lanes. The only way I could occasionally go to the theatre was to stand in the top gallery. Friends introduced me to their system. During the course of the first act we would note the empty seats in the front stalls and just as the first act came to an end would rush downstairs, avoiding the ushers, and spend the rest of the evening in comfort.

The 1960s were already promising a new freedom. Truffaut and the New Wave in French cinema had taken off. In the theatre Beckett, Ionesco and Genet had thrown off the shackles of realism. In the UK the Beatles were about to audition for the BBC and Bob Dylan made his first appearance. A few years before, John Osborne had created a furore in London with *Look Back in Anger* and the small world in which I moved began throwing off the old and looking towards a new non-conformist tomorrow. On the dark side was the war in Algeria. Army tanks stood on every street corner and terrible daily news of the death in the Seine of *Pieds Noirs* (French Algerians), dying from the hate and anger of a country losing its colony. I remember with dread thousands of students marching down the avenues shouting, *'Algérie Française!'*

Courage mounted in class as my understanding of both Lecoq and French grew through the winter months. Every class was exciting and every day a challenge.

So what was this passion of mine to endure this poverty? Anyone can be a student. All you need is to enrol in a course of learning and *voilà!* a student is born. Here was I, in the Paris of 1962, a thirty-year-old actor among eighteen- and nineteen-year-olds. As I swept and scrubbed my ten floors of stairs in the early hours, I puzzled about my motivation.

Every morning at the end of class, the studio would erupt with energy and purpose. A quick cup of coffee in the café below and then the students were off to the next class—drama, perhaps, or voice or dance—or even an audition with a major theatre company. The New Wave in cinema had begun to surge and the air was full of gossip. Life, for most of these teenagers, was brimming with things to do. It left them little time for contemplation, and certainly none for discussing the class just finished.

I found, to my mortification, that I needed to linger over my coffee, to go over in my mind and scribble in my perpetual notebook what the class this morning had taught me. What was the meaning of all those exercises and improvisations? Where did I go wrong? And how could I correct it? What was it Lecoq had said? What did he mean? As the café emptied I was left alone, scribbling, scribbling.

Lunchtime meant attendance at Alliance Française in a desperate effort to improve my French. My knowledge of mime was a much quicker process. My French was fine in the studio, where I became familiar with Lecoq's language, and in my favourite food shops. The problems always came in casual conversations where talk of other things required more attention to the grammar and vocabulary. Paris called constantly to be discovered and lingered over, but I reserved these explorations for the weekend. Weekday afternoons were spent in my little *chambre de bonne* going over the morning class, this time in front of my long mirror, and in inventing ideas for later use. My days were filled with questions and effort.

I made a pact with myself that for each class I would arrive prepared and with some form of improvement to show Lecoq. Young students would gaze in astonishment at *le petit vieux*, as my skills leapt ahead of theirs. When a Canadian colleague asked me how I did it, this 'little old man' confided his hours of daily homework.

'*Mon Dieu*,' he exclaimed, 'that is what I call obsession.'

Is that what it was?

'I don't want to become a mime artist,' he continued. 'I'm simply adding a skill to my repertoire of studies.'

'Nor do I,' I protested. 'But you appear to have difficulty even with some of the basic exercises.'

'Oh, yes,' he replied aimiably, 'but I have no intention of performing them, just using the ideas.'

I said no more but began to study the other students. Some were as serious as I seemed to be, but many improved only slowly and with much frustration. Instead of pursuing their efforts, they were inclined to give over and leave the technical skills to others. Whenever Lecoq called for partners for improvisation I would head for a tiny Japanese student who was as focused as myself. Her face would light up at my approach and we would work together, knowing that between us hours of solitary homework would follow.

My age, of course, contributed to my becoming obsessive. I was now nearly thirty, and studying a difficult physical discipline needed good health and a co-ordinated body. For younger students mime was just another subject to be given attention among their many pursuits. In retrospect I wonder at the pain and suffering I inflicted on myself.

One winter's night, I was shivering in my inadequate bed as the freezing wind moaned across the attic window, when a knock came at the door. I wrapped myself into my dressing gown and opened the door to my old friend Glen Balmford, a poet and folksinger from Adelaide. I apologised for the dark and lit my kerosene lamp with freezing fingers. As the flame lit up my tiny space Glen sighed and murmured:

'Oh, George, it's *La Bohème.*'

'Sod *La Bohème,*' said I. 'Do you have any money?'

Laughing at the absurdity of it, my lifesaving friend took me down to the biggest slap-up supper I'd enjoyed in two years.

Later in the year, Lecoq began to teach us the correct way to tumble. For this *petit vieux* the work was a nightmare, resulting in many a clumsy fall onto the soft mats. At times I felt like an old clown providing entertainment for the kindergarten. Once a week Lecoq sent us to the Modrano Winter Circus to see how we fared. What a thrill it was, even with a heart full of terror, to cross the threshold of this famous building, birthplace of the great European clowns. I would watch a family of brothers who were aerial acrobats, fascinated by their relaxed yet totally focused practice. Every movement, controlled by a safety harness, was repeated until the technique became as natural as a bird taking wing. To watch them soar and glide above was hypnotic.

'Is that obsession?' I asked my Canadian friend.

'*Mon Dieu, oui!*' he replied.

I smiled and continued with my obsessive need to defy the fear as I did a back flip in harness. I was never able to rid myself of the nausea I felt when showing our skills at the studio, but nothing stopped me from trying. Arlecchino is a natural acrobat and my small but compact body was a perfect vehicle for this immortal character.

It soon became obvious which students had succeeded in understanding and absorbing Lecoq's teaching. This required a great deal of attention and concentration and if you fell by the way Lecoq would soon begin to ignore you. Watching the process I would silently sympathise with this great artist, trying to instil into reluctant hearts his vision for the world of physical theatre. Regrettably, at the end of their time these students would leave Paris with the satisfaction of completing a course with a great teacher and pass on their shallow technique to others.

To be a good student, I learnt, is to give one's full attention to the training, not only in order to master in detail the techniques necessary but to understand why. If this is obsessive, so be it. In hindsight I have not a moment of regret for what I put myself through in Paris. Personal comfort meant so little compared to the stimulation of the life led in the studio. But then, I had experienced this before in the Jimmie James Company—the daily discomfort balanced by the thrilling life on stage. Pain and suffering mean very little if the soul is fed. Perhaps they are even essential to it.

As the long summer break loomed I knew I should take a bus to London and work at some job until September, but a notice in a travel agency window changed my mind. That summer the ancient amphitheatre at Epidavros in Greece would open for the first time in over twenty years and promised an extraordinary season. I had enough money for a third class return train fare to Athens and a few theatre tickets. If I slept in my sleeping bag out in the open air, ate olives, cheese and bread and hitchhiked, I could make it. Without thinking about the following year or how I would survive, I began drilling myself in the Greek language and at the end of June took the train out of Paris, heading south-east.

I hoisted my rucksack and waved goodbye to my Greek friend who roared and clanked his truck on towards his farm somewhere in Sparta. Then I turned towards a long avenue of trees and began walking. It was well into the afternoon and the cicadas were already deafening the day with their shrill calls. From time to time small huts revealed uniformed men yarning together. They stopped to stare at the sight of a traveller in shorts and sandals, but did not interrupt my casual walk towards a wooden building at the end of the avenue. Trees gave shade in the still, hot afternoon and at times I paused to breathe in that subtle herbal air that I will always associate with Greece.

Finally, I approached a shabby hut where a grizzled, uniformed man was working. He looked up at my approach and stared as if I were some apparition. In my eagerly practised Greek I told him I wanted a seat for tomorrow's opening night. He continued to stare at me, then smiled broadly and gave vent to a stream of Greek. He soon realised I didn't understand a word.

'American?' he asked haltingly.

'Ochi,' I replied, 'Avstralia.'

'Avstralia!' he said excitedly, and went off on another stream of Greek within which I heard the word 'Melvourni' and knew from my experience in Athens that he had relatives living in Melbourne and that meant I knew them personally.

Being Australian had opened friendly doors from the moment I touched foot on this old and sacred land. Tears formed in his eyes. He slowed down, trying to make me understand, and I was able to discern that his son was there living in Richmond with his young family. In halting Greek I told him that I had lived in Richmond too but that I did not know his son. That did not seem to matter; I was already a relative, and he leant over his wooden counter to give me a bear hug. He then wrote down his son's name and address and pressed it on me. He sat beaming at me, and I had to remind him of my request, adding that I was an actor myself.

'Malista, malista,' he said and brought out a ticket from a small pile in a drawer. I pulled out some money to pay, but he casually gave his head a reverse nod, which means 'No' in Greek, and pointed me smiling towards the teatro. I waved him goodbye and walked up the hill towards a high, ruined wall. This must be it, I thought, but where?

My thoughts collided in mid-conversation as the theatre revealed itself behind the wall.

Epidavros! It lay empty and sleeping in the hot afternoon like an enormous giant fan with sweeping rows of stone seats soaring up to the heavens. They seemed to stare at me like a hushed audience waiting for the play to start, waiting to be brought alive. I stepped lightly onto the sand of the arena. On this very semicircle 2000 years ago masked actors had enacted the very play I was to see tomorrow. I put my backpack down, stood in the centre, opened my arms, and began a speech from *Antigone.* Hæmon, with love in his heart but dread in his soul, tries to persuade his father Creon to have mercy on the sister who has defied tradition for love of a brother. I finished the speech and wondered if Sophocles could hear me; it was all so possible here in this most sacred place. Someone began to clap, and shading my eyes I saw figures standing at the top of the theatre. I was embarrassed and angry to have my reverie so interrupted. I hastily gathered up my rucksack and went forward to sit on one of the stone seats and look back at the arena, where the actors of fifth century BCE Greece performed their plays.

The wall I had first seen was the back wall to the stage, much of it still intact and I sat mesmerised by this holy grail of a place. The theatre had been built against a hill in an extraordinary natural setting, so that the audience could see beyond the stage to the plain of Argos stretching way into the distance. I heard chattering behind me as a group of tourists descended to the stage. I hurriedly picked up my rucksack and climbed the terraces on the other side.

I had been in many top galleries of many theatres in my time, but nothing like this. The tourist group was now far below me but their voices carried as if they were ten feet away. These were acoustics actors dream about. I would be one of 13,000 spectators at the opening night of this first season at Epidavros since before World War II and all of us would hear every word. How I envied the young actors who would take to the stage tomorrow night.

I was equipped to camp outside in the balmy summer evening, with a sleeping bag, small stove and bags of fruit, olives and cheese. That night I dined at the top of the theatre among the trees and fell asleep dreaming of the gods.

In the late afternoon of the following day I was the first who took my seat. People had been arriving all day and were dining at restaurants or picnicking by cars. My seat was halfway up in the middle, and I felt like a king waiting for the troupe to arrive. As the sun slowly sank in the distance the theatre began to fill; early arrivals were given a wonderful performance as the colour faded from the sky. Then huge arc lights replaced the fading light, bathing the theatre and giving the arena a strange glow. *Ajax* was the play for tonight. I knew it began with a prologue from the goddess Athena and an opening chorus of men. I began shivering in anticipation as the excitement in the huge theatre became palpable and the cicadas fell silent.

Suddenly, without warning, a helmeted figure began mounting stairs placed at the side of the stone wall. The audience became hushed and the goddess continued her climb in silence, with only a slight wind blowing through the arches and rippling her gown. She reached the top of the wall and turning towards the audience opened her arms and in a strong melodic voice intoned, '*O Pateras Mou*' (O My Father).

There was a moment of silence—and then the audience around me burst into tears. Like a human avalanche, 13,000 people leapt to their feet, the entire theatre rising as they shouted their joy. I turned my eyes towards the stars, striving to keep back tears. Athena stood, silent, with her arms outstretched. Their ancient theatre had opened again after so many years of conflict and civil war, and the goddess Athena, the divine patroness of Athens, had opened her arms to embrace Greece once more.

She stood silent until the audience settled back in their seats, and then continued her speech. I became aware of a rhythm, like waves on a beach. The audience became more and more conscious of it, until a gasp from some brought everyone's attention to the road seen through the arches and leading to the arena. There, slowly and ceremoniously, a troupe of young men, brushing the ground with their sandals and singing a ritual complaint, danced their way onto the arena. The play had begun.

Ajax is an early play of Sophocles and less known than the later dramas, but as the fortunes of this great Greek general were played out on the sands of Epidavros, the wisdom of its choice became apparent. The audience were instantly captured by what to them was a critique of Greece's catastrophic recent history: two leaders quarrel, bringing about a civil war within the country. As Ajax spoke his last speech of shame and fell on his sword, the audience groaned and wept for his terrible errors and fatal pride. The funeral rites for this fallen hero became a religious ritual, as the chorus chanted their last warning:

> Many are the things that man seeing must understand.
> Not seeing, how shall he know
> What lies in the hand of time to come?

I sat watching the stream of people slowly exit and then slipped up the aisle to the top and hid among the trees. I wanted to be alone with the night and the empty theatre. I sat down on some rocks to have my supper, making a careful cup of tea on my little stove. The evening had stunned me and the sudden memory of the opening ten minutes sent me into a sort of gulping, sobbing fit, swallowed down with bread, tomatoes and tea. An hour later all was quiet as I prepared to bed down.

Suddenly I heard cars arriving and voices filled the air with shouting and laughter. I crept to the top row to look down on the scene. Thirty or so men and women had invaded the theatre, climbing over one another to sit in the rows close to the arena. Lights were set up and they gathered to listen to a central figure. They were actors, I realised. They were here to rehearse a play.

With a thumping heart I sat down in the top row with my pullover wrapped around me to ward off the evening breeze. Some had put on garish head-dresses, while others had tails strapped to their backsides. This was surely a comedy by Aristophanes. I had no idea what play it was, nor could I appreciate any of the things they found funny, but the effect was magical. Fancy being able to rehearse in the theatre itself—and to rehearse at midnight, when the cool of the night made thinking possible. Their excitement rang out in the dark surrounding night and I could feel the joy and comradeship. To be playing out their own 2,000-year-old drama in the original setting; what more could an actor achieve?

Three hours later they called a stop and with the bang of car doors sped off into the dark, leaving me and the stars to dream.

'But you must stay. This year could be very important. You must stay.'

Lecoq's tone was insistent. He turned on his heel and disappeared into his office. Back from the magic of Greece, I was now facing my immediate future. On my hitchhiking return to Paris, having spent my return ticket wandering the islands of Greece, I had paid a call on Delphi and prayed to the gods for guidance and good fortune; but now I found myself very much alone in Paris.

I had money to survive for no more than a month or two. What to do? To work in Paris I needed a visa, which I did not have, and a *carte de séjour* which I did not have. What to do? I could not ask my family for more help. Somehow I must survive and remain with Lecoq. Fortunately I still had my room in the sixth and the staircases to clean. I asked the concierge if I could earn any money doing jobs for the building. She would try for me. She seemed surprisingly grateful to have me back. It would be years before I realised that two hours' hard work every morning and a weekly wash of ten floors more than paid the rent for six square meters without light.

I presented Lecoq with two months' fees, promising to pay the rest as soon as possible. He looked at me severely; fees in advance were a rigid rule. But after the first class of the new year he called me over. He had been asked to present a *commedia* sketch on television, he said, and I was to play Arlecchino.

'It won't pay for the rest of the year but it will help,' he grinned.

I danced home along the Boulevard Raspail. The gods of Delphi had answered my prayers. We had special rehearsals for the *commedia* sketch in which Lecoq cast old friends and actors. It still gives my heart a lurch to remember my entrance, from a window twelve feet high onto the concrete floor of the television studio.

Following this, Lecoq asked me to join the senior students who were presenting a private performance of their work in a neighbouring studio. I was to devise a sketch involving pure mime. It was very exciting to be able to create my own sketch; it would last only a few minutes but took many hours to prepare, many nights in front of the mirror in my cold little room. It was a macabre little story of a man asleep in his bed, disturbed by a party going on next door. He proceeds to take dreadful revenge on his neighbours. The performance pleased Lecoq and brought me to the notice of his assistant teacher, Isaac Alvarez. Isaac was a volatile, super-energetic Israeli who decided I was the funniest thing he'd met in many a year.

As my second year progressed the problem of money yawned once again. (The television experience was exciting, but in the end gained me very little.) One day Isaac invited me to a meal with his French wife Isabel, also a student with Lecoq. We were joined by two other students: Pierre Byland, a young Swiss with remarkable agility and the potential to be a very fine clown; and Julian Chagrin, a dry, rangy Englishman with a bizarre, comic talent. By the end of the evening *Les Rigaudons* were born. The word means 'French country dances'. We were five artists of varied talents and backgrounds, from France, Israel, Switzerland, England and Australia; and we contrived a program that included dramatic mime, poetry and comedy sketches. We later changed the name to *Les Comédiens mimes de Paris*.

Julian and I began working together as a comic mime duo and found we were able to play off each other very compatibly. Julian's wife-to-be, Claude Niderkoén, also a student at the school, began working with us and revealed the fine teacher's talent that would take her to Britain's National Theatre. Working closely with these performers, I was now no longer isolated and began to feel less like a foreigner and more like a European. What is the difference? I've tried to define it; something about connecting with the past? And accepting it as part of living now? Europe might be a vibrant living entity, but it lives as if the past coexists with the present.

Isaac, working feverishly, pulled us together and managed to arrange performances during that autumn and winter. They saved my life at a time when my health was deteriorating and put me back on the stage to relish again the actor's life. The money was poor but enough to keep me breathing.

During the winter season we were invited to play at the famous St Moritz resort in the Alps. The excitement of the train journey over, a picture-postcard scene presented itself as we taxied up snow-covered roads to be enveloped in the hotel welcome. Our performances were well received and in the comforts provided we rehearsed new work. But

I knew I was not well; the months of hard work and too little food were taking their toll. During the performance I would be almost overcome with dizziness. Mime technique requires complete focus and the others noticed my faltering steps. By sheer willpower I survived until our final performance, when, climbing on board the train for the journey home, I collapsed and became delirious. When I awoke I found myself in bed in Julian's hotel in Paris. This good friend had taken charge of my life and continued to pay for all the care I received over the next three weeks as I gradually recovered from the effects of malnutrition.

This was a turning point. I knew I could not complete the next five months with Lecoq without help. Once again my dear mother came to the rescue. Appalled to think I was lying ill on the other side of the world, she made sure I had enough to eat properly over my final months with this strange French teacher I had discovered. For someone who had been taught never to become financially dependent, my plea to the family was a shameful act, but to stay with Lecoq was imperative and I determined that one day I would pay it all back.

As winter turned into spring, Paris became the most perfumed city in the world, with hundreds of florist shops exploding with spring flowers. Everyone was walking their dog and the pavements required careful negotiation. The cafe owners pulled back the winter screens and their outdoor tables became crowded once again as Parisians enjoyed their favourite pastime. Truffaut's *Jules et Jim* filled the cinemas, along with Visconti's glorious *The Leopard*. My world on the rue du Bac continued to excite and inspire.

By this time my French had greatly improved and the daily improvisations for Lecoq transformed from moments of farce to open and unafraid experiment. Lecoq ventured out of his studio and arranged a performance, which we gave in a small exquisite theatre on the Champs-Elysées. Among the spectators was the great Jean-Louis Barrault, whose performance in *Les Enfants du Paradis* has never been surpassed for its poetic inspiration. Meeting him was a great honour.

One morning in May, Isaac announced that we had a contract to play at all the Club Méditerranéan holiday venues during the summer. With whoops of delight we tackled rehearsals and new routines. Four bell-ringing monks became our signature piece to open the new program.

Using all our technique we were able to persuade the audience that bells were actually ringing, and the clowns came to life as harmony gave way to cacophony and disorder. The laughter from the audience became the sound of the bells.

I greeted the end of June with mixed feelings. The Club tour would begin in Greece and I was looking forward to it, but this summer meant saying goodbye to Jacques Lecoq. Despite looking forward to the prospect of money, I knew I could not afford to return to the little studio that had become so important to me.

His last words to me were, 'Take this mime and use it to direct theatre. There lies your path.'

He had recognised the longing I had to apply to theatre everything he had taught me. Through the summer I enjoyed the life of a wandering performer, but these thoughts of the theatre were not far from my mind.

Les Comediens mimes. George, Pierre and Julian farewell Isaac who has ascended to heaven.

Led by a somersaulting, capering Pierre, Isaac pounding a big bass drum and Julian, Isabel and myself with an assortment of cymbals and cowbells, we paraded through the startled village, passing out leaflets for a performance that night in the village square. *Les Comédiens mimes de Paris* were taking a night away from the holiday-makers in their safe and carefully-tended enclaves to entertain the local people. Nothing could have been more like the ancient *commedia*, nor more appropriate on this Greek island. Our stage was a raised platform with improvised curtains and lit by large Tilley lamps.

By the time the show began the square was packed with people. Employing only our bodies, accompanied by music, we gave of our best. At times I would glance down at the silent audience, wondering if they had fallen asleep, but their eyes were wide and their mouths open as they watched the mime come alive. Julian's and my clown fight set them laughing. This mime began with two fearsome masked figures fighting to the death and ended as vengeful but harmless clowns. At last the evening took off. After the performance a huge supper of local Greek food was served and we took the boat back to the Club Méditerranéan resort, pleased with our diplomatic venture. Such experiences were repeated throughout the summer.

With a week off from performances in Yugoslavia, we took a boat up to Venice and spent a few days wandering through the streets and canals of this fabulous city. Our entrance into Venice was made through the Grand Canal and, as the sun set over the golden domes, I leant over the deck rail dreaming of the past and murmuring to myself, 'All we need now is Vivaldi.' An impeccably dressed old man was standing nearby, reading a newspaper. He thrust it in front of me and pointed with a fine manicured hand to an advertisement. That night the famous I Musici string ensemble from Rome was giving a concert on the Isola di S. Giorgio Maggiore.

I dumped my bag at the hotel and took a gondola to the island, where I found myself an incongruous figure among the superbly-dressed Venetian audience. The startled lady at the box office took my money and dubiously handed me a ticket. I followed the crowd down an avenue of cypress trees towards an ancient monastery and took my seat in a large, open, formal garden. In the centre a large platform was erected and as the breeze softly blew through the square the musicians took their place and filled the air with eighteenth-century grace. A rare evening such as this remains with me and is always recalled by the Venetian masters on a visit to an art gallery.

Our tour included clubs in Greece, Yugoslavia and Spain; finishing up in Sicily. Everywhere we found time to set up a stage and a show for local people. On one magical evening in Barcelona we met Salvador Dali when he was the guest of the Club. Artists had built enormous ten-foot puppets from his designs, and they played out an old Spanish tale on the side of a brilliantly-lit mountain, accompanied by the Concierto de Aranjuez by Rodrigo. As the puppets appeared from behind the great trees their story was broadcast in Spanish through huge speakers. Watching it we became children again, excited and terrified by the giants of old fairy tales. It was an evening that echoed in my dreams for many years.

In Sicily our performance was a very special event. We were offered a magnificent location in a ruined cathedral where, lit by arc lights and in front of an audience of a thousand, we performed our full show of mime, poetry and song. Here our work took on a different dimension. With the holiday-makers it had had a breezy lightness. But on this night the huge lights, the towering stone walls of the cathedral and the attentive, quiet audience inspired every one of us with a deeper meaning. The awesome, physical work of Isaac and Pierre became a poetic expression of mortal combat, and our clowning took on the epic joys of the great circus clowns. This was my first opportunity to use my voice and with a trembling heart I read French poetry through giant speakers as Isabel danced and floated over the stage. It was a wonderful night under the stars and supper awaited us, hosted by Sicilian society. It was only much later that I learnt the whole night had been arranged and paid for by the Mafia.

Life was good. We were performing only two or three times a week and my health improved with the sun and the wonderful Club meals. The amazing natural settings of these resorts, filled with young people from all over Europe, were relaxing and pleasurable. We became minor celebrities.

As September loomed and a tinge of autumn could be felt in the air, it became time for decision-making. Isaac wanted us to continue together but Julian was keen to return to England and pursue his career. I was pulled in both directions. Europe had seeped into my bones and I was strongly tempted to remain and work with the team. On the other hand my career as a director, which had lain dormant for two years, was becoming impatient. My fruitful new association with Julian offered a chance to develop it in England and provide much-needed finance. In the meantime a contract for the group to appear in Geneva, followed by a television appearance for the BBC, was a welcome way of evading a decision for a few months. We said goodbye to Sicily and travelled north.

The forgotten pleasures of London included hearing the English language again. For two years I had battled with the French tongue without a single excursion across the channel. I had faithfully attended the Alliance Française until I could no longer afford it and, at a party before leaving, actually made a joke in French. The accolades for such daring convinced me that I was on the long way round to fluency. But the English language, I knew, was where I belonged. Then, going to the rue du Bac for the last time, M. Lecoq almost undid me by asking me to stay with him, as his assistant, to tour certain cities and demonstrate his teaching.

Three careers were now offered. To continue working with Lecoq meant a career in teaching and in mime. It also meant remaining in Paris and continuing to work with Isaac and Pierre, fashioning ourselves into a group of European poetic clowns. To pursue, with Julian, a comedy duo on the English stage meant a new career, an English comedy partnership, which could develop in many ways. To forgo both would free me to return to directing, should I gain the opportunity after two years away from legitimate theatre. As *Les Comédiens mimes de Paris* prepared for their act on BBC television, I needed many rides on the top of London buses to think it all over.

But what had happened to the London I had left almost ten years ago? I now saw it with the eyes of a 32-year-old, very differently from that of the young hopeful in 1952; a walk down Carnaby Street confirmed my age as crowds of seventeen-year-old Beatles fans screamed their new identity. But this was only one aspect of change. My apprenticeship had been informed by a long-established way of life. The London of 1963 was wrenching itself away from this world, turning its back on old values and old architecture and opening its arms to a new multicultural age, as the heirs of her old colonialism poured into the city.

In the fifty years I have known London, it has changed beyond recognition, except for a few great buildings around Westminster. Paris, on the other hand, has kept its façade almost unaltered in the forty years of my love affair with that exquisite city. Perhaps here lay the meaning of 'being European', that had haunted me. In Paris, where changes were also happening, the past remained ever present, ever influencing the new.

In 1963, however, London had other things to think of. The British Empire was coming home to roost and her far-flung children had begun pouring in, to change forever the face of the country. I watched, as English society slowly began its painful transition into a global society. Anti-nuclear marches brought the world into Trafalgar Square in a way Nelson could not have imagined. This newness was exciting.

John Sumner now seemed a far-off, almost forgotten figure, particularly when I turned the pages of *The Stage* once again and found a regional theatre movement exploding in the capital since the advent of television drama from the North. The small screen was full of exciting new work with actors using their regional accents. Playwrights such as John Osborne, Arnold Wesker and Bernard Kops were being fêted for attacking the established order. Britain was shaking off its old values; a new generation sought a new beginning—and no more so than in my world of theatre.

Three countries were now pulling me: France, emotionally; England, intellectually; and Australia culturally. All this left me feeling at a loss. My heart went to my family in Canberra, none of whom I had seen for over two years. Babies had been born, a young sister had grown up and joined the Navy, a young brother was now a journeyman in his father's trade and I missed them all a great deal. I would see my mother soon as she and her headmistress friend, Helen Freeman, were planning a trip and I would be in London to welcome them.

In my world, George Devine and the Royal Court Theatre Company were turning tradition upside down with a constant stream of new writing from every corner of the UK. Young directors such as William Gaskill were bringing new visions of the classics to the stage. The satire of Peter Cook, Dudley Moore, Jonathan Miller and Alan Bennett in *Beyond the Fringe* had just exploded, shooting satirical laughter at the old world. Nowhere was this revolution better displayed than by Joan Littlewood's company at Stratford East in the political musical *Oh, What A Lovely War!*. The sixties were under way and I needed to be part of it.

Old friends were already installed in this exciting environment. Leon Lissek was a member of Peter Brook's Theatre of Cruelty project and Patricia Conolly had joined the Royal Shakespeare Company. Neil Fitzpatrick was soon to become part of the new National Theatre and my old friend Peter Kenna was breathing in this birth of new thinking.

Our BBC performance meant goodbye to *Les Comédiens*. When the day arrived, one decision had been made. I would remain in England. Goodbye to Isaac, Pierre and Isabel and goodbye to Paris and all that it implied. This was not like other decisions I had made. This was irrevocable. I knew I would never return to Paris to live and work as a European.

Years later, in moments of reflection I would return to that decision and wonder what might have been—because I cannot, for the life of me, work out how I made it. Certainly, the seduction of London and new beginnings contributed greatly; the love of my own language also; and the career that followed would seem to have made it the right choice, but the Paris I had discovered to be part of my soul would remain. The betrayal I had felt in leaving the Family was something done just too soon; this one, an emotional one to be sure, was forever.

My friends have always suspected it was a love affair that had driven me away from France. I did fall in love in Paris and that experience gave my whole being a sum of pain and ecstasy that would always affect my work. What's more, it was a love unrequited, as is the motif of so much poetic invention. I experienced all those sleepless nights; mad days spent searching for a glimpse, a word, a gesture and many a walk along the Seine contemplating the unbearable nature of such love. It is, perhaps, the reason why it would never happen again in such a flamboyant way. How amazing is memory when it can bring alive every moment of such a time. Forty years later, I still find myself walking remembered streets of Paris, half expecting to catch sight of a familiar walk, a look, and a sudden easy grin.

Was this the real reason for not returning? I do not believe so. A lover can never turn his back on the beloved to avoid pain. No. Whatever the true reasons were for leaving Paris behind they were not emotional. For my twin, Jim, the answer was easy. 'Become French? What rubbish, you are Australian.' Perhaps, but even as Australians we have a Scottish heritage and all my youth was spent dreaming of 'home'. A permanent exile. I must leave it like that and turn to London and the immediate excitement of the following weeks. Almost before Julian and I set out to conquer London, a phone call from an old friend gave me the chance I had been waiting for—to direct once again, this time at a major drama school in London. The truth of my feelings I could not ignore as I took hold of the opportunity with all my heart.

'How would you like to direct some students?'

Would I? Clem McCallin was back in England, soon to take his place with the Royal Shakespeare Company once again. He had known about my move to directing and found the change from acting not surprising. He introduced me to the Central School of Speech and Drama at Swiss Cottage, where I began work with drama students in their third and final year.

Among them was a girl called Sara Kestelman and I had the joy of directing her in her graduation play for the school. I still remember the experience as a highlight of my career. Sara played the leading role in a one-act play by Jean Anouilh called *Madame De*, adapted from a novel by Louise de Vilmorin. It had been made into a famous Max Ophuls film starring Charles Boyer and Danielle Darrieux, but the play was written, with music by John Hotchkis, to be a stage piece. I leapt at it. It allowed me to use my years of work with Lecoq on a play of delicate French manners, involving the loss of a necklace and a consequent drama in diplomatic circles.

Mime and improvisation became rehearsal tools, as a delightful group of students, using only minimal props and furniture to maintain the musical flow of this bonbon and bring to life the Paris of the 1780s on the stage of the Embassy Theatre. The result was very pleasing and we received a fine notice from a London critic. Sara was exquisite as Madame. She left us in no doubt that this young actress would go far in our profession and, indeed, she later gave me a wonderful evening as Titania in Peter Brook's famous production of *A Midsummer Night's Dream*. I look back with great affection and gratitude to this group of young actors, who later made good careers in theatre and film. Our success also generated more work for me at Central during this first year back in England.

Side by side my two lives prospered as my comedy career with Julian began to take shape. Polly Adams, a young actress who owned a charming house in Hampstead, made a welcome home there for a group of Australians: Leon Lissek, Neil Fitzpatrick, Patricia Conolly and myself, together with Maggie McCourt, another English actress. As autumn turned into winter, this cottage became a real sanctuary from the struggle to make a living in this tough profession. It was in this house that we witnessed an event together that shook the world. On 22 November 1963 President Kennedy was assassinated. Like so many others, I remember the moment of the news flash, how we were seated around the television set, the silence that followed, the quiet weeping. For days the world reeled with shock—but in our corner the show must go on and panto laughter twice nightly climaxed the year.

During 1964, an unexpected offer came, through the school, from the RSC's theatre director and scholar John Barton to join a group of directors to work on a selection of scenes from modern and classic texts with the less-featured actors of the company. By now work with Julian would soon be full-time, but this was an opportunity with Britain's leading classical company and I was determined to take part. Julian accepted my decision with a long sigh and wished me luck.

I arrived in Stratford in fevered excitement. It was my first visit to this historic shrine to Shakespeare and to his theatre on the Avon. The Company was in the middle of a massive project: John Barton had conflated Shakespeare's history plays into the epic *The Wars of the Roses*. Here was an inspired example of a challenge for a new world. Out of history they had wrenched a living documentary of man's inhumanity to man. My first nights were spent watching this achievement and sitting in the actors' café, meeting such idols as Peggy Ashcroft and Hugh Griffiths and making new friends in this huge and prestigious company.

The first, not-altogether-pleasant, surprise concerned the plays I was to rehearse. With my experience and training I had expected texts that would incorporate mime, mask and *commedia* technique. Instead I was given four densely-textual classical works. I knew only one, *The Alchemist*, which brought a rush of memories of Canberra. Sophocles' *Antigone* brought with it thoughts of Epidavros, the others were unfamiliar: John Webster's *The Duchess of Malfi*, and Molière's *Tartuffe*. I had seen the latter in Paris and even with my colloquial French I could tell that this was a very bad translation. Four formidable plays. Each play had a different cast and was to receive only a few rehearsals in the time allotted. Despite the fact that only one or two scenes from each were being rehearsed, it still meant having a good knowledge of the play. The whole idea was impossible. The pleasures of *The Wars of the Roses* had to be curtailed as I wrestled with these texts. Performance was not the goal, we were assured, rather the study and experiment.

With great trepidation I began rehearsals. I was allotted some delightful actors with whom to share the joys of these great authors, among them a young actress, Susan Engel. I immediately fell in love with her and we became friends for life. As work progressed, more and more it began to feel like fast food: gobbling down the lines and hoping they'd stick. The performance day seemed to loom from the first rehearsal, but, as I kept on assuring the actors, it was to be a day for the Company to catch us in rehearsal, not performance. Poor fool I.

Nevertheless, working with the actors was exciting and the occasional visits from John Barton to help us unravel meaning, particularly from the intricacies of Webster, were much appreciated. Here was a scholar truly in love with the text. He reminded me so much of Ralph Wilson—they both had a propensity to fall off the stage in their eager concentration. Too quickly the day of showing arrived. How naive of me to take the instructions literally! Other directors were clever enough to know that any audience, no matter how small, wanted a performance; and so they had rehearsed their actors as if it were weekly rep. It made me angrier than I had ever been in my life and left me deeply suspicious of the phrase 'work-in-progress' ever since. I felt huge sympathy for my actors who, on seeing what was happening, put on their best efforts. The company director's verdict, I was told, was: 'What a pity the most interesting man produced the least interesting work.'

My answer to that was: 'What a pity the company felt the need to keep the actors busy. A footy match might have been more appropriate.' The criticism, nevertheless, has stayed with me as a reminder that my work can always, always, be better.

It made me see how much I love the rehearsal process, maybe because my early life in the theatre had had none. My experience and love for my profession had been born and developed through intuition. Without any training I had been taught my craft by my audience. But if a great play is to be studied, rehearsed and performed, time must be given to it, otherwise the result will be cockeyed, as was my work at the RSC. It was a salutary lesson. Ever since that time I have been reluctant to have people watch rehearsals while there was a chance the actors might respond to them as audience and discard the process.

I was relieved to be back with the students of Central later in the year directing the latest third-year students in Molière's *L'Amour Médecin*. Perhaps I should be grateful that the setback at Stratford-upon-Avon spurred me on rather than deterred me. Lessons must constantly be learnt and, if disappointment and anger are part of the experience, then so be it.

So often in our theatre life friendships develop, are cut short by work in other parts of the world, and then picked up again in fresh circumstances. One of my happier memories of Stratford was my meeting with a New Zealand actor, Rhys McConnochie, who was performing in *The Wars of the Roses*. Goodbye to Stratford meant goodbye to Rhys, only to find him again in Sydney twenty years later in the cast of one of my first films. Fifteen years later we met again,

TUESDAY, AUGUST 25, 1964

Late night revue   *by Coia*

Coia caricatures the cast of the late night revue, "Chaganog," which opened last night at the Royal Lyceum Theatre. Left to right are: Sheila O'Neill, David Toguri, Patsy Rowlands, Julian Chagrin, and George Ogilvie.

Cartoon by Coia. The *Scotsman*, 25 August 1964.

teaching at the Victorian College of the Arts Drama School. Time has no meaning in our business; reunions with like artists are an accepted part of living and catching up on the in-between years a pleasurable pastime. My visits to London from Australia and Paris always mean a reunion with Susan Engel and her husband Sylvester Morand, two actors who, for me, represent the best in the English actor—people who love the theatre not because of personal ambition but because theatre celebrates life and can teach us to be better human beings.

Following my stint with the RSC my career with Julian took wings. *Chaganog* was born.

The combination of Chagrin and Ogilvie created first a name, then a late-night revue at the Edinburgh Festival and a season at the Vaudeville in London's West End. It was redirected for a season at the Hampstead Theatre Club and then moved on to St Martin's in Cambridge Circus for a short but spectacular season.

It was a heady time. My memory of Hampstead is overlaid by the experience of standing in my underpants one night after the performance, when, with a knock on the door, Princess Margaret walked in and, with a great smile, shook my hand and congratulated me. At the Vaudeville another knock brought in Sir Malcolm Sargent. I still remember the feel of the handshake from that distinguished conductor. Another great musician, Yehudi Menuhin, sent a letter of appreciation, a copy of which I treasure. In Edinburgh we were followed into the Lyceum Theatre by Marlene Dietrich and exchanged notes of welcome and birthday cheer.

All this excitement occurred at the time I was also directing in London and Stratford. How I managed to do this is almost beyond my memory. It meant rushing from one city to another, squeezing in rehearsals wherever possible. The result was a split life that I knew could not last. But I take this opportunity to celebrate a partnership which meant so much to me and which was also the last period of my life as a performer.

It all began in the studio in the rue du Bac in late 1960. My impressions were riotous on that first day with Jacques Lecoq. Who were all these students? And why were they studying such a subject as mime? In 1960, this was a mysterious word for which there seemed no use in the real world. The only mime artist known outside esoteric groups was Marcel Marceau, who was only just beginning his extraordinary world tours. I was not at all sure why I was there. I had no intention of trying to become another Marceau. Coming from the spoken theatre, language meant too much to me. I was dying to know if other students felt the same, but without a common language communication between so many foreigners was awkward and we slipped in and out of class with a perfunctory nod. One day I heard an unmistakable English accent underlying some French conversation in the change room, and found myself facing a tall, thin student from the class above me. As I was a new student and humble in front of someone already expert, I remained silent and watched as he met his fiancée Claude and swept off to Parisian delights.

So it was not until months later that I saw Julian's work for the first time. I was very impressed. Later a London critic described him as, 'a tall, lean young man with a variety of expressions ranging from the lofty and disdainful to the amazed silly ass.' This describes him so accurately I need say no more. His timing was impeccable and you could not take your eyes off him. Within a short time Isaac Alvarez had brought us together and we began to work on sketches as a duo.

Having the same native language was, of course, an advantage, particularly in negotiating moments of timing and the climax of a physical joke, but perhaps the most important common ground was our sense of humour. Although under Lecoq's tutelage the basis of our work was strict physical control, his classes on the Clown became the foundation for the work ahead and for the birth of *Chaganog*. The essential world behind all these classes, as Lecoq would stress, was the world of childhood; to put aside the layers of sophistication and world weariness of which adulthood was composed and see the Clown as a creature of hope, an innocent who could turn *malin*, that lovely word meaning shrewd and naughty. Here lies the basic nature of Arlecchino, an innocent with a mischievous streak that would always land him in trouble. There is always hope in the clown's world, no matter what horror awaits his unsuspecting curiosity; when he burns his fingers, he sucks them better and tries again.

The game of 'Hat' became a lesson in clowning which had to be understood if the life of the clown was to progress. Julian and I spent many, many hours using this game to create our world. Two clowns meet. A is wearing an unusual hat. A is very proud of the hat and shows it to his friend B. B thinks it is a wonderful hat and asks to try it on, but A does not want to take it off. The game is for B to use his wiles to seize the hat from A until in triumph he has it, for a moment. The essential rule to grasp and to follow is this: the game is more important than the triumph. If B does not lose the hat before his triumph sets in, the game is over. Neither party can continue. That was how our partnership worked.

Work together began to tie us into a clown duo but our arrival in London meant facing a different future. In late 1962, after two years in Paris, Julian was determined that we should continue to further our professional life in England. This was his dream, the chance to reveal the clown in him to his own people. For me the decision was more complex, but for the moment I followed.

Julian took me to meet his parents and younger brother destined to become an actor. I found a small flat nearby and we set about selling the idea of silent mimed comedy. But where to begin? A young English actor and director, Tony Tanner, and his partner Alan Edwards, had seen our BBC performance and proposed incorporating us into a second edition of an experimental revue called *Mis-shapes*, together with the folk singer, Isla Cameron, and a jazz dancer, Sheila O'Neill. We did several of our sketches from Europe and the audience reaction was pleasing and hopeful. Tony and Alan produced another soon after, called *Five in Eights*. It was presented in Oxford at the Century Theatre. Comedienne Margaret Jones, soprano Pamela Charles and a young actor, Jonathan Elsom, joined us in new sketches. My friendship with Jonathan Elsom was to be renewed thirty years later in Australia. These revues were praised for introducing this Continental form of clowning to the London stage.

As we moved into the profession, the camaraderie between artists brought new friendships and we gained in confidence. Pam Charles joined us again in a delightful revue at the York Festival during the summer of 1963, directed by Ronnie Stevens. *For a Change* had successful seasons in York and Hull and gave me a chance to work on other sketches with comedians like Gordon Rollings and Graham Armitage. Pam sang the 'Jewel Song' from *Candide*, which introduced me to Leonard Bernstein's impressive musical. She and our mezzo, Anne Carr, also whipped me off to an early performance of Britten's *War Requiem* at York Minster—an unforgettable event. This shattering work brought my frenetic life back into perspective as it moved the huge audience to tears in that historic cathedral.

Making use of our training, Julian and I, with his new wife Claude, put together a lecture demonstration of Lecoq's work, which helped us into the autumn. Claude was then offered a post with the new National Theatre, where she established an international reputation as a movement teacher. It was at this time, too, that I was invited to the Central School and my work as a director began to assert itself.

Towards the end of the year Tony Tanner and Neville McGrah announced that they had written a pantomime, *Puss in Boots*, for John Counsell, manager of the Theatre Royal in Windsor. The result was our first pantomime, as a comedy duo, Costa and Brava. That Christmas was one of the happiest. The mad world of English panto, given full justice in a theatre where pantomime had been a tradition since the nineteenth century, gave us a great opportunity to test out jokes and sketches on the happy holiday audience. A young Elizabeth Counsell played Puss and Louie Ramsay, Pedro. An old trouper, Duncan Lewis, played the Dame, and our villain, Dan Thorndyke, completed the troupe of wonderful variety artists.

Back in London, an Edwardian music hall revue was being mounted with a bizarre selection of stars, and Julian and I were offered places in the cast. We were able to introduce a couple of our own sketches into the program as well as becoming part of other numbers. Among the artists was the wonderful Australian-born comedienne Cicely Courtneidge, with whom I had the joy of doing a sketch, and the great tragedian, Donald Wolfit, who recited 'The Eye of the Little Yellow God' with resounding solemnity. Another comedienne with whom I worked was Joyce Grant and we became firm friends over the run, which lasted many weeks, twice-nightly.

During this season we were introduced to the producer, Peter Bridge. To be welcomed into the inner sanctum of a genuine West End producer seemed to be the height of theatre romance. This was the place where dreams came true or were shattered. Peter was determined to steer us towards bigger things and 1964 ushered in plans that would take us to the Edinburgh Festival with a newly-created late-night revue.

One of England's bright young theatre men down from Oxford, Braham Murray, would be our director and pour ideas into the work of two mimes from France, two dancers of lyric beauty, Sheila O'Neill and David Toguri, and a comedienne of rare quality, Patsy Rowlands. With Patsy I would do a sketch called 'La Dame au Caramel' in which the gift of chocolate became more seductive than making love. I grew to adore this item. David Toguri was to become a big success in London musicals. His optimism, his poetry, his kindly mind and friendship would add considerably to my life. Such meetings with artists are rare and precious.

Our own clown work was developing quickly and we continued to improve each sketch. 'The Two Princes', that began life on the Club Méditerranéan tour, was our funniest routine and would always bring the house down. Two masked oriental warriors would engage in a fierce fight with massive scimitars, and it was important from the start that the audience be persuaded it was a serious display of skill. Then, when Julian in a great lunge trod on my feet, extracting a squeal of pain from behind my mask, it was taken as an accident, until my revengeful retaliation some seconds later. Like a classic Laurel and Hardy sketch, control quickly disintegrated and the fight gathered momentum until Julian broke his sword over my head, I burst into sobs and he rushed to comfort me, placing an arm around my shaking shoulders. We then left the stage, conveying to the audience that it had all been their fault for laughing at us.

In another, more detailed sketch we were two sculptors working together on a large statue. Both the statue and the tools were mimed, so it took days of work to achieve the illusion of a lifesize figure and its reality in space. Once again competition between us wrought havoc to the work, which finished up as a wreck with our arms and legs trapped within it.

Occasionally we worked on individual sketches and Julian was achingly funny as an incompetent farmer attempting unsuccessfully to milk a huge cow that kept fighting back with tail and legs. With the permission of a young student at the Lecoq school I developed an idea that became 'The Matador' in which a meek little clerk is assaulted by a fierce dog while having his sandwich lunch on a park bench. Gradually his terror is transformed into aggression and he becomes a matador whirling his jacket and umbrella at the snarling animal.

It was decided to make the show approximately 75 minutes long and to integrate the three ingredients of mime, dance and clown without a word being said. The music would come from two pianos and Don Lawson on drums. The work of young Braham (he was twenty) was indicative of his great future as the progressive young director of the Exchange in Manchester. I loved the format of late-night revue and we left for Edinburgh excited and hopeful at sharing in a Festival filled with great artists, from the British mezzo-soprano, Janet Baker, to the pianist Sviatoslav Richter, many Shakespeare productions and for me one special event, the great German baritone Dietrich Fischer-Dieskau giving a Lieder recital with Gerald Moore. Edinburgh did us proud. We opened to notices ranging from 'an audience helpless with laughter' to 'pure bliss' and a cartoon in one of the dailies. We were a very happy group of revue artists.

This was my first visit to Scotland since meeting my grandmother more than a decade ago. To hear daily the accents of my parents' early life and see faces of my heritage brought about that nostalgia within me of something gone yet still breathing. She had now passed away and life was at present too busy to be able to go north. I promised myself a visit to Elgin as soon as possible.

In the months ahead, Peter Bridge continued to work on our behalf, determined that we would be seen in London. Finally, success crowned his efforts and *Chaganog* would live again at the Vaudeville Theatre. But it would be a much larger show and much new work and thought had to go into it. When the evening was extended to a full program I felt a little lost and over-cooked. Nor was Braham available to direct. I was sure a mistake was being made.

Opening night, at the beginning of December, was a terrifying experience. The audience seemed bemused by it all. The applause was not bad but the after-show party was not a triumph. So this was what it was like, to have a show doomed by 'not a good opening'. The papers were surprisingly positive but for the West End something more was needed. Peter, being the honest man he was, let us know that *Chaganog* would have a short, short season.

Christmas 1964 was a sad affair. I began to realise by what store we artists set our goals. Was our partnership doomed because of one half-hearted response? Fortunately, we were made of sterner stuff, as was Peter himself. The New Year brought new energy to this show of ours, and the *Daily Express* critic, Herbert Kretzmer, commented: 'This lively corpse just won't lie down.'

In the course of this adventure a thought kept battering at my mind. 'Was I losing the need to be an actor?' This was a shocking thought for someone whose whole life had led to performing. My life with the Family had been, for me, absolutely right and I have no doubt that, had I stayed with them, I would have continued to walk on stage. Admittedly, my early directorial excursions in Melbourne had awakened a new ambition, and working with students had furthered this; but to stop performing altogether? I pushed down these thoughts and injected renewed energy into *Chaganog*.

Peter was as good as his word, and Braham took over the direction again. To my great sadness, Patsy called it a day and took other work; but we discovered in Vivienne Martin a worthy successor. Having

Braham back also lifted our spirits as he put his clever head to work on our program. The result was a triumph. We toured to Brighton and then on to the Hampstead Theatre Club, which became my favourite venue for the show. It was modern and intimate and suited our detailed mime to perfection. And so thought the critics, who drenched us in compliments. Princess Margaret's visit was the highlight of this celebratory season. We transferred to St Martin's Theatre in Cambridge Circus and did well, but I missed the intimacy of Hampstead.

Towards the end of the season at St Martin's it came time to be honest with each other. Revue has a short life. Our mime sketches certainly had a future but in what format? Julian was well aware of my disposition and I finally confessed to him my profound wish to follow a path that was beginning to mean more to me than performing.

'Not perform again? Are you mad?' was Julian's response. Perhaps I was.

Then, as if in answer to this turmoil of indecision, John Sumner arrived in London. With him came an offer to return to Australia as the associate director of the Union Rep, soon be called the Melbourne Theatre Company and based in the little Russell Street Theatre. I would begin directing immediately: November 1965.

I took myself off to Greece to assess my nomadic life, find an answer, and face the future. Now there was only one choice left to make—to stay in England and pursue my life as a director or return to Australia to do the same thing. I took a bus from Athens to the ancient city of Mycenae and then to Epidavros. I sat night after night, swept away by the power of Sophocles' *Electra* and Euripides' *The Trojan Women*. Assessing my professional life over tea and rice pudding under southern Greek skies seemed much easier and far less fraught than among the fevered ambitions of London.

Two years with the Family had given me the foundation of all my work as an intuitive member of my profession. Two years in Canberra among the scholarly amateurs had begun my love of classical drama and of research. Two years with the Elizabethan Theatre Trust had meant being part of a revival in Australia but without a true identity. Three years at the Union had given me the chance to work with young actors of my own outlook and introduced me to the excitements of directing theatre. Two years in Paris with Jacques Lecoq had brought together all the previous experience, and begun building a philosophical method of work for the future. Three years in London had allowed me to begin this work, tempered by the salutary experience of the RSC, and to experience with my beloved Julian the mime and clown world that France had given us.

Fourteen years of wandering and learning since that morning in 1952 when I had boarded the *SS Otranto*, heading towards a dream. Since then I had never really stopped to reflect and some decisions had been outside my control. Now, however, was that time. The adventure was turning into purpose. Melbourne would give me that purpose. Like a constant companion, thoughts of Paris and the life there would haunt me until I resolved it decades later. But this time I made up my mind without any 'however' and returned to London to say 'yes' to John Sumner and the Melbourne Theatre Company and goodbye to Susan Engel and friends.

Saying goodbye to Julian was one of the most wrenching things I've ever experienced. I knew he tried hard to understand me, but he honestly thought I was insane to give up the clown work. Perhaps I was, but I held firm to my resolution. Julian continued his career as a solo performer and in 1976 settled in Israel. He formed his own film production company, Julian Chagrin Films Ltd, and continued to work as a performer internationally on stage, film and TV until a back injury forced his retirement. I left the UK for the second time but with hope in my heart that the future held new horizons, knowing that I would leave the actor behind.

As I look back on these pages I am amazed that I can remember such detail. With some performances I can visualise every moment and hear the reaction. Perhaps all artists can do this as every performance is a time when we are super-conscious of the now, living in the very moment, clear in mind and heart of past and future and only aware of the breathing present.

After fourteen years as performer I now exit the stage to become its witness.

Patsy Rowlands and the author in their sketch *La Dame au Caramel*.
Illustrated London News, 26 December 1964.

Five

THE DIRECTOR

The Golden Years

A knock on my new office door brought in a slim, dark-haired young man with haunted eyes, clutching a large portfolio.

'Kris?'

He opened the portfolio, spread it on my desk, and I sat gaping at the series of exquisite costume designs for the staging of Tolstoy's *War and Peace*. This was my introduction to Kristian Fredrikson, who would be my friend and favourite designer for the next forty years.

Later he would begin another partnership with the choreographer Graeme Murphy and together they would dazzle the world with their creations. Now it was 1965, and Kris had already joined John Sumner to design his last production at the Union Theatre of Pinter's *The Homecoming*, before John moved the Company permanently into the Russell Street Theatre. John was determined that they should move away from the University grounds in order to create an independent company of artists. I was joining him to share this future. We began to produce work with a superb group of actors and a production company unrivalled in Australia. It causes me unabashedly to call this second half of the sixties the Golden Years.

To return in memory to 1965 is to feel an immediate surge of excitement. At long last something was happening which might grow and become part of the ritual celebration of life. Hitherto, such a grandiose phrase belonged in church or on the sporting field, but now the arts were beginning to be recognised with State government money and within two years Federal money. New theatres were being designed; permanent companies of actors were being established to perform, for a growing audience, new and classical work from all over the world. The country's first drama school, NIDA was now six years old and others would soon follow. To be a member of such a band of artists was beginning to mean becoming a respected member of the community.

For me, these years were spent in a small miracle of a building: the tiny Russell Street Theatre, situated on the edge of the city of Melbourne. On a stage without flies above with very little wing space and only two long, narrow dressing rooms, we played to an audience of 416. The production department was an old wooden warehouse in Lennox Street, Richmond, filled with makeshift workshops and offices. Our plan was impossible: a permanent company of over twenty actors—and more needed during the year—to play a season of works better suited to Drury Lane. To try and squeeze Rolf Hochhuth's *The Representative*, Tolstoy's *War and Peace* and Peter Shaffer's *The Royal Hunt of the Sun* into a tiny theatre like Russell Street was laughable—and yet we did it. There were two major reasons for our success. The first was our poverty, both of space and material, which drew on resources of improvisation on a massive scale. The second reason lay with the artists themselves.

Where do I start in this homage to a time now lost, but which remains in the memory as the best of times? We must start with John Sumner. This indefatigable man coaxed, urged and prevailed upon both State and Federal governments to keep our little theatre alive year after year, building a loyal audience. In 1968 he would confirm the status of the Company by changing its name to the Melbourne Theatre Company; the same year it emerged as Victoria's State theatre company, selected by newly-formed Australian Council for the Arts. And at the same time, with the architect Roy Grounds, he was laying the groundwork for Melbourne's Arts Centre. As I write these words so many years later a knot of anger rises; I feel ashamed for Melbourne that this man's immense contribution has been so little recognised. Over the years John has been awarded an AO, a CBE and a Green Room lifetime achievement award but nowhere do I see his name attached to a theatre in permanent recognition. John Sumner spent the creative part of his life working for a city and a country he had come to love and call his own. All of us who call ourselves Australian actors owe a debt of gratitude to his far-reaching vision.

Of this time the memory bank teems with people and plays, many moments of inspiration and others of such tiredness as to make the world stop. Around Betty Druitt circle actors changing into one costume after another as she pins and cuts, while designer and director discuss the play, the scene, the moment. Her wardrobe was a hive where business was conducted at every level. Peter Roehlen's workshop was another place that required a daily visit from the directors. Our two designers, Kris and Richard Prins, worked day and night with Peter to bring to life the designs for the burning of Moscow in *War and Peace*, the rape of the Sun God's world in Peter Shaffer's *The Royal Hunt of the Sun* and the great railway girders of Arthur Miller's *Incident at Vichy*. Every member of the production team was an artist, whether in construction or finishing, and had an intimate role in each play. Opening night was a celebration for every member of the Company.

Let me try to recall some of the treasured moments and perhaps explain why these memories are so precious; try to describe the manner of work and the dedication that was given to every play. All these plays were produced within the years of 1965 and 1970, a time of change and conflict in which the Vietnam War was causing civil strife at home and abroad. It was the time of the flower children calling us to make love not war. The arts, too, were seeking freedom from censorship and the domination of imported mass media. Theatre seemed a good environment in which to begin to understand what was happening to our country.

War and Peace (1966)

The audience was gathering in the foyer and Arthur Hynes, the stage manager, waited nervously to signal the front of house to open the doors—there was no front curtain in Russell Street. It was the opening night of this adaptation of *War and Peace* and I was standing on stage with Dennis Miller who was to play Pierre. We were waiting in tight, anxious silence for the armies of the opposing forces to arrive from the workshop.

Kristian Fredrikson's ikon designs for *War and Peace*. Melbourne Theatre Company 1966. (Photo: Henry Talbot.)

At the last moment Kris Fredrikson, his eyes black with tiredness, staggered from the wings with a large box. Not a word was said as he extricated the intricate soldier models and guns, only just dry after the final coat of paint, and placed them carefully onto the small covered platform, ready for Pierre's 'war games'. As Dennis helped him arrange them in the order he needed, I looked around for a long moment at the twenty rows of neat seats waiting to be filled. I had a flashback to Epidavros and that great empty theatre sitting in the sun, also waiting to be filled. Those moments before audience and cast combine never fail to fill me with shivering anticipation. We gazed down at the splendid war field. Dennis and I looked at each other and knew it would be all right. I nodded to Arthur who lifted his arms in triumph and gave the signal to open the doors.

Twenty-five minutes later, as the Berlioz trumpets blazed from the corner, two great doors swung open and the cast swept on stage and seated themselves facing the audience, like a grand painting by Jacques-Louis David. As the last trumpet sounded, Edward Hepple, dressed in evening wear, walked on to greet the audience and introduce the play.

'Good evening,' he said, and then—dried.

I was suddenly and wrenchingly back with the Family and my first test. Was this an omen? I shrank down in my seat. John was seated beside me and patted my hand with an 'it'll be all right,' as Ted in a superb gesture moved past the cast as if inspecting them, arrived at the prompt corner, turned as if this was intended and spoke the first speech of the play. Later the cast would talk of the surge of adrenalin that ran through them all; and with this unexpected excitement the play proceeded without a falter.

Led by Brian James as Count Rostov and Jan Leeming as the young Natasha, this newly-formed company of actors brought the story alive. The burning of Moscow was achieved by Kris with a glorious icon which dominated the stage until it was reduced to a burnt and blackened frame. It made a most disturbing symbol of the destruction of war. I can still hear the waltz from Berlioz's *Symphonie Fantastique* and see the beautiful white figures of Natasha and Andrei, played with simple nobility by Michael Lawrence, dancing together while Pierre stands to the side, totally in love with this young heroine, murmuring,

'That girl, that girl, that girl.'

That night I was aware of a promise I had made to myself: to make the experience of all the years before lead to this moment. I felt both elated and nauseous, two feelings that would always accompany me— elated at doing the work I loved and sick with the desperate hope that the audience would appreciate what they had come to see and hear.

The three most important words in a director's armoury are knowledge, passion and surprise. By knowing not only the play but also the circumstances surrounding its creation in the life of the author, a director can help the artist to realise the world of the play and their character within it. Secondly, his knowledge must be conveyed with passion. If a passion for the work is caught by the artists as rehearsals progress, the result will never be boring or indifferent. Thirdly, it is essential for all artists to understand the importance of spontaneity on the part of the actor. Each speech and situation must be performed as if for the first time (as Mary Martin had shown in *South Pacific* so long ago) and therefore become unexpected and urgent, conveying to the audience the same urgency. Sometimes accidents or unexpected moments will do the trick. Ted's dry at such a heightened moment certainly pumped adrenalin into the cast, but not even the director can provide for the unexpected. I recall an evening during the long run of our Edwardian Music Hall show in London when the chorus girls were becoming lax. My comedienne friend Joyce Grant began a rumour that Marlon Brando was in tonight. The response was immediate and the audience, without Brando, was treated to a grand show. These moments are rare and the actors themselves must ensure that all their preparation is left behind as they step on stage to be newborn.

The Royal Hunt of the Sun (1966)

As the weeks progressed, while war against Napoleon played itself out on stage, another war was being constructed in the workshop. The armour of the sixteenth-century Spanish forces and the glittering gold prizes of the Inca nation gradually took shape as I watched. Kris was surrounded by a great team and he lived out his life twenty hours a day in the workshop in Lennox Street, while above them Betty Druitt with her team created more miracles, and on the side artists like Marjorie Head made hats and bonnets, and Kathy Dennis wigs worthy of a great theatre. Later, two young designers, Hugh Colman and Anna French, would expand the team and add to the MTC production unit's enviable reputation.

Royal Hunt was the first play in which I used the mime I had mastered. This great invasion had to be performed almost standing still on our tiny stage and our constraints required many imaginative ideas. As we prepared the Spanish soldiers for their march to war, I found my knowledge of the physical stress placed on the body in action to be of great benefit. The ocean of blood that was spilt in the Spanish conquest of the Incas was another problem; Kris gave me the ideal way of conveying this. The set was a semicircle of stone, and as the signal for attack came, the soldiers charged the walls and hammered their fists through the paper-thin fabric of which they were made. From behind the walls they grasped handfuls of blood-red ribbons and ran across the stage with them, criss-crossing each other into a crazy pattern of blood. The effect was electric. The genocide of the native population became a tragic conclusion to an epic evening.

Melbourne Theatre Company, 1966. The Spanish army advances in *The Royal Hunt of the Sun*. Paul Caro, George Mallaby, Peter Hepworth, Edward Hepple, Michael Duffield, Dennis Miller. (Photo: Henry Talbot.)

War and Peace and *Royal Hunt* pose particular problems for the director and for the actors playing the roles. In each case the characters are well-known historical figures or fictitious personalities of epic proportions. How do you play characters involved in great social change and who appear to represent an entire generation? One thing is certain. No audience wants a history lesson unless it is presented with excitement, emotion and above all, drama—by which I mean played out by characters with whom the audience can identify.

I believe that in plays like these the director must be quite specific about the research he asks his actors to do. In R.C. Sherriff's *Journey's End*, for example, set in the trenches of the Great War, a study of that war is useless to the actors. They are playing characters who know nothing of the political circumstances in which they are fighting, nor do they know anything about the military force of which they are part. The war-torn world that surrounds them may be in the minds of the audience, as it was during early performances of this play, but what the characters do know is the school they went to, the family they came from and their attitudes to friends and country. The play itself is a domestic one, not an epic one. So here lies the research that will help the actors bring to life a group of loving, caring human beings. The outcome for the audience is the realisation that, even under extreme conditions, human behaviour does not change. I am reminded of the appalling mistakes I made in my first venture as a director with *Blood Wedding* when I gave the cast a huge history lesson on Spain, confusing them and turning them away from the immediate family situation in which the drama is set. The play's theme is sexual jealousy and revenge.

The Russian or Spanish soldier carries similar domestic needs to war, not the imperial ambitions of the powers that lead him. The director must know this in order to understand the play: that the actor's world is tiny, more concerned with his toothache than the complex and useless reason for his death. The background of the characters in *Royal Hunt* is more elusive than that of *War and Peace*, but is nonetheless worth searching for, in order to give the actor a world in which to exist.

War and Peace and *The Royal Hunt of the Sun* are not great plays. They are narratives from history fictionalised by their authors and adapted for the theatre. The playwrights have provided texts that allow the director and actors to find their own way into the action. No two productions of either play could be similar, for the texts require the imagination of actor, director and designer to realise. Neither is a play that the profession could call director- or actor-proof. My next play, for all its simplicity, was better constructed than either of these two adventures into theatrical storytelling.

The Knack (1966)

I loved directing this play. To begin with, it is extremely well written, was contemporary and set in a familiar environment, and it featured my first set by Dick Prins which inspired me to rehearse the quartet of young actors as though the text were a piece of music. Ann Jellicoe's dialogue has a musical rhythm; all we had to do was follow the cadences, pauses and the sweep of events—a good play. And what a quartet we had in Robin Ramsay, John Gregg, Clive Winmill and Lyndel Rowe, I had a perfect cast. For me there was also great relief in directing a play with four actors instead of twenty, and to become absorbed in the intimate and detailed minutiae of ordinary life.

Dick's setting was the large basement of a London tenement, with two huge, half-whitewashed walls which revealed the outside world through a large window and stairs mounting towards the street. With the floor jutting out towards the audience, it looked like a painting by a contemporary artist.

Rehearsals became an absorbing pleasure. Because the play was not long we could spend time listening not only to the dialogue, but also to the sound of the paint brush on the wall, to footsteps on the steps and traffic passing by. Every sound heard in rehearsal was considered and used. The window, set level with the street, gave glimpses of the legs of passers-by. The squeak of the old bed with its badly-sprung base became a counterpoint to the text. Tiny details were as important as every word. We all felt as if we were creating a breathing corner of contemporary life in London.

The Knack opened the new season of plays at a time when outside the theatre a contemporary tragedy was being played out. It was now 1966, the conscription ballot for Vietnam was on its way and twenty-year-olds' lives were being gambled on their birth date. Already the protest marches were in full swing. I think it was Peter Brook who said that actors should have no political allegiance, but be a filter through which ideas were expressed. Here in Australia this was difficult advice. The American President Lyndon B. Johnson was about to arrive, seeking our further commitment to the war.

'All the way with LBJ!' cried our Prime Minister, Harold Holt. For those of us who hated war in any form, this was a shameful time.

One evening our performance was under way and Robin was up the ladder starting to whitewash the wall when Clive, as the young teacher, made his entrance. Instead of beginning a conversation with Robin, he advanced towards the audience, pulled out a paper and began to read. Robin, who knew nothing of Clive's intentions, looked around, rested his paint-brush, leant against the ladder and gave his attention to Clive's impassioned anti-war speech. The audience took a while to realise that this was no part of the play. They too listened as the young actor, barely able to keep from breaking down, continued reading. Soon, a restless murmur spread through the audience and a man rose from his seat.

'Excuse me, young man, but I think you'll find that we all agree with you.' The audience burst into applause, and Clive retired, tears streaming down his face, to re-emerge, after a deal of fraught activity backstage, in character. It was not the end of Clive's protest, however. He followed the LBJ motorcade and, taking aim, landed an egg on the windscreen and himself in court. I took the stand as a character witness for him and we all returned, gratefully, to work.

In the weeks that followed, we debated whether theatre in any form could influence thinking on serious public issues. Political theatre was a topic in actors' coffee shops, but its practical application remained in the street where groups of young activists played out their anti-war protests. Activist theatre was well established in the United Kingdom and the United States, but even there it remained largely a fringe activity. In the same way, in Australia, it was easy to see that, for our audiences, theatre was essentially an entertainment. Over the years people have spoken to me of the pleasure certain performances have given them, but their pleasure has been of the spirit, not of social consciousness. I used to muse about what might have happened on a night in Athens in 415 BC, after the Greek armies had laid waste to the island of Delos. That was the night Euripides presented *The Trojan Women*, which deals with the aftermath of such a slaughter and the pitiful, tragic end of the women prisoners. History does not tell us what took place but years later, when I witnessed Sophocles' *Ajax* at Epidavros, the audience rose in vocal anguish over what to them was a re-enactment of the recent atrocities of their civil war.

I did produce a real piece of political theatre in 1971, *The Trial of the Catonsville Nine*. The production caused much self-analysis among the artists as well as the audience. It is a documentary piece, based on the trial for civil disobedience of the Catholic priests Daniel and Philip Berrigan and their colleagues, who in 1968, at the height of anti-conscription rage in the United States, broke into a government office in Catonsville, Maryland, and took hundreds of military draft records. Despite a storm of popular support they were found guilty and sentenced to gaol. It was an act of courage that I found both fearful and inspirational.

But, to be honest, I wonder now if my admiration stemmed from the act of disobedience itself, rather than from any fuller understanding I gained from working on the play. I had to recognise that companies throughout the world that presented political theatre were composed of actors who chose to participate because of their politics. In Melbourne, student activists were taking their protest against Vietnam into the street, with marches, speeches and agit-prop theatre. For me, on the other hand, and for so many like me, the theatre was a means of exposing and celebrating life in all its aspects. It has made me an observer of life, from the sidelines, entering into the main arena for a short scene, then retiring to wait for my next entrance. I sometimes cursed the British Army for the way it invaded my life, not allowing me to remain an observer, pacing in my corridor, but forcing me to join the march.

Of all the modern plays that deal with an awareness of social justice Arthur Miller's *Death of a Salesman* and *The Crucible* are two of the most lasting. In productions by John Sumner both plays proved landmarks for the Russell Street Theatre in this period. They were also a personal triumph for their leading actor, George Whaley, who had worked closely with Wal Cherry and who remained a major actor with the Company throughout these years and a good friend. These are plays of the heart, and any actor will tell you that the experience of working in the theatre is mostly one of the heart. The mind is fed by a well-written play and a strong argument but the emotional experience is the most powerful.

As successful as *War and Peace* and *The Royal Hunt of the Sun* might have been, my work on *The Knack* taught me something about my own nature: for me small is beautiful and the grand sweep of major events is best left to someone with the talent for it. I love the detail and subtle change of people and events and in hindsight, had I taken this advice, it might have saved myself some heartache.

Melbourne Theatre Company, 1967. Jennifer Claire, David Turnbull and John Gregg in *A Flea in Her Ear*. (Photo: Henry Talbot.)

A Flea in Her Ear (1967)

It was 1967 when John decided I should bring to the stage what I had learnt in Paris, and so we introduced the French author Georges Feydeau's *A Flea in her Ear* into the season. This is a complex three-act farce of early twentieth-century bourgeois manners in which Madame Chandebise, in her attempt to prove her husband unfaithful, finds herself in a dubious hotel along with her entire household. I worried, not only over how a young Australian cast could cope with the frighteningly-accurate timing and rhythm demanded by the script, but how our conservative Melbourne audience might react.

The cast was assembled on stage, seated and ready for the first reading, and I began talking, conscious of a vacant seat. I began to talk, not so much about the play but the life led by successful bourgeois families of the period: the prudery, the fear of scandal within their small circles and the jealousy and boredom such restrictions caused. Just as I came to the point of signalling the reading to commence, a slim, lithe figure ran down the aisle, leapt onto the stage and slipped into his seat with a furtive look of apology. This was how Dennis Olsen entered my life. Dennis was to become a major figure in Australian theatre and a man whose work I loved.

The reading commenced and, following my instructions, the cast was reading to get the sense, not to attempt a performance. Dennis, having just arrived from Adelaide, had not received these instructions and, when he made his first entrance as an insanely jealous Spaniard, a full-blown performance exploded across the stage. The rest of the cast were delighted and followed suit. At the end of the reading I halted their laughter and gave them these notes:

> As actors, you obviously found the play a delightful comedy in which you could share the jokes, but for the characters in the play their every moment is one of crisis, fraught with shame and possible discovery. Life for these bourgeois people is anything but funny. So, from this moment on, let the characters take over your thinking. Feydeau said once that he deliberately set out in his writing to make sure that the two people who should never meet do so as soon as possible. Find out what is important to these people and what they must do in order to keep their reputations in society. When these imperatives are broken, shame and ruin are the result.

This they did and, from the first rehearsal, the cast took on the serious nature of comedy work, valiantly trying to follow my obsessive instructions. By now they were totally at ease in the rehearsal room. David Turnbull led the cast, in the double role central to the plot. We had discovered him playing in Adelaide some time before and asked him to join the Company to play Atahawalpa in *Royal Hunt of Sun*. He transformed into a glorious vision of young manhood, standing in the Sun circle of the Inca Empire. His performance in *Flea* would establish him as one of the finest actors to emerge from these years.

I was anxious to find ways of countering the fact that the cast was young but the major roles were all middle-aged. Kris Fredrikson helped me solve this for the women by designing hobble skirts—long narrow skirts that forced the women to walk like ducks; both set and costumes were designed in the emerging Art Nouveau style of the period. The poor young women—Lyndel Rowe, Elaine Cusick, Jenny Claire, Elspeth Ballantyne and Bridget Lenahan—had to learn to manage this monstrous restraint as well as the play's fiendish timing. But they proved more than adept. The very restriction became a comic device. At the dress rehearsal, Lyndel, as Mme Chandebise, wearing the hobble for the first time, began her entrance down steps leading to the hotel. In the process she would see someone she was not meant to see and would run down the steps to hide. Finding herself trapped inside the hobble, she had no choice but to hop like a rabbit. We kept this moment and even today people remember with joy her attempts to hold onto her dignity.

Whether or not to show their awareness of the comic effect of their character is a crucial choice for the performer. In the English tradition audiences often expect actors to laugh at themselves. But with Feydeau it is essential to convey an obsessive gravity. Our cast achieved this brilliantly. When John Gregg brought the first act to an end playing, with fiendish enjoyment, a young clerk with a cleft palate and an effervescent joy of life, the first-night audience went wild. It became a 'must' to see and was brought back for a second season followed by a tour. *Flea* would be our last production before we emerged as the Melbourne Theatre Company.

To sit in an audience and watch rows of people helpless with laughter is, for a director, an exhilarating experience; but if we are honest with ourselves, it is also a puzzle to be solved. How did it happen? What was it that made the audience love this play more than another? Immediate answers include the writing, the acting, the design, the direction. But I believe the true answer is more complex and lies within the lives of those who come to see the play. Whatever private concerns bring them to this point of release will remain a mystery to us in the theatre.

Melbourne Theatre Company, 1967. Robin Ramsay as Pantalone in *A Servant of Two Masters*. (Photo: Henry Talbot.)

The Servant of Two Masters (1967)

As if Feydeau was not difficult enough, I then took on Goldoni and *The Servant of Two Masters*. And to do it I needed to teach the actors the art of *commedia* masks. In Robin Ramsay I found a Pantalone to equal anything I had seen in Europe, and the whole cast embraced the masks as if born to them. Australians being such physical creatures certainly helped in the classes I gave to achieve the musical flow of the *commedia* characters and the large gestures that give the masks their life. Kris and his team made the masks, accurately designed from old drawings; his overall design for this play has never been bettered, in my opinion, anywhere in the world. It also gave me an opportunity to work with my old mate Alan Hopgood, who was brave enough to take on, with great success, Arlecchino. Lyndel, with her instinctive feeling for the clown, brought magic and silly, funny life to the young heroine.

For many in the audience this play was a new experience. I was determined to give the audience an insight into the play's European origins and invited them to witness the Company preparing for the performance. Actors tried on the masks and responded to them with acrobatic exercises practised behind gauze curtains. The *commedia* world proved to be a curiosity and I was proud of bringing a touch of European theatre to Melbourne.

The actors responded with a sure touch, but it was work that had no future for us unless *commedia* could be translated into an Australian idiom. Twenty years later I was present when Nick Enright's and Terence Clarke's musical *The Venetian Twins*, starring the superb comic actor, Drew Forsythe, exploded into the theatre. Here, the whole tradition of *commedia* was brilliantly located within the Australian context and Arlecchino, as *malin* as ever, came to life as the larrikin Zanetto/Tonino.

Of all the forms of theatre I have experienced, it is comedy with which I have been obsessed, and its extreme expression, farce. The word 'comedy' is difficult to define beyond saying that it is an entertainment that makes people laugh; but when it encompasses plays as varied as the ludicrous pranks of *Rookery Nook* and the comedy of life in *The Three Sisters*, the range is wide indeed. My predilection for comedy began with the Jimmie James Company, of course, who in very short order taught me a sober truth: that preparation for a night of laughter required much more intense work than any drama.

The magic word in all comedy is 'timing' and this involves every actor in the play. Some have an instinct and talent for it, which gains them an enviable reputation. Others must work at it. The greatest 'timer' I ever saw was Jack Benny; he made me helpless with laughter just with a ten-second pause.

Timing became the most important skill, to be tried and tried again, to arrive at the perfect rendition of a line, a word, a pause, or even an inflection. Being aware of an audience was essential for this study; to know when and how to deliver the line to set off the laughter. Comic 'business', or *lazzi*, as the *commedia* expresses it, is usually not inherent in the situation but embroiders it. It therefore needs very careful planning and executing, so that it will appear to be a natural outcome. A play like *The Servant of Two Masters* is written entirely around *lazzi*, to display the skill of the performers.

Most importantly, within every actor/comedian, there must breathe the clown. Of all the actors it has been my pleasure to work with, the one who for me most embodied that lovable, innocent wisdom was that great actor/comedian Leo McKern. McKern would enter the rehearsal room with the eager innocence of a schoolboy, and, as his character blunders through the life of the play would wonder why on earth people were persecuting him in this way. In the play *Patate*, by Marcel Achard, which I directed in 1972, he played a rather old-fashioned gent who enjoys a good pint in a comfortable chair. When he has an appointment in an ultra-modern office he sits himself down and leans back comfortably. But this sofa has no back and he falls into a full back somersault onto the floor. He stands up in a bewildered way, aware that his future here holds hidden terrors. This one piece of business, rehearsed to perfection, sets the path for a character who is finding it difficult to cope with modern life.

Together with the principal comic, most comedies have characters which I call 'witnesses'; those who watch other characters become participants in the affairs of the play. The witnesses are usually intelligent, thinking people, with a sense of humour or a sense of the ridiculous and can therefore voice the audience's own response to the events unfolding. They are allied to the audience as their spokesperson and become a benchmark by which the absurdities can be measured. One of the principles of drama is that characters learn from experience. In farce, as every actor must remember, there is no development in character, only in situation. Characters are fully established from the moment of entry. The witness is therefore powerless to forestall the disaster that he forsees so clearly.

The capacity and willingness to make a fool of oneself is therefore essential in any actor. This brings me back to the situation in the rehearsal room. Most actors, if they are strangers to the other cast members, are reluctant to release the clown within until they feel safe with their fellow artists. It is essential for the director to see his first job as creating an environment in which his cast can relax in each other's company, to give them permission to release the child within.

By creating such an environment the director will then find the actors do the work, willingly and with inspiration. I have seen rehearsals ruined by actors who refuse to let go, who remain on the fringe of the work, unwilling to expose their vulnerable natures to their fellow actors. To evoke this necessary willingness is the first step towards an ensemble. Actors are boring only when they refuse to play the game. It was a great lesson for me to realise how serious I became in the early rehearsals of *Blood Wedding* and how inhuman the drama became because the foolish was excluded. To direct a drama with a group of actors determined to keep their dignity will always be a doomed enterprise. To do drama with a group of comedians willing to play the game will produce a vulnerable, recognisable slice of life.

I think of the moment in Euripides' *The Trojan Women*, when the women of Troy are finally confronted with Helen, the cause of their tragedy. They hate her for the betrayal, but they also envy her for her beauty and Paris' passionate love for her that brought about their destruction. In the production I saw at Epidavros the audience was encouraged to laugh at their envy even as they cried. When we are without foolishness we are no longer human.

Incident at Vichy (1967)

As the dress rehearsal finished, I thanked the stage management and the actors for their patience and dismissed them to rest and have a meal before the show. It was the day of the opening but an extra dress rehearsal had been necessary as Dick Prins' set was complex and involved quite dangerous clambering over huge railway girders high above. I had also invited a special group of people to see this dress rehearsal. They were members of the Vieux Colombier Company from Paris, who were touring Australian universities with a production of Molière. Our play was Arthur Miller's *Incident at Vichy*.

I found them riveted to their seats; a few were sobbing. Miller's work has always been highly thought of in France, but this play would, I knew, strike a chord of personal anguish with the sensibilities of these French actors. It dealt with the betrayal of Jews by the Vichy Government at the beginning of the Second World War.

They were intensely moved by the play and by the performances; and the cast, led by George Whaley as a Jewish psychiatrist, Robin Ramsay as a Catholic intellectual, with John Gregg, as a German officer, did it great justice. In 1967 it was now twenty-five years after the event, and Vichy was still not spoken of in France. The play had not been seen there and the French actors enthused about this production being presented at the next festival of Théâtre Internationale in Paris. Much later I learned that an invitation had been offered but allowed to lapse. It would have been an experience '*assez extraordinaire*'.

The opening of any production requires special preparation by a director. The audience usually arrives in a state of general anticipation and the director wants to focus this as quickly as possible. At the opening of *Incident at Vichy* a disparate group of men are being held at a railway siding. They are terrified, not knowing why they are there but conscious that all of them are Jewish. In order to heighten the expectancy in the audience, I instructed the guards to begin bringing in the men one by one from the half-hour call. This meant that people coming into the auditorium were discomfited to find that the play had apparently started without them. Their chatter stopped abruptly and they sat in uneasy silence watching frightened men being ushered down the steel staircase into the siding. Finally, the full cast was assembled and with an apologetic cough, David Turnbull, as a perplexed artist, began to speak. As he did so the audience let out a sigh of relief and the tension mounted again from this moment.

Some plays require a longer time than others to capture the audience. With *Incident at Vichy* the characters speak with suppressed terror from the opening words and it was important they should hold the audience from the first moment to the last, so no interval was allowed. Sometimes music can do the job of establishing the right mood, sometimes appropriate use of documentary film. A good director will always find a way for the actors and audience to come together in understanding as soon as possible.

So many good plays are too-quickly forgotten. In all the years since *Incident at Vichy* I have never seen another production. It's a play that deserves revival. Like the best of Arthur Miller, it stays in the mind.

Kristian Fredrikson, in his setting for *The Heiress*, 1967. (Photo: Henry Talbot.)

The Heiress (1967)

'Guess what! Sumner wants me to do *The Heiress*! That piece of boulevard nonsense. It makes Henry James look like a writer of soap.' I raved on with rubbish like this. The moment I had the news I was on the phone to Kris, who was having a weekend in the mountains.

'Sounds good,' said Kris, 'the sort of play that can deliver a good piece of theatre. Just down your alley. We'll probably make a good job of it.'

And we did. How easily we turn our backs on good stories. They have upheld the theatre for decades since Galsworthy and would continue to do so. Each time I find a warm satisfaction in the expertise that brings these plays alive. The well-made play is in many minds a derogatory term for an old-fashioned three-act drama of suspense with curtain lines that cause talk at the interval bar. And indeed there are many such plays not worth a second glance, but if they are written by expert craftsmen and women of the theatre they can enthrall and hold an audience to the final moment. In her review in the *Australian* (19 September 1967) Katharine Brisbane agreed: '*The Heiress* is the solid bread and butter of theatre and with plenty of meat in-between. It has a three-dimensional, nineteenth century setting, strongly realised naturalistic characters, a real and absorbing plot and a satisfying resolution.'

Such plays as Terence Rattigan's *The Winslow Boy*—Did the boy steal the postal order?—or Daphne Du Maurier's *Rebecca*—Will Mrs de Winter wrestle successfully with the image of the dead Rebecca?—are good yarns superbly written. As in all good mysteries, we do not witness characters developing through three acts but rather how these characters, established early on in the play, will react to the events which unfold. So I found in *The Heiress*.

The authors of *The Heiress*, Ruth and Augustus Goetz, knew the theatre, and this play cunningly brings the drama to an extraordinary climax. Michael Duffield, a great friend and major actor in the Company, played the role of his life as Doctor Sloper, and Maggie Millar, playing his daughter Catherine, the prey of fortune hunters, revealed with aching sensitivity the appalling circumstances of this plain girl's tortured life. Such plays as this require a highly detailed set and costumes to help bring it alive. These Kris supplied.

Never had the theatre been so well served by Betty Druitt's wardrobe and Peter Roehlen's workshop. Russell Street Theatre became Washington Square. David Turnbull revealed his versatility with a haunting performance as the young adventurer and Monica Maughan was a delightful Aunt Penniman. It was truly an actors' play and the audience packed the theatre for the season. So much for my first reaction! I will never stop learning with the theatre as my teacher.

When Catherine finally mounts the staircase, lamp in hand, leaving Maurice banging at the front door below, the first-night audience stamped their ovation. As I sat watching on opening night I thought of Jimmie and the Family and how they would have loved this play. All their choices were well-made plays. My apprenticeship was within the construction of the well-told story and never again would I turn my back on this foundation of good theatre.

In hindsight, from a great distance in time, I think suddenly of the ovation Daphne du Maurier's *Rebecca* received twenty-five years later, when I directed it at the Marian Street Theatre in Sydney. When the curtain rose revealing the mists from the sea rolling into the English living room, and the whispered voice of Mrs de Winter floated through the auditorium, there was an audible sigh. Like children being told once again a favourite story, the audience watched a mystery unfold that they knew and loved. The cast did not let them down.

The Magistrate (1968)

By this time I had gained a strong conviction that my role as a director was that of interpreter; someone who brought the writer's work to the stage faithfully, without embellishment. It is therefore with a certain hesitation I confess that in the next two plays I broke my rule and all because of music.

The Magistrate was new to me. I was delighted to find this late Victorian farce so beautifully constructed and so English. It made me fall in love with the work of Arthur Wing Pinero, seeing him as the beginning of modern comedy as we know it. Later, I would direct his great comedy *Trelawney of the Wells*, about the decline of the old touring melodrama troupes. In Pinero's time the piano was integral to English domestic life, and a piano was required for an early scene between Cis, the young son, and Beattie, his pretty music teacher. I recalled the colourful music hall and parlour songs I had uncovered years before in Canberra and consulted our musical director Sandra McKenzie. The songs, we felt, could reinforce the context and provide added enjoyment for the audience. As rehearsals progressed, the combination of play and song confirmed the broader style of English comedy that has its roots in the Music Hall.

Research into the manners and social mores of the period revealed essential differences between English bourgeois society and that of late nineteenth-century Paris. Feydeau's society was much more cruel, witty and sophisticated. The English drawing-room centred on the piano and the sentimental songs of the time. The English pantomime with its easy jokes and audience participation invokes the community singsong and a world ripe for Gilbert and Sullivan. The world of childhood lasted much longer in late Victorian England than in Paris.

Where the plot of *A Flea in Her Ear* evolves around illicit assignations, the adventures of the little magistrate and his family in a Soho hotel are brought about by the goodwill and innocent misjudgment of the central character. Michael Duffield mirrored this quality perfectly in the playing of this essential Englishman in much the style of ArthurLowe's Captain Mainwaring in the TV series, *Dad's Army*, written sixty years later. England has remained faithful to the silly ass in all his guises.

With the same group of actors moving from Paris to London, rehearsals revealed interesting differences. While the French characters' fear of 'what others might think' demanded serious and concentrated work on the rhythm of the dialogue, *The Magistrate* maintained an easy, rather homely atmosphere. The English did not mind making idiots of themselves; the French abhorred it. The cast had great fun as Sandy taught them the great songs of the period and we fitted them into Pinero's comic world.

I recall with great pleasure Dennis Olsen's silly-ass rendition of the love song 'Ever of Thee'; George Whaley's brusque clown Colonel Lukin, Martin Vaughan's Mr Bullamy providing the perfect figure of the music hall MC with his bawdy songs, and the fresh-faced antics of John Gregg as the boy who never grew up. Jennifer Claire, as the Magistrate's wife, gave that vague, lovely woman a specially endearing trait. To cover a scene change, the whole cast marched on stage to sing 'There'll always be an England'. Bets were taken nightly on how many keys Jenny would contrive to hit as she gave battle to this anthem.

My heart dedicates this time to Michael Duffield, no longer with us, who gave our audience and us, his fellow artists, a grand time.

Melbourne Theatre Company, 1968. Helmut Bakaitis, Sean Scully and George Whaley in *Burke's Company*. (Photo: Henry Talbot.)

Burke's Company (1968)

The writer Bill Reed sent me his play, *Burke's Company* while he was working abroad. His treatment of this classic story of Burke and Wills' doomed attempt to traverse Australia from south to north excited John Sumner and me and we decided to schedule it immediately. Kris met the challenge of conveying the vast landscape surrounding the 1861 expedition by producing one of his most evocative sets. He designed a floor of corrugated earth, raked fairly steeply and moulded into rigid curves like a contour map. Hanging behind the men as they journeyed was a steel sun, which shone and sometimes dazzled as the fatal trio tramped their way to death.

I then set about incorporating into it my two personal passions, mime and music. I had been listening to the music of Peter Sculthorpe and in particular his Sixth String Quartet, which seemed to me to hold all the tragic sounds of this epic journey. I rang him to ask if he would agree to his music accompanying Burke's journey to his death.

'Go for your life,' he said.

For the actors, his music became part of their voices, their vision, and inspired the choreography of their bodies, as they battled on in the blazing sun.

Led by George Whaley as Burke, Helmut Bakaitis as Wills and Sean Scully as King, the actors spent tortuous weeks learning the body control needed to express the agony of their journey. All my physical work with Lecoq came to fruition in their dedicated practice. At times, they resembled a memorial to the expedition sculpted in bronze. Other members of the cast were Dennis Olsen as Brahe and Simon Chilvers as Wright, the two men who survive to carry the guilt for the tragedy.

On opening night, as their army boots stamped their way down from the dressing rooms to stage, lamps began to glimmer and the first cello note of music began the drama. Using mime for everything from props to animals concentrated the drama on bodies and faces and I was well pleased with my students. It was interesting to observe the audience, most of whom had never seen mime used in this way. I remember the blank look on some faces as the play began. For some it was altogether too foreign, but generally the audience responded well. Such work has become familiar since then, but in 1968 it was a new experience for most who came to see it. Some critics thought our meticulous work simply disguised the undramatic nature of the play. Perhaps so, but I did not begin preparations thinking this. I thought, as John did, it was a fine piece of writing and the mime and music supported the drama.

I recently picked up my old copy of the play with photos of George Whaley's face on its cover, caught in the last terrible moments of Burke's life. As I read the text it occurred to me that here was a libretto for a modern opera. Reed's rhythms and poetry seemed waiting to be expressed by the power of great voices; that Burke, Wills and King would make a wonderful trio. My choice of Sculthorpe almost forty years ago did not seem such a bad idea in retrospect, particularly as in later years he was commissioned to write the score for the 1985 film.

Martin Vaughan, Graeme Blundell, Lyndel Rowe, Dennis Olsen and Gary Wastell in *The Three Sisters*, 1968. (Photo: Henry Talbot.)

The Three Sisters (1968)

'I came to a matinee as I was on my way back to Adelaide,' said the actor. 'I'm not a very good audience but friends said I should see it. At the end, I walked out of the theatre and danced down the street.'

Chekhov's *The Three Sisters* contained the finest work I've ever done. Why I should believe this is difficult to say, but I will try to reason it out, from the countless emotional souvenirs I have of this extraordinary play. I believe it to be the finest play translated into the English language. It is a Russian play, about Russian people at a certain time in Russia's history, but this does not lessen the effect it has on people in any country. It speaks to the young and to the old. It reveals our dreams, our stupidity, our selfishness, our indifference towards others, our unwitting cruelty, and finally, our desperate optimism—in other words, our humanity. All this is revealed, not in great speeches, but in ordinary encounters between people, as three sisters live out their lives in their provincial home, visited by friends, neighbours and occasionally by officers from the military barracks. The years roll on through four acts, as they grow older, a little wiser, more disappointed, even despairing, but always hoping for better times to come.

The casting fell into place fortuitously. We were about to go on a lengthy tour of *The Crucible* and *The Magistrate* and the cast was assembled from these two plays that had already taken up the lives of all the actors for many months. This circumstance provided the most unexpected and unplanned bonus for the rehearsal of Chekhov: we had an ensemble. Knowing each other well created a trusting environment, and the fact that we rehearsed on tour, in temporary premises as we found them, gave the rehearsals a family feeling. Adrift in unfamiliar towns, the actors were happy to come together each day. *The Three Sisters'* house became our home.

These factors became significant in the weeks that followed. Much preparation is required by a director before rehearsals begin. The design is usually complete and the text familiar from study. In this state of preparedness I faced *The Three Sisters*, but something happened from the first rehearsal. As the actors began speaking the lines and confronting each other in scene work, a world of feeling, of dreams, of secret desire began to be exposed. Gradually, a hidden life was revealed: lying behind the social chatter and the lies lay the pain of vulnerable human beings. This momentous discovery required time, patience and support for the actors and myself. I no longer felt like the director, instructing from the stalls, and became someone walking with them, uncovering the dreams we all have as we wander through life. The play began to take shape as we toured from one town to another, setting up our few props and makeshift furniture where we could.

In Canberra we were given a beautiful room in which to rehearse, with great windows along one wall. The sun shone and the breeze blew through, as the old servant Anfisa spread a spotless white cloth to begin Act One and the sisters, with their guests, came laughing to lunch. This play and our work together took over my life and it returns in my dreams. If there is one playwright who has taught me that the truth about a human being is seldom to be found on the surface, it is Anton Chekhov.

By the time we returned to Melbourne, the play was ready. Kris gave us a slatted wooden house, a garden of birch trees and simple, subdued costumes, allowing this family drama to ebb and flow like life itself. I never wanted to direct this play again. Most times a production leaves you wanting to have another shot, to take the play further, but my memories are so strong of the cast of this production I can only see the characters through their eyes. I list them in grateful memory of an extraordinary time. Olga, Jenny Claire; Masha, Maggie Millar; Irina, Lyndel Rowe; Andrei, Helmut Bakaitis; Tusenbach, Dennis Olsen; Vershinin, George Whaley; Solyony, Alan Hopgood; Natasha, Elaine Cusick; Chebutykin, Michael Duffield; Anfisa, Patricia Kennedy; Kulyakin, Martin Vaughan; Arthur Hynes as the old man Ferapont and two soldiers, Rode and Fedotik, Graeme Blundell and Gary Wastell.

As Tusenbach stood beside a silent Irina, muttering with desperate need, 'Say something,' I could feel the waiting world breathe. And as in the last moments Andrei wheeled his young son into the garden, escaping the harsh voice of his wife Natasha, we became aware that the play, like life, would never come to an end. Chebutykin would go on humming his old music hall song, accepting the world as he found it. As they left the stage for the final time, someone in the audience was heard to whisper 'Oh, don't go. Don't go.'

To this day, friends and strangers remember affectionately the three sisters and their visitors. For me, they represent that time in my life when all was right with my world, even as the world outside was in turmoil. During the course of writing this memoir so many years later, the opportunity came to direct *The Three Sisters* once again with students at NIDA. Despite my vivid memories of the MTC production, I agreed. It gave me unexpected pleasure, not just revisiting the text but also learning more and more about the man Anton Chekhov. In my old age he remains unsurpassed as an artist and a human being.

Life, of course, was a little simpler in 1968, particularly for the performing artist whose career was not beset with many choices. Television drama was being made but to no great extent and the film industry was just starting a revival. For those actors who were part of the MTC during the late 1960s, their whole life was dedicated to the work at Russell Street. Over coffee and drinks concentrated voices talked endlessly of the work at hand and very seldom was there a glance over the companion's shoulder to see who more interesting might have entered.

The wickedly erudite Frank Thring, despite his success abroad in theatre and film, became part of our family. If he was not performing at Russell Street he would be seen on opening nights surrounded by actors from the Company, drinking his moselle and enjoying the camaraderie and well-being of the actors' world, and at the same time ticking off any actor who did not in his opinion make Russell Street shine. Patricia Kennedy became our great lady of the Company, never afraid to stand up to her director and demand attention and care for the actors. Along with Brian James, they both remained fiercely loyal to the Company for many years. I recall their performances in John Sumner's meticulously-observed production of Edward Albee's *A Delicate Balance*. Sitting in Russell Street on opening night made me proud that this cast was part of our Company. Whenever I need to cast an actor to play 'a real gentleman', I think of Brian. When in later years he would join me in Adelaide I knew I had one obligation to him; to give him the opportunity of playing the father in *The Winslow Boy*, a role he was born to play. His courtesy and energy during rehearsals would be a standard younger actors were obliged to meet.

Old friends from the Union days, Monica Maughan, Lyndel Rowe, Neil Fitzpatrick and Robin Ramsay, became leaders of their profession during this time, playing major roles and becoming favourites of our loyal subscription audience. Monica's performance as Jean Brodie in the adaptation of Muriel Spark's *The Prime of Miss Jean Brodie* was a highlight of the season, as was Neil's portrayal of Christ in Dennis Potter's *Son of Man*. In later times I directed Neil in Christopher Hampton's *The Philanthropist* with a cast that included the exciting new talents of John Allen and Matthew Burton. The play concerns a university professor who hides his terror of life behind wit and urbanity until, in the last minutes of the play, the terror explodes. Neil was brilliant in the role and Richard Prins brought technical mastery to his set for the climactic suicide. The way the blood and brains splattered the back wall brought cries of horror from the audience. Together they gave us a most rewarding night in the theatre. A landmark production by John Sumner was Shakespeare's *Henry IV, Part I* with Frank Thring as

Falstaff and Robin Ramsay as Prince Henry. This swaggering production went on tour to open the Octagon Theatre in Perth, spreading the news further that the MTC was a formidable force in Australian theatre

New Melbourne friends like Jennifer Claire, Simon Chilvers, Maggie Millar and George Whaley all developed their skills with plays chosen to engage their talents and natures. Simon's home became a second home for me as our friendship developed over these years, made possible by the constant work of the Company. The young Graeme Blundell joined us for a while before becoming a foundation member of the Australian Performing Group in Carlton. At Graeme's invitation I gave classes on the Clown to the group and was impressed by their willingness to experiment.

From interstate came a group of actors destined to become major players on the Australian stage. Dennis Miller from Tasmania, Dennis Olsen and Elspeth Ballantyne from Adelaide, Elaine Cusick from Queensland, David Turnbull and John Gregg from Sydney. Elaine's talents took her from *Flea* to *The Magistrate* to *The Three Sisters* with that enormous energy and goodwill that seems to be born in people from the North. Dennis Miller provided me with one of those moments of which directors dream. John and I were holding auditions before the Company was launched and a young untried, untrained young man strode on stage. 'A real find,' we silently said as he opened his mouth and took over the tiny space. From the moment he joined us Dennis proved us right. His performance in Alan Hopgood's *And the Big Men Fly* was sensational and, when he played Pierre in *War and Peace*, Tolstoy was well served.

From the Young Elizabethan Players came Helmut Bakaitis and Peter Hepworth. The Young Elizabethans were founded by the Elizabethan Theatre Trust and run with love and dedication by Malcolm Robertson. Since playing Andrei in *The Three Sisters* Helmut has remained beside me as artist and friend. Peter Hepworth now writes for television, but I have a photograph of him as a boy soldier, playing the drum in *The Royal Hunt of the Sun*. It remains hanging on my wall as a reminder of those young days.

The older generation, with Patricia Kennedy, Brian James, Michael Duffield, Bridgit Lenahan, Martin Vaughan and Edward Hepple, provided a healthy balance for the younger members of the Company, offering their experience to help create a standard of work that brought many people from interstate to enjoy their performances.

For all these artists, there was always a chance to experiment in rehearsal, and try out new ideas without the fear of disapproval. The Company belonged to them and they were at home in the rehearsal room above the box office or across the road at the YWCA hall. It was in this hall that we wrestled with the masks and the extravagant body language of so many iconic characters. George Whaley, Helmut Bakaitis and Sean Scully endured weeks of exhausting exercises in mime to suffer the journey of Burke and Wills. My last memory of this generous hall was rehearsing Ionesco's *Rhinoceros*, not as director but as actor under the direction of George Whaley, playing Berenson with Frank Thring in the title role. The experience was hilarious and frightening. Becoming an actor again after all this time was a challenge and I determined not to let it happen again. I was terrified of forgetting lines (this in the man who could learn 45 pages in one night in earlier years) and of breaking up on stage—which I did constantly to Frank's malicious enjoyment.

My years in Europe lived and breathed with me in Melbourne, and those strong memories affected everything I said and did. I was determined to pass on that legacy to every actor who would listen, and in that way soon assuaged any regret I might have had about my departure from Paris.

Soon after I arrived back in Melbourne John Sumner introduced me to Margaret Scott who, after a career as a principal with the Ballet Rambert and the National Theatre Ballet, had founded the Australian Ballet School. She invited me to teach mime at the school and my love of the ballet began. I continued to teach for several years twice a week after rehearsal at the MTC.

As I took my place in front of twenty young students attired in their tights and soft shoes, I recalled Lecoq's reproof, '*La danse n'est pas la vérité.*' Here I was, about to teach young artists movement founded on reality and far from their abstract and romantic world of placed gesture. To be an actor requires a very different aptitude from being a dancer. Those who intuitively combine both are rare. Mime requires the talent of an actor rather than a dancer and I had to find ways for the dancers, whose natural direction lay in movement rather than words, to discover the real world. It did not take long to see the difficulty. Every movement I gave them was translated into one of grace. I knew I had to find another way.

Among the students were three young men, Richard Hayes Marshall, Ian Spink and Paul Saliba. In later classes Don Asker and Graeme Murphy appeared. These dancers, I noticed, were more adventurous than others and I determined to think of new approaches. They listened intently and showed they were willing to try anything that might help their creative work. I brought a cassette player to the following class and played a familiar ballet melody, which at once brought a dance response. I stopped the tape and divided them into small groups with instructions to devise a different scenario: eating in a restaurant, stealing from a house, taking the bus home, a day in the office. The results were hilarious and began to make connections to their daily lives.

Before long the students found their own choreographic themes and brought many ideas into the classroom. Ballet dancers, I discovered, were rather shy artists and found it difficult to confront the idea of clowning, but those who did made a real breakthrough. At a school showing in a city theatre all of the students presented a Kafka-like sketch of lost people, using pure mime and figuration, that is, using their bodies as objects. The ballet audience had never seen anything like it and many found it ridiculous, but others were fascinated by the ideas and the possibilities it provoked. On another occasion Richard Hayes Marshall, Paul Saliba and Ian Spink brought Lecoq's teaching alive with five minutes of expert artistry in a sketch we called 'The Three Thieves'. Without any urging, Richard later left the school to join Lecoq in Paris; to study with him, become his assistant and finally to open his own school. Paul, after studying in America with Martha Graham and Alvin Ailey was closely associated with NAISDA for many years. Ian continued study and work in the United Kingdom, before joining the RSC as movement coach. Soon after our classes, Graeme Murphy began his distinguished choreographic career and has now been artistic director of the Sydney Dance Company for thirty years. Don Asker went abroad and achieved fame with the Netherlands Dance Theatre. He returned to Australia in 1980 and founded the Human Veins Dance Theatre in Canberra. Other future choreographers such as John Meehan and Robert Ray, later principals of the Australian Ballet, showed a real talent for mime. I look back with pride that they too were among my students in their early training years.

During these busy years of the late sixties, while directing plays at Russell Street, I continued to teach and give workshops to both dancers and actors in the art of pure mime and clown. It was satisfying to see how many young people were captured by Lecoq's work and ventured, as I had done, to Paris. Many artists working in Australia today are creating new theatre which puts to use their knowledge of Lecoq's methods. His school now has new studios and is a very large establishment.

My association with Margaret Scott's ballet school continued for the next decade before I joined the Australian Ballet Company and Marilyn Jones to direct their three-act ballet, *Coppelia*. Margaret gave me a never-to-be-forgotten opportunity to dance the Headmistress in *Graduation Ball* with the final-year students of the Australian Ballet School. As in the dream of a small child, I skipped and waltzed among real dancers and took a dancer's bow.

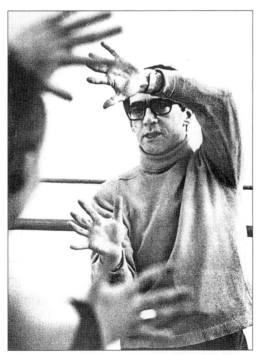

The author teaching mime at the Australian Ballet School, 1960s.

One morning I woke up and thought to myself: 'Wouldn't it be lovely to make some money? Not a lot, but enough to buy a little flat and put something aside for the future.'

Poverty was a condition of life in those days for all of us at the MTC. Money was always short and we lived almost like gypsies on the fringe of the good times. Occasionally it hurt, but our work together more than compensated. I had never given more than a passing thought to money before this time; perhaps I was having mortal thoughts. After all, within a couple of years I would be forty years old and I was still living in a room in a rented house. My modest salary with the MTC was just adequate to live on and was part-subsidised by the fees for the mime classes that went back to the Company. Saving was out of the question.

My thoughts persisted. 'Half my life is over and I do not even own a car.'

A thought can grow like a canker, crowding out everything else. I began to have secret 'commercial thoughts'; silly to think them shameful when it was the commercial theatre that had trained me. On the other hand I was by now embedded in a system of government grants. We were a privileged group, our purpose was 'the pursuit of excellence'. Our theatre company was free to experiment with new and rare plays and present the classics for the higher good, regardless of their popularity. We could also keep a large company of actors. Those actors whose lives were spent in the precarious commercial world considered our lives to be cushy. This attitude was unreasonable, of course. New work has always depended on patronage. Even in the days of *commedia dell'arte*, troupes depended totally on the favours of the rich.

This argument has, I know, been raging in our country ever since the idea of arts grants was introduced. Patronage had been rare and experiment confined to the amateur theatre; so, for the general public, theatre has been entertainment and little else. A young country is more concerned with present issues than with traditions it does not have. However, as I write, I can now see a rising recognition of our origins and our need for self-expression.

There was no getting away from the fact that ambition was knocking at my door. An urge for freedom began to fill me; to be cast adrift from the safety-net of government-assisted drama companies, to test my skills on the open market; to find my own space, to see what might happen. Nights of talk with friends and days of ruminating provided me with a catalogue of possibilities; but, of course, this meant once again leaving Australia.

Ever since I could remember, London had been the goal. However, I had now spent ten years of my professional life in Australian theatre and the Melbourne Theatre Company had been my home for the last five. How did I feel about London now? Was it still the prize? Or was that prize receding from view? I recall vividly the panic that set in as I tried to answer this question. When I turned my back on Paris I knew I would not return there to work. Leaving London for Melbourne had been a very different decision. I would return after gaining more experience as a director. The panic I now felt was the fear of having left it too late. I had to test myself and find as honest an answer as I could. I must return to London. Good fortune, after five years of hard, satisfying work, delivered a small arts travel grant into my hands. With John's blessing once again I took a plane to London.

For the third time I arrived in London, this time a little more prepared. My agent had introduced me to the London Management Agency, who were ready to help me gain a foothold, as long as I had the patience for the long haul it promised to be. Old friends had shifted and married during those five fervent years in Melbourne; London had also changed. What had been new and exciting six years ago was now established. Julian Chagrin was living in Tel Aviv, carving out a career in his new country of Israel. Leon Lissek had become a film actor; he was married to the actress Heather Canning and they lived in Buckinghamshire. Lyndel Rowe was back in London, working from time to time, but mainly in television. Patricia Conolly was enjoying a career in American theatre and my friend Susan Engel was playing with the RSC at Stratford. London no longer felt familiar and I discovered an unexpected impatience in me. How long would it take me to become established and be allowed to do the work I was doing in Melbourne? Was the long haul worth the wait?

An important change had taken place in my heart that went beyond ambition and I needed to be here to feel it: the realisation that I was an Australian, that I loved working with Australian actors and that I was proud of the work we had done in Melbourne. London had some new and exciting theatre, but work was waiting for me back home and I was aching to return. My youngest sister, Caroline, arrived and we spent time together, mainly going to concerts at Festival Hall. This great city offered so much. Who knows, if I had been a little more patient I might have been able to start again, but my life as an Australian director was now established and new opportunities were already being offered.

I turned my back with a willing heart and returned to Melbourne. There had been a quick visit to Paris and old, familiar cafés and streets, but John Sumner had offered me a masked production of Gogol's *The Inspector General* and my mind was preoccupied with the play and the rehearsals and the company of actors whose work and dedication matched anything I had seen on any stage.

It was now 1970. Back in Melbourne the work gave me much pleasure, but the need to earn more money and expand my experience continued to haunt me. The opportunity came quite suddenly. Robert Helpmann was to direct *Conduct Unbecoming* by Barry England for the producer Harry M. Miller, but had had to withdraw. Miller offered the production to me and without a moment's hesitation I said 'yes'. I had taken no time to consider the consequences and my exit from the Melbourne Theatre Company proved painful in the extreme; in fact, I felt as if a moment in life was being repeated as I confronted John Sumner with my decision. As with Jimmie James all those years ago, it would take John many months to forgive my betrayal of him and the Company. But I was determined to follow my obsessive need to find a market for my skills. And indeed, 1971 did lead to interesting new horizons.

Conduct Unbecoming is an English military thriller in which the dark deeds of an Indian regiment in the 1800s are exposed. It was one of those plays of the 1960s in which the British were breast-beating about the loss and mismanagement of the Empire. I hated it. The rehearsals confirmed a fear I had held ever since my first itch to break free from a permanent company. This freedom meant assembling a group of actors who had no connection with each other beyond the play they were rehearsing and little to say to each other beyond 'good morning'. They were good actors, good people, willing to work, but in the time available there was no possibility they could create a breathing world on stage. We had a bearable time. Everyone was quite pleased with the result. But the show did not last very long. I did not make much money.

The idea of creating an ensemble had been a natural goal for me and in Melbourne I had come close to achieving it. But it had required time to develop. In the commercial world, such time is unprofitable. I was sadly disappointed that my fears had been so quickly confirmed, and realised that they were to a large degree the same fears I had felt when considering a future in London. Actors are used to it, of course. They work all the time with other actors whom they meet at the first reading. They adjust their feelings, concentrate on their role and play as the director sees it. They skirt around each other, negotiating their relationships, the roles, the director's instructions and hope that somehow the result will be satisfactory. It sometimes is.

I was saved by the Old Tote Theatre Company, the Sydney equivalent of the MTC, which appointed me to work with Robin Lovejoy. I was back with a company of actors. I was delighted with them. Ensemble work was their aim and, with Pinero's *Trelawney of the Wells*, we came close. In hindsight I perceive a fundamental difference between Melbourne and Sydney in their respective attitudes towards theatre production, both then and now. In Sydney the actor is primary. There is a strutting peacock in the beauty of Sydney and leading actors are singled out as prizes. In Melbourne the text is considered the most important element. Melbourne is a much more reflective city with its colder weather, and has a more appreciative attitude towards the author. Actors are there to interpret the play, not to use the play to display themselves.

The *Trelawney* cast reads today like a Who's Who of Sydney theatre; Ruth Cracknell, Robyn Nevin, Melissa Jaffer, Kirrily Nolan, Doreen Warburton, Christine Amor, Coleen Fitzpatrick, Tim Elliott, John Gaden, Drew Forsythe, Gil Tucker, John Walton, Michael Rolfe and Arthur Dignam. I cast three Melbourne friends: Lyndel Rowe, Brian

Old Tote Theatre Company, 1970. Marion Johns, Martin Vaughan, Lyndel
Rowe, Drew Forsythe and Tom Farley in *Trelawney of the Wells*.

James and Martin Vaughan, together with two old-timers, Tom Farley
and Marion Johns. Neil Fitzpatrick, back from London, led the cast
as the aspiring playwright. Anne Fraser's evocative set featured as a
backcloth a print of 'The Railway Station', by William Frith, depicting
a Victorian family leaving by train. Opening night was a delight and
Sydney enjoyed the perspicacious Pinero.

One real pleasure in Sydney was the Parade Theatre which, like
Russell Street, was small and intimate but was also equipped with
proper wings, and later flies were added. One could be a little more
adventurous here. It was a lovely theatre which was torn down to
make way for the present NIDA complex. Like its counterpart in
Melbourne, abandoned after the opening of the Arts Centre, it is still
missed by many.

After *Trelawney*, I was offered *Uncle Vanya* with a cast led by John
Bell. It was well received but left me disappointed. The work was not
organic. It did not emerge from any real company ethos but employed
the actors for each production. With only a couple of years separating
this Chekhov from *The Three Sisters* in Melbourne, comparison was
unavoidable.

192

At last a call from John Sumner came in his familiar breezy voice—as if nothing acrimonious had ever occurred between us—with the request to return to work with him and Leo McKern. I sped back to Melbourne with a glad heart, my exile was over. I admit that my exit from Sydney was made with some relief. I was known throughout my short time there as someone 'from Melbourne'; that peculiar schism at times seems to amount to their being different countries. My year in sunny Sydney had its rewards but I found an inner joy at being back in a colder clime. It would be close to a decade before I returned to Sydney to work in a new and vibrant scene at the Opera House and the Wharf theatres.

As an established director, I am expected to have worked with many famous people, and in opera and film I have had my share. But celebrity in the Australian theatre is a modest thing, confined mainly to the musical theatre; on the legitimate stage internationally-famous names seldom came my way.

My mother once provided me with a very sweet lesson in notoriety. She was bedridden for the last years of her life and television provided an occasional enjoyment. By this time I had been a director for many years and had carved out a successful career. However, to my mother, my life continued to be precarious, without permanence and therefore without security. To someone like her, who had endured the Great Depression, the question was always on her lips:

'Are you doing all right, son?'

One day I came on a visit to find her sparkling with her news. She had seen an interview on television with Warren Mitchell, with whom I had recently worked. It appears he spoke kindly about our work together. To my mother this meant that not only must I be earning good money but, on reflection, I was probably fairly famous myself. Her satisfaction lasted for the rest of her life.

Two other famous people came my way in the early seventies and provided me with some salutary lessons in theatre craft. The first was Leo McKern, who from time to time during his illustrious career returned to Australia to keep in touch with a country he loved. Late in 1971 John Sumner invited Leo to join the Company for a year and perform in two plays, Ray Lawler's *The Man Who Shot the Albatross*, a drama about Captain Bligh's period as Governor of New South Wales, to be directed by John, and Michel Achard's comedy *Patate*, which I was to direct. Both plays went on a national tour so that my association with this great actor continued for twelve months. From the first rehearsal he taught everyone around him what it was to be an actor par excellence.

On the first day of rehearsal the door flew open and what appeared to be a smiling young boy bounced into the space. At least, that was my immediate impression. Leo loved experiment. Everything was worth a try. Any suggestion was worth not just thinking about but putting into practice—if it did not work, throw it out, try another one. He was inexhaustible. No idea was so valuable it had to be preserved. What delighted me particularly was his ability to keep an open mind about fixing comedy business. Day after day we would try new ideas and, if they worked, use them. Like all great actors, Leo was aware that the overall effect was the goal, and any detail within it could be sacrificed to attain this

Leo is no longer with us and I reflect with nostalgia and love on his joy of being an actor. He never wanted to talk about his art. He was an intuitive man who lived for the moment and responded to it. I would regale him with stories from my days with the Family and he would roar laughing with recognition. By the end of the tour he would force me into another life-changing decision.

The second famous person was Googie Withers, whom I met immediately after *Patate*. John had chosen *An Ideal Husband* to display her dazzling talent. This production would be designed by Hugh Colman and presented at Melbourne's Comedy Theatre. The cast was to include Frank Thring, Dennis Olsen, Simon Chilvers and an old friend from early days of the Trust Players, Dinah Shearing.

When I was a young man I fell in love with a young star who was carving out a career in those thrilling black-and-white English movies of the 1940s. Googie Withers, with her huge expressive eyes, a sense of humour that played constantly in her face, lips which seemed carved

Melbourne Theatre Company, Comedy Theatre, 1970. Betty Lucas, Leo
McKern and Frederick Parslow in *Patate*.

like a Nefertiti's, hypnotised her audiences. Beginning her career as a
dancer, she turned actress in the 1930s and became a long-standing
success as a stage actress as well making a stellar career in film.

To work with Googie was to work with a born actress. What do
I mean by this? I believe those who are born to act are a rare breed.
Television and film have produced great entertainers who spend
their whole career playing themselves—or a personality invented by
themselves. Born actors, on the other hand, transform themselves at
will into whatever character they choose. In so doing they come alive
and grow in stature. They enter the stage with a feeling of fulfillment,
like coming home. Off stage they appear nice ordinary human beings;
once on stage something happens which brings them vibrantly alive. It
is difficult to take your eyes off them.

Googie was like this. She placed herself entirely into my hands, and
it was up to the designer and myself to create her environment. She
did the rest. No matter where I placed her on stage or who I placed
her with, the character of Mrs Cheveley grew within her, to explode

across the footlights on opening night. Hugh Colman's glittering Victorian, upper-class world framed her perfectly and the men who surrounded her danced superbly to Wilde's caustic wit.

To be born to it. In watching and listening to a great musician one can see how the artist is born to play the instrument. I have been in cars with motorists born to drive, completely at home with their vehicle. Perhaps that is it. To be the master or mistress of the stage, effortlessly commanding attention. Such mastery delivers great performances.

So it was with these two great artists, who, at home on their stage, displayed such generosity of spirit towards those who joined them. They were actors among actors, working towards a common purpose.

Adelaide

A new move was now on the horizon that seemed to answer my recent preoccupations with financial security and the yearning for my own company of actors. Colin Ballantyne, chairman of the Board of the new government-backed South Australian Theatre Company, invited me to apply for the position of artistic director. The position offered the opportunity for a professional company, and eventually a home in a new theatre complex under construction.

My first acquaintance with Adelaide had been on tour in 1956 with the Trust Players. Now I was in the market for any work which would keep me financial and it became a period of wandering from one major city to another. I had met Colin when, at the invitation of the current artistic director Peter Batey, I had directed a production of Ben Jonson's *The Alchemist* with Dennis Olsen, Edwin Hodgeman and Jennifer Hagan. These three actors had superseded my happy memories of the play from Canberra, and far less happy ones from Stratford-upon-Avon, with a vibrantly vocal performance. The extraordinary speed with which they delivered Jonson's superb rhythm, and communicated each line with panache and meaning, left me breathless.

Peter had been with the Company for several years. Before him the founding director had been John Tasker, under the aegis of the Australian Elizabethan Theatre Trust, whose work established Adelaide as a new and lively venue for professional actors in a business struggling to survive. Now the reforming young Premier Don Dunstan had restructured the Company as a statutory body with handsome State funding and was building it a theatre. It suddenly seemed a very exciting prospect. So I said 'yes' to Colin Ballantyne and began planning my new troupe even before the job was offered.

Just at this time the tour of *Patate* was coming to its end in Adelaide. One night as he drove me home after a performance, Leo asked me to go back to England with him and work at the successful new Exchange Theatre in Manchester where Braham Murray had established his talent. However, I had already accepted the new venture and the idea of my own company was too good to let go. With great regret I said goodbye to this remarkable actor.

Two friends were directly part of my plan, Helmut Bakaitis and Rodney Fisher. Helmut's dream was to make theatre with young people and I was impressed by his theories and ideas. Rodney I knew as a scholar and writer who displayed over the few years of our acquaintance a passion for theatre and the spoken word. The three of us spent a great deal of time in discussion and had begun to compose a working structure for a company. Colin gave us that chance, and the idea I put to the Board of a triumvirate, myself as artistic director and Helmut and Rodney as associates, was accepted. By mid-1972 our appointments were confirmed and the three of us headed out west. Before leaving I contacted two designers who would become an essential part of our adventure, Michael Pearce and Shaun Gurton.

Crammed into my impossibly small Fiat, luggage and all, the three of us set out on our adventure across the Hay plain and down into Adelaide. Plans and hopes for the future kept our conversation lively, until, some miles from Balranald on a highway that stretched from nowhere to nowhere, the valiant little Italian drew attention to the fact that it was running out of petrol. Uneasy silence, mixed with hysterical scenarios from disaster movies, kept us focused, as the little engine chugged on and on until, with relieved squeals, we saw the corrugated iron roof of a building shimmering in the hot distance. Much, much later, on the final run into the southern city, a grating sound announced that the engine was dropping out of its frame. In a search around the car Rodney found an old wire coat hanger and repaired the holding apparatus. We drove gently into Adelaide as the sun was setting, its dying rays making the Adelaide hills shimmer.

'Oh,' said one of us in a glow of romantic hope, 'it looks like Florence.'

We were to remain in Adelaide for four years from late 1972 till 1976. It would be the best of times and the worst of times and from the experience I would earn friends for life, see good theatre achieved, and a dream shattered by mutual misunderstanding.

Two abandoned church halls stripped for rehearsals and joined together by a green-room and kitchen, a large house on the same property to become our home and office, a company of fine actors and we were ready. Our company, our responsibility—backed by Don Dunstan, whose personal commitment to this venture ensured funding at a level of which other States were envious.

We were given enough funds to work with the actors for three months, to develop the beginnings of an ensemble, to commence a structure of community involvement, and to get to know Adelaide as we prepared our first season. Our longer task was to prepare a company for the wonderful new Playhouse, part of a Festival Centre on the Torrens River. This would be our future home within two years. The plans of this centre were already advanced and we were invited to help with advice. This was to be a splendid edifice. It would house visiting artists and build a world-wide reputation. All of Adelaide was excited by the prospect of a beautiful building with which to focus the biennial Festival of the Arts. As a home for the South Australian Theatre Company, however, I had grave fears for it; fears which mounted over the first months, but which I kept to myself in the light of the general optimism.

Adelaide had a number of amateur groups, which had long established themselves as the main artistic outlet for both actors and audience. These groups had their own theatres and a tremendously loyal following among the theatre-going public; which I discovered to my dismay was comparatively small. Adelaide was a big, comfortable, country town; a comment from one resident rang in my ears:

'Why have another theatre company when we already have several good ones?'

Peter Batey had warned me of this amateur culture before I took office. This man, with very little help and a tiny staff, had done much to keep a professional company alive in Adelaide, touring to many towns in South Australia. I was grateful for his input and advice before he left.

However, with Don Dunstan's sincere encouragement we continued, undaunted. For the first two years we were to live like a band of gypsies, our home being the rehearsal rooms where we planned and rehearsed, had coffee and readings, workshops with the Company and local performers. To perform we booked ourselves into whatever theatre was available. I was in bliss. It was like being back with the Jimmie James Company, but with a bigger future. Our company of actors responded with all their talent.

Helmut, as our director of youth activities, was immediately at work and began the Saturday Company of young performers, based at a beautiful old heritage house called Carclew, today the home of the Carclew Youth Performing Arts Centre. Here he was inundated by enthusiastic teenagers eager to make theatre. The result during the next few years was original and exciting work. Many of his young people later joined the profession. He also made contact with schools, and so began workshops which the actors took to the children. These workshops were the outcome of the first weeks in our home where every morning we gathered to experiment with different approaches to theatre. Telling stories became a major work, using word, gesture, mask, sound and mime. These experiments were then used to create theatre in the schoolroom. Scheduling had to be carefully plotted as there were plays to rehearse as well.

As a preliminary to my appointment I had visited Adelaide earlier in the year to meet with the new Board and the Premier. While I was there I directed a new play by David Williamson, *Jugglers Three*, as a way of introducing myself to Adelaide as the new artistic director. The cast was composed of four Adelaide actors, Julie Hamilton, Leslie Dayman, Don Barker and Martin Redpath, and three Sydney actors, Barbara Stephens, John Hargreaves and Martin Phelan. *Jugglers Three* was a most successful production of one of David's finest plays. At the end of the opening performance Don Dunstan turned to me, smiled broadly and said,

South Australian Theatre Company, 1972. Don Barker, Martin Redpath and John Hargreaves in *Jugglers Three*. (Photo: Grant Matthews. By permission of the STCSA.)

'I think you have a company there.'

And so these actors became the foundation of a company. Everything was set for its completion. Included, from Adelaide, were Patrick Frost, Khail Jureidini, Barbara Dennis and an actress who would become important in my life long after Adelaide, Daphne Grey. Daphne and her husband Jimmie Kirkland opened up their home to me and it became a haven of welcome in the years that followed. They are no longer with us but their laughter and love remain close in my memory.

Adelaide is an animated society. Eating out was a popular activity with friends, sitting at home under grape vines or in restaurants. Dinner with the Premier himself was a special night and invitations to Adelaide's homes were frequent. It was during this early time in this pleasant city that I discovered how necessary their amateur theatre was to community life. Interestingly, some of Australia's finest actors have come from the Adelaide companies including Ron Haddrick,

Edwin Hodgeman, Dennis Olsen, Elspeth Ballantyne, Barry Pree, Audine Leith, Barbara West and many others. Our chairman, Colin Ballantyne, had been a leading director in the amateur theatre for many years. Don Dunstan had been one of his actors. As the Canberra Repertory Society had been, this theatre culture was a major force in local artistic endeavour, joined socially to a strong literary culture. To so many people a professional company seemed superfluous.

Completing our immediate company were Vivienne Garrett, George Szewcow, John Cuffe, Alan Becher and Shaun Gurton, who would also begin his career in design. Others who would join us later included Carol Burns, Carole Skinner, Jane Harders, Ken Shorter, Brian James, Dennis Olsen, Neil Fitzpatrick, John Walton, Michael Quinto, Ian Dyson, John Currey, Edwin Hodgeman, Paul Weingott, Greg Zukerman, Alan Andrews and Patricia Kennedy; a page of names but of Australia's finest. Our principal designer was Michael Pearce and our stage manager Laraine Wheeler. Music was important to develop skills and a young Adelaide composer and teacher, David King, joined us to workshop the actors and compose for us.

Then with the cry of 'It's Time' it was December 1972 and a Federal Labor Government led by Gough Whitlam took office. The first change in the Federal Government in 23 years. Inspired by this welcome news, and the Labor Party's platform on the arts, we leapt into our workshops and rehearsals for our first season, designed to take place in two theatres. I've rarely been so nervous as on the day we gathered in our green-room and I began to outline our plans for the future of our company.

How to create an ensemble? How to bring a group of actors drawn from all over Australia to a point of ease with each other where they could expose their talent and vulnerability? I had plenty of ideas, as did Rodney and Helmut, but they needed to be tried and tested. Actors, after a certain time in the profession, fix their way of learning—as I myself had done years before. I had no intention of destroying their practices, particularly as our company had within it so many experienced practitioners.

With all this in mind we set about searching for ideas that would relax the actors and allow them to get to know each other in an easy way. Daily exercises began and we experimented to find those that would release the actors rather than exhaust them. We found new ways of telling stories. With storytelling the actors could boost their self-confidence in conceiving and sharing ideas. By employing their imagination in small groups they became active participants in creative work.

The day before the first workshop, John Hargreaves approached me and asked: 'What character am I to play at these workshops?'

Taking no notice of his gimlet stare, I replied: 'No character, just be yourself.'

Between tight lips John hissed: 'I don't know who that is. I'm an actor!'

Collecting myself quickly, I silently cursed my mistake. 'Why don't you play a man who suspects everything we do today and objects to its truth, meaning and usefulness?'

With a grin, John accepted my advice. He became fiendishly argumentative, as did all the other actors, who now had someone with whom they could really argue. The day was a triumph. Ten years later I conducted a similar workshop for film people in Sydney and John was a major participant.

My own expertise in mime was put to use, including figuration exercises, using the body as an object: objects as something other than what they are; shaping objects in the air and telling the story with minimal gesture and word; searching always for the centre of the story, whether it was a fable, a poem, or an incident reported in a newspaper. Rodney began collecting stories and poems that would lend their telling to a small group, who in turn would entertain other groups with improvised performances. At times the tale would be told straightforwardly, at others it was used to comment on the present day. Fairy stories and nursery rhymes came under scrutiny and inspired hilarious improvisations. David King proved himself a great teacher of actors and within days had the whole group making beautiful music and using it in their storytelling.

All this practice forged a close working community and gave the actors material with which to work with the children. Rehearsals for the plays in our first season led a separate life and the mode of rehearsal was left to the director. Rex Cramphorn, whose work with his own group, the Performance Syndicate, was starting to change the way our contemporary theatre interpreted the classics, was invited to join us and to direct Shakespeare's *Measure for Measure* while I rehearsed a new English play by John Antrobus, *Crete and Sergeant Pepper*, recounting the escape of prisoners-of-war from a Nazi prison camp. This was told in mime, song, sketch and dialogue coming directly from our workshops. Rodney was to direct Trevor Griffiths' play *Occupations*, Rex also translated a Feydeau farce, *Certified Marriage*, for me to direct; and finally a program called *All of Us or None*, with the folk singer Margret Roadnight, was arranged and directed by Rodney from the writings of Bertolt Brecht and the music of Kurt Weill.

Five performances. That's all we gave of *All of Us or None* at the little Arts Theatre in April 1973, and yet it reverberates in my mind still. It was our last offering in our first season, a night of songs and the short plays Brecht wrote in the 1930s before he left Germany. I was a performer myself, as was Helmut. Here we were, a group of well-fed Australians trying to understand the fear and betrayal in the lives of ordinary people as their country headed towards the Third Reich. By hard work and good direction, I believe we came very close. My own experience was echoed by others, as I sang 'Mack the Knife', beginning in German and sliding into drunken English as a street *clochard*. One memory stamped into my mind was the night of the dress rehearsal, when at midnight, Rodney demanded we do it all again, right now! Exhausted, angry and muttering revenge, we did it. At two o'clock we stood on stage, feeling wrecked but excited and aware that something had happened. Some understanding of Brecht's angry polemic had been reached. I began to realise how scared I had been of touching this dramatist's work. The alienation theory Wal Cherry had attempted to explain was quite beyond my understanding; this experience allowed me to bypass it and find the greatness within the plays. I have never been afraid of Brecht since.

Daily visits to schools became a feature of our lives alongside the workshops and rehearsals. It was a very busy and I believe, highly creative schedule. Within all this, Theatre-Go-Round was also established. As its name implies it was a simple idea: to get performances out of the theatre and to as many people as possible without incurring the expense of a full play production. Of all my memories of those four years, this work remains the most vivid, a direct outcome of the months of workshops conducted every morning.

We began by sitting around while the folk singer Margret Roadnight sang one of her songs. I cannot remember which song it was, but I know that every one of us fell under her spell that day. Without hesitation she had accepted Rodney's invitation to join us in a 'people show'. This was an evening of poetry, mime and song researched, collected, arranged and directed by the triumvirate and the actors, and we first presented it at the Art Gallery of South Australia. It was a simple evening without interval that could be adapted to the venue and the audience. It allowed the Company to go to places the theatre never penetrated. Later, in another season, we performed versions in department stores. When Margret could not be with us we would add *The Woman Tamer*, a one-act low-life comedy by the early Australian playwright, Louis Esson; or introduce another singer we found in Adelaide, Robyn Archer, with her distinctive voice. And what poetry we read, from Robert Louis Stevenson to R.D. Laing, and songs performed by the actors under David King's tutelage and accompanied by the guitar of David Thomas.

Or the evening might be taken over by the work of James Saunders in *Games after Liverpool*, or it might become an anthology of Adelaide with the soprano Wendy Parsons singing a song by David King. Yet again, one-act plays by Alma De Groen and Jack Hibberd would fill the bill. These programs went on tour all over South Australia and into the Northern Territory, bringing unfamiliar work to many people. Rodney and the actors injected into them not only research and talent, but a belief in the possibility of small miracles.

Our first season of plays opened without fanfares and without great support. We were playing alternately in the alienating Union Hall that reminded me of a university cafeteria without the tables, and the little Arts Theatre which was the home of the Adelaide Repertory Society, a group with a history going back to the beginning of the century. But people came and we began to build a small, loyal following.

Measure for Measure, with Helmut as the Duke walking through a blaze of sacred light, and Julie Hamilton as a ravishing Isabella, in

Renaissance costumes designed by Rex himself, radiated a quality that lit up the Union; as did the dancing and singing of the male company in *Crete and Sergeant Pepper*. The scarifying, comic talents of John Hargreaves provoked warm response from the audience in both plays. Playing the fantastic Lucio or a rebellious prisoner-of-war, John was so completely at home on stage and showed such a feeling for the spontaneous that he made the other actors nervous. Feydeau's *Certified Marriage* was given a warm welcome at the Arts Theatre with Julie, Don Barker and George Szewcow playing three country yokels in the big city; and Khail Jureidini, accompanied by Daphne Grey and Les Dayman, gave me, in *Occupations*, a thrilling experience, as the tiny Italian socialist, Antonio Gramsci, fought the oncoming tide of Fascism. With a return of *Jugglers Three* we felt proud of our first season and of our Company.

But unease was settling on my heart. Even after the first season we remained strangers in Adelaide; eastern-staters who had arrived to teach and deliver to the locals something they did not really want or believed they already had. Adelaide critics continued to see us as visitors and not for a single moment was I encouraged to believe that our work could be of value to a community already perfectly satisfied with itself.

One aspect of our life became a cause of aggravation to some. As director of the Company, I was expected to play a part in the social life of Adelaide. But we were three directors and the strength we displayed together caused many people to see us as a ghetto, barring others from entering. We did nothing to eradicate this impression, which grew during our second season. I received many invitations, but I was busy eighteen hours a day with rehearsals, workshop, office, planning and even performing. I was not a diplomat and was beginning to feel more and more alienated from this Athens of the South. I buried myself among the actors, in the end, by focusing on achieving excellence in our work we failed to take the time to study the needs of our audience.

South Australian Theatre Company, 1973. Paul Weingott, Dennis Olsen, Alan Becher, Les Dayman and Shaun Gorton in *Journey's End*. (Photo: Grant Matthews. By permission of the STCSA.)

As the curtain came down on the body of Shaun Gurton as the dead Raleigh, his own design of mud and trenches collapsing around him in the final moments of R.C. Sheriff's *Journey's End*, I sat in the stalls, marvelling at how appropriate the old Royalty Theatre was for this play. In just such a theatre the play was first performed and now the old wreck seemed a perfect background for the story of the death of that generation of men in the Great War and the passing of its way of life. Led by Paul Weingott as Stanhope, looking exactly like the images we have of the poet Rupert Brooke, the cast gave full focus to the minutiae of the life in those tragic trenches. Later in the year we brought back the laughter to this old vaudeville house with Ben Travers' 1920s farce *Rookery Nook*, presented in a perfect period setting designed by Michael Pearce with a cast led by Dennis Olsen, Edwin Hodgeman and Barbara Stephens.

In our second season of plays we continued to scramble from one theatre to another. The vast horror of the Union seemed to defy any play and we escaped it when we could. One play that did survive there was

E.A. Whitehead's *Alpha Beta*. Daphne Grey and Neil Fitzpatrick remain in my memory as two actors capable of tearing each other to shreds in this new and frightening dissection of a marriage while remaining their charming selves off stage. The audience sat shivering as their domestic tragedy unfolded. Both Daphne and Neil had the same childhood dream—to become a professional actor. But the lives that led them to meet and work together in Adelaide could not have been further apart.

Daphne Grey was born in England and spent her childhood in foster homes. An ambitious young actor, she secured a place at the Central School of Speech and Drama and found work with the Dundee Repertory Company. There she met and married a medical student, Jimmie Kirkland, and, following Jimmie's appointment to Flinders University, they and their two sons moved to Adelaide. As her sons Adam and Mark grew so did the chance to take up acting again. With the encouragement of Jimmie she became a full-time member of my company, an indispensable actor and friend.

And indeed did Jimmie. One bright morning I arrived at our rehearsal rooms after two hours in the office and joined a movement class given by Tessa Steel. I leapt around the room with them until my enthusiastic jumping was interrupted by a pistol shot from my ankle. I fell in a heap having split my achilles tendon. A pair of crutches from the props room made me mobile again and I continued the rehearsals of *Alpha Beta*. Some days later, Jimmie Kirkland arrived to take Daphne home from rehearsals and asked to examine my leg. His grin widened as he did so. What magic, he asked, was I applying to bring the tendons in my leg together? He then packed me off to hospital, an operation and three months in a huge cast.

Neil was brought up in what was then the working-class town of Williamstown, a port outside Melbourne. Neil showed a precocious talent but drama schools were non-existent and the only opportunity for training lay with amateur groups. His career began in 1956 when he won the juvenile role in Robert Anderson's *Tea and Sympathy* co-starring with the English actress Dulcie Gray, at the Comedy Theatre in Melbourne. My first association with Neil as a fellow actor was at the Union playing together in the musical *Lola Montez*. In the same cast he met his friend for life, Patricia Conolly.

In 1960 he joined the Trust Players, and among his roles played Edmund, the younger son in Eugene O'Neill's *Long Day's Journey into Night*. In Adelaide he would play the elder son. When the Trust Players folded Neil left Australia to join the new National Theatre and in 1969 Robin Lovejoy invited him back to lead the Old Tote Company in its new role as the NSW State company. He took the lead in my production of *Trelawney of the Wells* and we worked together from that moment on.

As different as their backgrounds and journeys might have been Daphne and Neil had something in common; they were born actors, filled with the joy of performing. The sound of their laughter is something I still hear. They both revelled in comedy but were also obsessive about the detail of their work. When, in 2005, Neil died in Sydney, a designer friend at the packed requiem mass commented that the meaning of torture was discussing the colour of the socks required by the character Neil was currently playing.

Jimmie Kirkland died suddenly not long after I left Adelaide, but Daphne continued to work. She came east to be in several plays and films I directed, including playing Russell Crowe's alcoholic mother in *The Crossing*. When she died, in 1998, we gathered in the Playhouse at the Festival Centre to remember a great artist and friend.

Six plays were presented at the Union and the Royalty in our second season. At the Union they were performed in repertoire which was also something quite new for Adelaide. For us they represented a pleasing outcome of our work together. James Saunders' *Hans Kohlhaas*, *The Comedy of Errors*, *Alpha Beta* and *Long Day's Journey into Night* at the Union; *Rookery Nook* and *Journey's End* at the Royalty. *Hans Kohlhaas* is an inspiring story set in Germany in the Middle Ages about a man who whose loyalty to his beliefs brings tragedy upon his family.

Patricia Kennedy had long been a leading actress in Melbourne. As a young woman she had toured Australia with Sybil Thorndike. She and Brian James were given a great welcome by the Company when they arrived to lead them in *Long Day's Journey into Night*. They would return again and again as associate actors during the next three years. This production of Rodney's was the first to travel interstate. It had a highly successful season at St Martin's Theatre in Melbourne. *The Comedy of Errors* was my first production of Shakespeare. From that time on I would take every chance to direct his work, learning more with each experience.

Our Theatre-Go-Round activities continued whenever the cast had time and our visits to schools under Helmut's direction became a regular program. His Saturday Company was building enormously and Dame Ruby Litchfield, one of Carclew's trustees, and Jim Giles from the South Australian Education Department encouraged and supported its growth. I began to feel envious of the local support Helmut was receiving. In due course he began to undertake huge productions with fifty to a hundred youngsters, who would invade the new complex with their vibrant energy. These productions are still remembered in Adelaide.

The year 1974 began with more work to prepare before the opening of the Playhouse in August. For the Festival in March Rodney presented *The Bride of Gospel Place* (1926), the work of Louis Esson. In reviving Esson we sought to demonstrate our determination to honour the past just as we were trying to shape the future. But Adelaide was not concerned with our motives. It was not a success. Nevertheless, for those involved in these activities our workshops also continued to feed the imagination. On one such morning I found David King with the entire Company, exploring the sacred in music and movement. Their work that day revealed what can be achieved with focus and dedication.

As we began work towards the move into the Playhouse some activities had to be curtailed. The Company was being stretched to its limit and rest times became imperative.

Only with hindsight have I realised how well the designs for the Playhouse suited Adelaide. It proved the ideal theatre for plays like *The Winslow Boy*, with Hugh Colman's set of intimately observed middle-class comfort; and Robin Lovejoy's production of Noel Coward's *Blithe Spirit*, with its high-class style of 1930s living. These plays belonged to this audience. They were tremendously popular. As our third year began and we continued to plan programs to feed a growing following and prepare for our new home, it began to dawn on me how unobservant I had been. My first impressions of Adelaide had been made through the men who led the artistic community. They were strong-minded and proud of their record in literature and art. What they did not tell me or rather, what I did not ask was: 'Who else lives in this provincial capital behind this fine, Georgian facade?'

A State theatre company, particularly if it is to be housed in a new complex in the centre of the city beside its beautiful river, and with a publicly-funded brief to present classical music, ballet and drama, needs to feed a community with plays which engage and reflect their own lives and dreams. Or, to put it another way, it needs to celebrate life in such a way that it uplifts the spirit or reminds the ego of what it is to be human and how difficult it is to be just. As successful as several of our productions had been, none was described as a triumph or recognised as relating to their experience.

The Playhouse and Festival theatres rose like a white ghost on the riverbank and I was invited to visit from time to time and gasp at the design and construction. Kevin Palmer, an Australian production manager, was invited back from England to help transfer the Company into its new home. I saw very little of him but he kept in touch with the Board while Rodney, Helmut and I planned the opening season with the administrator Wayne Madden. Led by Kevin, our Board members would be seen threading their way through the different stages of the complex, talking to architects and city dignitaries, but not to us. Wayne had been the administrator from day one and had always been approachable and amicable, but he and his staff led a different life from the Company. Though we worked side by side, we seldom met. It had been very different in Melbourne where John Sumner was the single head.

Excitement mounted as we advanced towards August, and I was questioning the triumvirate's ability to guess what Adelaide really wanted, particularly from us, the strangers. The certainties we had felt were losing ground and that special relationship which had brought about such creativity was in danger of disintegrating. Doubts between us rose like barriers, as we tried to decide on three plays for this very special occasion. Two plays were settled: David Williamson had offered us a new comedy, *The Department*, which Rodney would direct, with Neil Fitzpatrick in the main role. I would direct *She Stoops to Conquer*, with Patricia Kennedy, Brian James and Dennis Olsen, and designed by Hugh Colman to display the technical capacities of the new theatre.

But what play would open? We looked for something altogether different; something Adelaide would never have seen in all their years of amateur playgoing, something which would give a sense of the great tradition. We chose a script that came directly from the *commedia dell'arte*. *The Three Cuckolds* leapt into rehearsals with the actors employing all the workshop and clown work we had done together, and learning how to live and breathe in the *commedia* character masks. Our designer, Michael Pearce, created three colourful, covered carts which became the focus for a troupe of *commedia* actors. The entire Company took on the characters of a band of roving performers.

Opening night arrived. The curtain opened to a packed audience who sat stunned and uncomprehending—the curtain revealed an empty stage. There was no set to feast the eyes upon; just theatre walls with ropes and ladders and working lights glimmering over a vast, cleared, wooden stage floor. For a long moment there was not a sound. We could feel the audience breathing. Into the pale light strode one man. Premier Dunstan stood alone in the middle of the stage and spoke movingly of this building—his special dream. As he finished, mediaeval drums began to beat and out of the darkened wings, figures in old and tattered clothes pulled Michael's three carts onto the stage, placed them side by side with their doors facing the audience. The doors opened, music began and the actors burst out onto stage to play out the tale of *The Three Cuckolds*.

I sat in the dark at the back of the theatre, with a thumping heart. For me it was a singularly private moment in my life. Like the dream from another life becoming real, the Company sang, clowned and brought their early Renaissance world to poetic life with funny, bravura storytelling. The audience responded well and clapped brightly at the end; but it was not yet the triumph we were seeking. I was devastated by this, but aware, at the same time, that I had given the audience an unsettling evening because it was quite outside their experience. The following plays were much more familiar and proved quite popular with our subscribers. Not until May of the following year in the middle of our next season would I crack it. When the curtain came down on Peter Shaffer's *Equus*, the audience went crazy, calling the actors back with a standing ovation and the rousing applause of a triumph that brought our publicist bursting into the foyer shouting, 'We've done it! At last!'

It was a play I had been reluctant to include in the season.

That night, in the darkened theatre, I had a long chat with myself. *Equus* had been a popular play wherever it had been performed. There was no reason why it should not have had the same success here. The fact that I did not like the play, that I found it to be false in its mumbo-jumbo psychiatry, that I found the characters unreal and that nobody else seemed to think this way, convinced me that the trouble lay within me and what was going on in my confused mind. As usual, when trying to unravel an issue I would travel back to the beginning, to the James family. They would have had no trouble with *Equus*. With them I would have played in *Equus* as often as our audiences wanted

South Australian Theatre Company, 1973. Carol Burns, Alan Andrews, John Walton and Barbara Stephens in *The Three Cuckolds*. (Photo: Grant Matthews, by permission of the STCSA.)

it. I loved our audiences in the Wales of the 1950s. I relied on their simple good sense.

To almost the same degree, I loved the Melbourne audiences. I loved the strong Jewish element in our subscriber lists. They loved theatre with a passion and we served them to our best ability. Sydney was still a mystery. I had felt uneasy with the audiences and their adoration of leading players, but this was a superficial conclusion on my part and needed much more testing. In Adelaide one conclusion was reached that night. These audiences were my masters. I was there to serve them and in Adelaide I did not know how. Not until *The Winslow Boy*, late in 1975, did I feel at all close—and by then it was too late.

To take a deep breath and return to work was the only way, but several scotches every evening and the habit of chain-smoking helped me disguise the deep unhappiness settling in my heart. My troubles also mounted with the Board and with the large complex for which we were now paying rent. Arguments became frequent and opinions divided as we attempted to decide future programming. The Playhouse was the centre of our performance and income. Anything ouside that was extravagance.

Helmut had already separated himself and his youth work from the Company and Rodney and Kevin Palmer were at odds in their views of how a company should be run. I looked forward with dread to every Board meeting knowing that criticism of the Company was now vocal. The final date of my four-year contract was approaching and its expiration meant that I could, with a little dignity, put a stop to this merry-go-round of tongue-lashing. Nonetheless, and despite all the troubles, the actors continued to work well and delivered, over my last year, an array of performances to be remembered with love and gratitude.

During the years from 1967 to 1975, it was my privilege to direct Dennis Olsen in some dozen plays, and each one was memorable. He brought with him all the innate skills with which he was born and an unparalleled dedication to his art. From the moment he arrived at rehearsals for *A Flea in Her Ear*, I felt the challenge a good actor can provoke. The good actor will make the creative process easier but also sets a challenge to go beyond the ordinary, to create a great performance.

How often does a director have the experience of working with a difficult actor? They are a nightmare for both director and cast, as attention must be paid to them, to the detriment of the other actors and the play. There are those who gain a reputation for being difficult but who still deliver a great performance; but something vital still suffers in the process. The finest actors are the easiest to work with, I have found. They are the ones who join the team, who are prepared to try anything to find the right answer and throw away anything that is inappropriate to the whole.

Dennis is like this. His inspired performances in Gilbert and Sullivan made him a household name, but I have precious memories of his virulent Spaniard in *A Flea in Her Ear*, his sad and longing Tusenbach in *The Three Sisters*, his elegant man-about-town in *An Ideal Husband*, his moving, quiet soldier in *Journey's End*, his breezy toff in *Rookery Nook*, his ancient, masked fool in *The Three Cuckolds*, his perfectly-mannered young hero in *She Stoops to Conquer*, his biting, scrupulous lawyer in *The Winslow Boy*, and finally his piercingly funny, middle-aged, Shavian industrialist in *Major Barbara*. Such memories make a director's life worthwhile.

To dedicate everything I learnt to the Company I directed for four years, is something I do most willingly, but let me single out four actors who, like Dennis, also came from Adelaide and gave my life special and life-lasting memories with their welcome, their friendship and talents freely given.

Daphne Grey, Julie Hamilton, Patrick Frost and Leslie Dayman were with me through all our work, our hopes and our troubles and our achievements. Daphne's expertise extended from the raving troubled Mrs Elliot of *Alpha Beta* to the gracious Lady Britomart in Shaw's *Major Barbara*; Julie's Rosalind in *As You Like It*, gave Shakespeare a joyous and funny heroine in the same way she served Feydeau with her Laura in *Certified Marriage*. Patrick's work ranged from a sweet, funny clown in Ken Campbell's *School for Clowns* to the troubled young aristocrat, Ferdinand, in John Webster's *The Duchess of Malfi*; while Les played a multitude of roles from Admiral Juddy in Ben Travers' farce *Rookery Nook*, to the prisoner Sam, in Jim McNeil's *How Does Your Garden Grow*. Together they developed the Company into an ensemble of players, sharing with each other and the rest of the Company. I thank them for their humour; their patience, their willingness and their talent.

The Playhouse was and is a beautiful building—the foyer a sea of blue comfort, the theatre well designed and colour-coordinated, the dressing rooms modern and fully equipped. The production areas were state-of-the-art, the rehearsal room huge and private. So why did not I like it? Why did I feel, from the moment I set foot in this plush new home, that the very ambition behind the construction had institutionalised and controlled us before we had even begun? For me, no longer did the decisions rest with the artists, but with the building, its thick pile carpet, its monumental site on the Torrens River, and the enormous outlay now required to run a company of actors in high-class real estate.

And where was my company of friends? From our two rehearsal rooms and adjoining green-room in which constant meetings, conversations took place, in which we shared the knowledge of each other's needs, we lost ourselves in long white corridors that required us to make appointments to say 'hello'. As in Melbourne, our production unit in workshop and wardrobe now became our centre of creativity, not only producing beautiful work but remaining friendly and warm places of welcome for both director and actors.

There were moments. At the end of a long and soulless corridor, in a small rehearsal room, Patrick Frost and George Szewcow were joined by three young actors, Jo England, Peggy O'Brien and Doug Gautier, to present a children's show by Ken Campbell called *School for Clowns*. Their joy and hard work brought this concrete building to life.

Perhaps the source of the problem lay in my very nature. I remember an encounter with John Sumner when I asked him to teach me the business of running a theatre. He dismissed the idea.

'You shouldn't worry about such things. You belong in the rehearsal room.'

I was affronted at the time, taking the remark as a criticism of my intelligence. Only long after could I see the truth of what he said.

John Sumner had been right; all the instincts and talent I have belong to the rehearsal room. It was only there that I felt totally at home. In the office of artistic director I was playing a role—and not very well. The fight required to keep hold of personal integrity in the face of so many opinions, so much conflicting advice, was formidable; my nature is not that kind of tough, nor could I ever see myself as the kind of community leader Adelaide deserved.

Only months before, towards the end of 1975, Australia had been shocked by the sacking of the Whitlam Labor Government by the Governor General, Sir John Kerr. Their dream had begun with ours, and ended as unhappily. Adelaide had given me the chance to make theatre and to experience those occasional moments that transcend the mundane and give a glimpse into something immortal. But the decision to say goodbye was inevitable. I was relieved to be leaving this southern city in other hands.

Lyndel Rowe and George Ogilvie clowning in 'Old King Cole'.

Six

THE SEEKER

Emerging from Dark Places

Not again! Not ever again! I could not go through it again. I swore on everything I thought I believed in that I would not let it happen again. Being artistic director in Adelaide had left me drained, bitter and guilty without knowing precisely why. I began seriously to consider giving up the business that had inspired me for twenty-five years.

As an actor I remember the freedom I had to establish good working relationships. As a director I remember creative sessions with actors and designers to bring a play alive. As an artistic director I remember the Board, its members from business or law or medicine, all offering well-meaning views on artistic matters, on how to do my job. I remember the budgets, which commanded the choice of play, the clever and successful choice that ensured we never went into the red. I remember the critics and leading lights who in hindsight knew better than I what decisions should have been made; and finally I remember the theatre itself, that monument, not so much to artistic endeavour as to community pride in its architecture, its comfort, and its necessary business acumen.

I remember thinking that everything would right itself once I had shaken off the dust of Adelaide and mingled once again with the convict descendants in the east. Instead I found myself in dark places, smoking sixty cigarettes a day. It would be some time before I would emerge from the aftermath of these dark memories. It was so easy to blame Adelaide for my failure and the difficulties I encountered in that city, but I needed time and distance to consider my own nature and the difference between being a director and an artistic director.

They seem to be similar but in fact require very different skills and perspectives on life. I knew I had talent for the former and in time I learnt I had none for the latter. To be an artistic director requires an extraordinary talent, combining a good business head with a cool diplomatic nature and the ability to take the long view. His or her vision must extend beyond the theatre to the community, to be able to smell society and guide the theatre company in tune with the social attitudes of the day. Since those days I have come to wonder whether the artistic director need be a play director at all; whether guiding the company is not the more important responsibility, while the director, in charge of the rehearsal room, gives all their attention to the intense world of the play and the actor.

Thankfully, the last act of my artistic directorship in Adelaide was delivered in laughter. I played a clown called Twoo in a children's program. As I sang 'Old King Cole', getting all the words wrong, an audience of vibrant four-year-olds shrieked with laughter and carried me back to those wonderful innocent days with the James family. Self-pity settled into my doleful bones. I was now middle-aged and wondered if it was all over.

It was far from over. Over the next five years I would direct opera, ballet and drama leading to that day in 1982 when the Sydney Opera House belonged to me. And it came about through a meeting with a guru.

It is now a day at the beginning of 1978 when the life of a forty-six-year-old lapsed Protestant changed forever. Towards the end of that first terrible year after Adelaide I was persuaded to emerge from my gloom and direct Pam Gems' play *Dusa, Fish, Stas and Vi*. It was a good play concerning the lives of four English women, their love for each other and their subsequent very different futures. I had a wonderful cast of four women; Carol Burns, Pat Bishop, Nancye Hayes and Vivienne Garrett. The rehearsals would take place in Melbourne, my favourite city, and the Australian tour would begin at my old stamping ground,

Russell Street Theatre. All was thankfully set for a competent and bearable time. Little did I know that bells were tolling and they were tolling for me.

Vivienne had just returned from a sojourn in India where she had been living in the ashram, or spiritual home, of her guru, Swami Muktananda. She had hung a small photo of her guru in the rehearsal room and occasionally I gave it a glance. One day, after she had been having problems with the character she was playing, I drove her home and she asked me in for a talk. She was staying in the annex to a little ashram belonging to the Siddha Yoga Association of which she was a member, and I was curious. The house was ordinary but spotlessly clean and, as instructed, I pulled off my shoes at the front door. We went into a large communal kitchen where Vivienne made tea and we began talking over the problems of the play, immersing ourselves in the dialogue.

A moment came when I suddenly felt someone enter the room behind me. I turned to see who it was but there was no one. Instead I found myself staring at the photo of a smiling man who had his hand raised in greeting. I did not recognise him as the man in the rehearsal room photo until Vivienne's voice confirmed it. My heart began to race and I could feel myself blushing furiously for no reason. I felt foolish and soon took my leave. On my way home I began to laugh and then found myself sobbing as I manipulated the car through the traffic. I shook off these unaccountable feelings, fearing some sort of breakdown, and tried to put the incident out of my mind.

Some days later I found on my rehearsal desk an invitation to an evening of Siddha Yoga to be held at the little ashram in George Street. Curious to know what that incident meant I accepted and presented myself at the ashram. A group of us was ushered into the living room now transformed into a meditation room, where we sat on cushions on the carpeted floor.

Then followed an easy and pleasant evening, much of which I do not remember, except for the sudden recollection of myself as a child, listening to stories at Sunday school. The words of the speakers flew over my head, but I do remember the feeling of welcome and ease, and a Sanskrit chant that gave me much pleasure. A cup of tea followed the short program and then I said good night and headed for the door.

At a small desk in the hall a young man was taking reservations for a weekend intensive to be held in two weeks' time. Without thinking, I pulled out the money and booked myself in. Why had I done this? The play was to open in the next week and I had more important things to occupy my mind. We were within days of the dress rehearsal and, as the technical problems mounted, my smoking had risen dangerously close to eighty a day.

The opening night became the usual horrible experience of wondering if this time I would be found out and subjected to universal ridicule. However, the cast was very well received. I thanked my lucky stars that four such talents could control the audience as well as they did. I considered my contribution to be pedestrian, but the producers decided the play was ready for the long tour. With enormous relief I looked forward to a period without the stress of work. At moments of honesty I admitted to myself that the career I loved had now become a real burden.

On the second night, Vivienne reminded me of the coming intensive. I would not commit myself; all I wanted was a rest, and the thought of a strange and foreign experience only made me smoke more. As Saturday loomed I felt confused and angry that I had got myself into such a position. Only in hindsight can I say without reservation that my decision to attend was the most important decision of my life. Without any thought for the consequences I decided to go. After all, it was only a weekend.

I woke early on Saturday morning and lay still, wondering what the day would bring. Having paid for the weekend I felt compelled to go, but there was nothing spiritual about my attitude. On the contrary, I was nervous and began to feel foolish about attending something so cultish. However, I left early enough to walk and arrived on time at the terrace house. I had brought a cushion, as instructed, and, after taking off my shoes, was ushered into the meditation room where soft chanting and incense created an atmosphere totally foreign to me. I was reminded of my only visit to a Catholic church while a service was in progress; my early life in the spartan atmosphere of a Presbyterian kirk was a world away from this highly-coloured ritual.

The morning began with singing a Hindi prayer, and then we settled on our cushions. A pleasant young woman introduced the program, which involved talks about Siddha Yoga; about experiences of meeting the Swami Muktananda and about the guru himself. Whatever I heard, my busy mind contradicted. In between the talks we chanted Sanskrit words and it was while chanting that I found I could relax and forget everything but the beautiful sound. I was grateful for the chant, which allowed my mind to rest.

The sessions of meditation, however, proved my undoing. Our instructors encouraged us to make no effort to be calm but to let everything float away and sink our minds into a space. I began to feel restless and uncomfortable. All sorts of negative thoughts and feelings crowded my mind, preventing me from finding a calm centre. I felt exhausted and fed-up when the bell rang to bring us back from the meditative state to the reality of the room. By the time the day was over I was determined to hurry home and forget this failed attempt to find peace and tranquillity. I went to bed that night grateful that it was all over.

Why I rose early, got myself ready and walked back to the ashram the next morning I will never know. I only remember a compelling and urgent feeling that it was not over, that I needed to continue the search.

Somehow it was easier the second morning. Feeling less aggressive, without tension in my body and with a mind finally empty of busy thought, I began to enjoy the talks and chants. The meditation came more easily. I began to listen and understand the instructions to let go; to let thoughts float away. Later in the day a talk was given about the guru. The joy expressed by the speaker became infectious and laughter flooded the little room. A little later a video showed the guru talking to a group of devotees. It was the anniversary of the passing of his own guru, and as he spoke of him his tears flowed, introducing a fantastic energy into the room. The air seemed alive. It was in this atmosphere that the final meditation session took place. I settled myself as comfortably as I could, closed my eyes, and, repeating the mantra to myself, drifted away.

I have revisited the experience of that day many times. My chief remembrance is of the laughing speaker and the crying guru combined together to create a perfect partnership. Their faces, seen in the pupil of a perfect eye, seemed to float towards me and enter me, taking me deep into space. It felt familiar, as if I had been there long before. I seemed to gather knowledge as I floated and knew that we were all joined together; that within every one of us lies something that creates this union, something immortal.

Suddenly, after what seemed only moments, an hour had passed and the bell rang to bring us back to the room. As I did so I felt a dam give way and I began to sob. Tears in front of strangers, in my experience, exposed a shocking lack of moral fibre; but here today it did not seem to matter. Trying to share the experience with others brought more tears, but they were tears of energy and wonder.

I was sharing a house at the time with three friends—the designers Kris Fredrikson and Hugh Colman, and Liz Cross, an artist. When I interrupted their supper that night the tears flowed again with the telling, mixed with much laughter. They must have thought me a little mad. I fell asleep that night floating into a deep peace. The following morning I woke early and dressed quickly to take Hugh's dog for a walk. As I came down the stairs Liz took me by the hand and ushered me into her studio. Liz had been dry of inspiration over the previous two years and depressed by the loss of her talent. Now the room was filled with work she had been doing all night, unable to sleep and swept up with the energy I had brought home with me. The park, too, was filled with fantastic colours on this morning and the very leaves on the trees seemed filled with energy. My mind was in a riot over the weekend experience.

This state continued for days and I knew there was only one thing to do. I borrowed some money, booked myself on Air India and flew to Bombay and Ganeshpuri, the Siddha Yoga ashram, to its north. It was just one week after my life-changing experience. There I was told of *shaktipat*, in which awareness of an essential truth is made manifest.

Swami Muktananda (Baba). The photo that drew the author to Siddha Yoga.
(By permission of the SYDA organisation.)

The ashram walls and the temple domes beyond seemed to my eyes a setting for the Hollywood film *Lost Horizon*. The taxi from the little station careered down the dirt road alongside the wall while I clutched at my belongings and the copy of the *Baghavat Gita*, which a young friend had thrust into my hands at Melbourne Airport. A hair-raising journey in a packed train had brought me to the little station and now we were arriving. I had been smoking continuously during the journey and my heart was racing as I opened the little gate and entered a small courtyard.

There was not a soul in sight, but through a dark entrance I became aware of some sort of service going on in the temple and hundreds of voices were chanting. I rounded a corner to be greeted by a member of the Melbourne ashram. He had been waiting for me and became my guide and friend that day. Mac Gudgeon would later pursue a successful career as a writer for television and film, but on this day he welcomed me in a manner with which I became familiar in Siddha Yoga.

He ushered me into the main courtyard of the ashram and I nearly passed out. The atmosphere was heady and exotic; the very air seemed packed with the spiritual energy I had so suddenly experienced in the little room in Melbourne.

'You must make sure you rest for a day or two,' Mac said, 'until you get used to the *shakti*.'

He took me to the office where I registered my name and handed over some money for the month I intended staying. Then we walked down paths past glorious flowerbeds and banana groves, under huge shady trees and up stone steps to one of the many small buildings that dotted this paradise. A welcome glass of fruit juice, a small room all to myself, instructions to come down in an hour to meet the Swami Muktananda in the main courtyard, and Mac left me to rest. I lay down, dazed by my own feelings, which were in constant danger of boiling over. I could not calm my racing heart as I listened to my own breathing and perspired in the Indian heat of this February afternoon. I finally drifted off to sleep.

In my dreams a man sat on my bed, nodding at me with a gentle look on his face. It was the guru's guru, whose temple I had passed and from which the chanting poured. I woke, feeling relaxed and calm. I washed myself, changed into clean clothes and took out my gift for the guru, a woven blanket of Australian wool. I then wandered down towards the central courtyard and found it to be empty. More chanting from the temple accompanied my silent wait, seated on a low wall facing the entrance to a building. A raised platform was built outside the door shaded by beautiful trees.

Suddenly the door opened and a man walked out and placed some cushions on the platform. Moments later another man, dressed in an orange habit, emerged and sat on the platform. Several people hurried towards him and fell full-length at his feet. He smiled and extended his arm to touch them as they settled down, crossed-legged, in front of him. As he did so the gold of his arms seem to radiate, encompassing the whole courtyard. I found the scene dazzling and felt my heart pounding with a mixture of terror and energy.

The chanting finished and moments later hundreds of people of all ages poured from the temple into the courtyard. They hurried towards the guru—for certainly it was he—and sat down in front of him, women to the left and men to the right. I followed the stragglers and sat at the back on the tiled floor. But there was no smile of welcome for these people. His face clouded over and he began to lecture them in Hindi. A young woman standing beside him picked up a microphone and began translating into English. He was angry at their haste and general hilarity.

'This is a place of devotion,' he said sternly. He used the word *dharma*, which seemed to equate with 'behaviour within a spiritual place'.

A still, silent crowd heard his words. The wind whispered through the courtyard as the young girl translated. His gestures were simple and free of tension but as I watched, sitting among these devotees who sat like carved stone, I felt a shiver of fear. Here was an extraordinary power. This is what people meant about the influence one man can have over people prepared to surrender to a spiritual call. As a chant filled the courtyard, I wondered if my gratitude and respect would be enough for him without surrender. It made me feel disloyal, even petty, considering it was a Siddha Yoga *satsang* that had brought me to this ancient country. The chant finished and I found myself in line to greet the guru, clutching my huge gift and without any idea what I was supposed to say.

When I arrived directly in front of him I fell on my knees, not so much out of respect as because I could no longer stand without feeling I would pass out. A young girl beside him introduced me, and Baba, as everyone called him, smiled broadly and said in English,

'Ah, a director.'

He said it with such a droll look on his face that we all laughed. I thrust the blanket at him but it took two assistants to help extricate it from its cover. He looked at me again with a long stare and slapped me on the head with a peacock feather. I nearly keeled over and hastily backed away.

What it meant I had no idea and I sat, gratefully unnoticed, among other devotees, to join in another chant and calm my beating heart. That night I wandered alone in the garden. My mind was blank but my heart felt strong. I began to realise that I loved being there. Peace and energy seemed to breathe together and I could feel a serenity not experienced for years. There was something very special in this ashram.

My mother would ask, later: 'What in God's name were you doing there, son?'

My only answer was, 'Learning to live again.'

For the next two days I did not catch sight of the guru and for this I was grateful. I began to relax and enjoy myself. I attended all the chants and meditation sessions, along with hundreds of devotees, and ate the beautiful food cooked and served in a huge, cool dining room where we sat on the floor in front of mats. It was a time to be silent and simply absorb the atmosphere of this extraordinary place. Meditation became a natural practice and I began to sink deeply into that space every morning in the meditation hall.

By the third day I was given *seva* during certain hours in the garden, feeding compost to the banana trees and cleaning out the showers and toilets scattered around the garden. *Seva* was a word to appreciate and use in the years to come. It means service given without need of reward, the reward being the work itself. Later I joined the kitchen staff in their spotless quarters and began to love the simple labour of washing up and cleaning. It was *seva* that taught me the meaning of the phrase 'spiritual practices'.

Almost a week later, while I was working in the garden, the cry went up that the guru was coming, and Baba, with a small entourage, strolled down the pathways smiling and talking to the devotee gardeners. The very sight of him was enough to make me need to sit down, and with a racing heart I hid, like a reluctant schoolboy, to avoid meeting him.

I knew full well why. Already, that word 'surrender' was becoming an obstacle and every time I caught a glimpse of him, guilt and doubt would hold me back, just as the sight of him would draw other devotees to his side. In meditation I had no problem with the idea of surrender, of letting go of all fear and surrendering to the place within, where there is a freedom from any known identity. Years later I came across a quotation from the Trappist monk, Thomas Merton, which has remained with me as the goal of meditation:

> As long as there is an 'I' that is the definite subject of a contem-
> plative experience, an 'I' that is aware of itself and of its contem-

plation, an 'I' that can possess a certain 'degree of spirituality', then we have not yet passed over the Red Sea, we have not yet 'gone out of Egypt'. (*Seeds of Contemplation* (Wheathampstead, Herts. Anthony Clarke Books 1972, p.217)

Baba would say, in the years to come, 'It is the inner guru to whom you must surrender, not to me.'

These words gave me courage to pursue my life with Siddha Yoga.

In my third week I joined several busloads following the guru around the district of Maharashtra to towns where millions of devotees lived. It was an extraordinary experience to discover that Siddha Yoga was a way of life for so many people. Also, and perhaps most importantly, I saw Baba with his own people, Indian people who were of the Hindu religion. Just as I had learned to watch actors so I now witnessed the drama of Indian devotees with their guru. I felt a stranger in almost every way. In the ashram there had been a bridge to understanding with the monks who surrounded Baba. Most of them were Americans or Australians who had studied with Baba and taken vows to become swamis for the rest of their lives. These charming men and women had welcomed me, and taught me, through the *satsangs* and chats as we strolled through the garden, how universal meditation was; that it was not a religion but pointed towards a better life of understanding and compassion. I was grateful to be back in the ashram for my final week and to continue the practices and programs that by now were becoming a natural part of my life.

For all the doubts and questions that rose constantly in my mind, meditation held me firmly in the present. The more I practised the easier it became to clear my mind; to become empty of all interior dialogue and filled with the energy required for the now. Meditation was no longer a passive means of relaxing but a preparation for spontaneous energy.

In my last week I took an early bus down to Bombay and the airline office to confirm my flight. I arrived before it opened and retired to a nearby coffee shop. Something in the air made me suddenly nauseous, and I turned to see someone smoking a cigarette. Only then did I realise that I had not smoked for a month. Nor have I done so from that day to this.

I was due to begin rehearsals for *Don Giovanni* within a week. The usual nerves associated with starting a new venture were somehow absent, and on the plane back to Melbourne I kept wondering if my tranquil state would continue as I re-entered the volatile world of the theatre, directing what others with more experience than I have called the most difficult of all operas.

Don Giovanni was not my first opera. There had been two productions for the Australian Opera, Mozart's *Die Entführung aus dem Serail*, towards the end of my time in Adelaide, and Donizetti's *Lucrezia Borgia* at the time I was meeting Baba. Now I was approaching an opera in a new state of mind. Not for a moment do I suggest that my talent had been transformed by Siddha Yoga. I do not believe such things happen. However, just as I do believe a good teacher will help the talents of a good actor to fly, so I believe that Siddha Yoga and meditation helped me to do some of my best work without stress and with new feelings of self-confidence.

The year that followed my experience in India was filled with energy. I would direct *Don Giovanni* and Verdi's *Falstaff* for the Australian Opera, a production of Shaw's *Widowers' Houses* for the Old Tote and a new production of *Coppelia* for the Australian Ballet. These four major works surrounded another major event, the arrival of Swami Muktananda in Melbourne.

During his visit, I spent as much time as possible near him to learn and wonder. Every day began with a visit to the ashram, meditation and a chant. At least two evenings every week meant *satsang* at the ashram where I would sometimes talk of my experience in Ganeshpuri. From time to time, particularly when the guru was in residence, an intensive was held and these weekend events became fuel stops; filling myself up with the extraordinary energy I seemed to possess. I would walk to rehearsal whether to the opera, drama or ballet, chanting to myself. Nothing fazed me; when a problem of staging arose, clear thinking brought a solution quickly and effectively. If I needed confirmation that Siddha Yoga had taught me to live again, every day of my life offered proof.

My life in opera and ballet spread over five years of activity and I must set down some of the things that occurred and things I learnt on this small journey through these great art forms. But before I do so, I need to tell of a pilgrimage that began in a most unexpected way.

As I danced back and forth to rehearsals, I would often find myself in a spiritual bookshop. One day I bought a new Bible, took it home and began to read it. My days with the church fellowship poured back into my mind and I began reading a little each morning. I felt dazzled by what I read. When I asked a swami to explain this turn of events he smiled.

'Meditation will take you back to your roots.'

Then, as the year came to a close, I became ill. The accumulated stress of years had come to a climax in my gut and diverticulitis demanded attention. After a successful operation and a fortnight in hospital my doctor pronounced that six months' rest was essential. Friends thought I would follow the guru to America during this time but something more urgent was knocking at my door. I decided on a sort of pilgrimage to places of the spirit—like Ganeshpuri but also to those centres closer to my own heritage: to Israel, to Assisi in Italy and to a place in France called Taizé.

The author's tent pitched by the sea of Galilee.

SIMPLE GIFTS

A voice came over the intercom, informing us of our imminent landing. At once someone behind me burst into loud singing. I twisted around and was startled to see, over the top of my seat, a middle-aged man with his eyes turned upward and the cords in his neck rigid and straining as he lifted his voice triumphantly. His eyes began streaming with tears. It was a prayer of thankfulness as we prepared to land at Tel Aviv airport.

Other people had their eyes closed, listening to the singer, and some moved their lips in private prayer. No one seemed at all put out by the commotion, as if this was a usual occurrence in aircraft approaching Israel. Some even continued reading their newspapers, untouched by the sudden display of ecstasy. As the wheels bumped down onto the tarmac, several people leapt from their seats unhindered by safety belts and fell on their knees kissing the floor. Some cried out while others wept. It was at once both comic and profoundly moving. Jewish people were coming home. I suddenly recalled my mother's tears on her return to Scotland. As the train thundered across the border and sped towards Aberdeen, her admirable self-control failed her and she sobbed as the familiar landscape aroused long-buried memories.

The plane came to a halt and pandemonium ensued as passengers scrambled to be the first onto the Promised Land. I sat quietly and felt a moment of deep stillness, recollecting the experience of twelve months ago, when I knew in all certainty that my true home lay buried deeply and mysteriously in my heart.

I had decided to fly into Israel from Athens on the Israeli airline, which in itself was an experience. The passengers were held in the airport lounge until the last moment, waiting for the departure gate to be announced. The result was a stampede down the corridors, followed by a scramble through no fewer than three security checks before we landed in our seats. There was a general air of congratulation, as if we had won a long and dangerous battle without a single shot being fired.

More security checks made it slow going at Tel Aviv airport. Finally I emerged, having passed by many suspicious, unsmiling officials, to join the bus queue. My destination was Tiberius from where I would take another bus to the Sea of Galilee. Just thinking of these names made me shiver in anticipation. I knew, of course, that modern Israel had transformed this ancient land into new towns and prolific *kibbutzim*, but through it Jesus had once walked and it was His journey I proposed to make.

The bus queue lengthened considerably over the next fifteen minutes. We were the most extraordinary mixed bag of humanity I had ever seen. A large number of young men in uniform, all carrying rifles and with faces that ranged from freckled pink to pitch black; broad peasant faces and fine delicate ones—faces that seemed to come from every country on earth. Above the chatter American voices discussed problems at the *kibbutz*.

At last the bus slid into place. The queue was abandoned as everyone rushed forward, fighting to get on. Pushing and shoving, they called out to friends and family, some laughing, some shouting in anger. One old lady began punching a soldier to obtain her right of passage, and screamed in triumph as she succeeded. I could only stand and stare open-mouthed. The driver stood by the bus, nonchalantly rolling a cigarette. He saw my passive stance and shouted something at me. I jerked myself into action, picked up my rucksack and hurried over to the already packed vehicle. Strong arms shot out the door, hauling me into the inferno. There I found myself in the middle of a celebration. The boorish queue was now a smiling animated party. A good time had been had by all, as they fought for entrance onto the bus. The tensions of daily living in the Holy Land had been eased by what I would discover to be national therapy.

Instead of sitting comfortably by a window drinking in the Israeli countryside, as I had planned, I was, for many miles, wedged in between a huge soldier and an American, both talking animatedly to their friends. In adjusting myself I trod on someone's foot and apologised. That apology was all they needed; for the next half hour I tried to answer a multitude of questions from every direction, mostly of a personal nature. Unasked questions of a deeper kind played around in my mind but I let them go. Time would answer them.

I alighted from my second bus trip outside the gates. The land around was green and fertile with orchards as far as the eye could see and trees bordered the *kibbutz* I was about to enter. This working community hired out camping places during summer months and many city families drove here to camp and swim. I would join them.

Paying a small fee, I found a place to pitch my tent only feet away from the southern edge of the sea. I was astonished by its size; the northern bank only just visible in the far distance. It was a hot, quiet afternoon, and a couple of large tents near me were empty of life. The water quietly lapped onto the shore as I made my temporary home. To the far right soared the Golan Heights, the site of recent warfare It would be my first experience of living in a country at war within its own borders.

As I sat down to a light evening meal, a large Israeli family drove up to occupy the empty tents and with many curious glances towards my camp site, set up their own meal. From my bus experience I knew what was expected of me as the stranger and moved forward to say 'hello'. To discover an Australian ten feet away from them was a holiday bonus to this group from Jerusalem and I was immediately invited to their fire and wonderful Jewish food. As I sat waiting to be asked to start, my host looked over at me with his mouth full and grinned.

'In Israel we do not have time for niceties. Dig in.'

So I did. After the meal others joined us and soulful Israeli songs rang through the night air.

For two weeks I wandered alone by the sea while around me the *kibbutz* kept its occupants busy all day long. Evenings were spent with my neighbours, hearing them talk of their problems, their hopes and fears. I would soon discover that every Israeli was a political creature and would defend their beliefs passionately.

In later times, I would revisit my memories of this country by reading everything by the great Israeli writer Amos Oz. In him I found a voice of reason and tolerance far removed from the fundamentalist views of so many. During the hot, quiet days I was left alone to discover the places that as a child I had learnt to respect as the geographical source of our Christian religion. My walks around the north shore of the sea brought me to the old city of Capernaeum, where many of the ancient walls still stood. I took my Bible with me, read the New Testament again, and found within me a powerful response.

Every time I looked up from my reading I would recall my experience at Ganeshpuri. Superficially, it was a world apart. And yet I recalled groups of young *swamis* walking, talking and laughing together on a river bank in Maharashtra and they reminded me of the group of Franciscan monks I saw by the shores of Galilee. They had the same joy and exuded the same aura of goodness. Despite their different beliefs, both groups seemed to me to advocate the same life of service and meaning. As each day went by, Ganeshpuri began to merge with Galilee. Instead of feelings of betrayal about either, I began to see in each the same journey.

There was a little church on the north shore, built by monks of the Franciscan order. This church commemorated the place where the crucified Jesus was seen by the disciples cooking fish on the shore. It was cared for by an old Italian Franciscan monk and for many an hour I would join him and, sitting on the rocks by the sea, meditate on the sacred nature of the place, just as I had done among the banana groves of Ganeshpuri.

I left Galilee with the same regret with which I had left Ganeshpuri, and boarded another crowded, animated bus heading for Jerusalem.

I was standing in the old city, savouring the busy atmosphere. The mixture of Arab and Jewish created a multi-coloured background to the purpose of the moment. A number of Franciscan monks leading a group of tourists were about to walk through the crowded lanes, stopping at all the Stations of the Cross.

After the peace of Galilee I found the Holy City anything but spiritual. The city exuded the feeling that an eruption of aggression could occur at any moment. This day I was feeling particularly vulnerable, having been the target of young Arabs the day before as I walked beyond the old city to the Garden of Gethsemane. A group had begun pelting me with stones and I had to take refuge in a small church. The experience had been unsettling. Looking back from my refuge, the city of Jerusalem was peaceful, shining like a diamond in the midday sun, but hiding inside itself its dark and angry inhabitants.

I stood on the perimeter of the group as the Franciscan began a prayer and felt a gentle tap on my shoulder. An Arab in his mid thirties was talking to me. Like any tourist I shied away. However, he persisted and when I turned on him in exasperation I found tears coursing down his face.

'Please, sir' he pleaded in stilted English, 'My mother needs blood. Very sick... has rare blood... please help.'

My bewilderment continued until I understood that he was asking for my blood type. His mother was in urgent need of a transfusion and the clinic did not have blood of her type. I had to confess that I could not remember mine. With a beating heart I found myself being led through a maze of lanes until we arrived at the little clinic. He presented me to the Arab doctor who quickly scraped my thumb to test the blood. Within moments I proved a disappointment. I left with the disconsolate man, conscious of how little chance he had of finding a donor.

What happened next I still recall as a sort of madness on my part. I took the man by the arm and, retracing our steps to the main gateway to the old city, proceeded to stop every male tourist with a request for their blood type. They listened and politely gave me the information. Then the miracle happened. A young Scotsman revealed himself as having the right type. Would he give blood at the clinic? Without hesitation he agreed, and in triumph we returned to the clinic where smiling doctors tended to the young man. The Arab was beside himself with joy and gratitude and I left them wondering by what miracle I had dared to beg in the streets of the Holy City.

Looking for a tranquil spot in Jerusalem was looking for the impossible. This city was alive with tension as the occasional bomb exploded in a nearby street. Loud talk in the cafés trumpeted with complaints about the state of things. But one day I came upon such a place of tranquillity. I began a habit of going every day to sit beneath quiet trees with a cup of English tea and some postcards—for it was a very English spot. It had become known as the Garden of Joseph Arimathaea, for a tomb had been discovered within the garden which some believe to be the tomb in which Joseph had laid the body of Christ and from which He rose from the dead. The place was run by a group of genteel English ladies who served tea and maintained this sacred site in strict and absolute quiet.

Up in Galilee I had felt close to the mystery as I walked the quiet shores and sat in the little church. Here, in Jerusalem I was as foreign as I was when on tour with Baba. There, the poverty and way of life divorced me from contact with the people; here, Israelis lived in a state of siege. Here was an urgency about living that had never existed in my safe life. When the young man at the desk of my hotel asked me my intentions in Israel and I told him, he nodded sagely.

'You have to have leisure and money to do such things. We do not have time.'

I went away chastened, worrying if that was all it was—idle curiosity born out of enforced rest. However, in the next moment I was wondering what might happen if all the busy people of the world took fifteen minutes each day to meditate on the mystery within. I began to see the journey to the spirit as an intensely inward, personal one that had very little to do with the social or political conditions that prevailed.

Further wanderings around Jerusalem revealed a small travel agency that took groups in a desert truck down through Israel. I immediately subscribed, wanting to leave this disturbing city. We took sleeping bags, slept in the desert and were fed by three enterprising young Israelis.

An assortment of some twenty people from all over Europe made up our party. For the most part we were quiet and kept to ourselves. We appreciated the almost unearthly silence of the desert at night. Sleep was only given a cursory few hours. It was much more interesting to wander a little from the camp and sit and meditate in the silence. I began to understand why so many people had a passionate love for the desert, and why so many religious communities existed there.

The ten days were spent travelling through desert, sleeping on the sand, swimming in the Dead Sea. One evening we had a splendid meal with a group of nomad Arabs; and the tour came to a climax one night as we set up camp at the base of Mount Sinai. Next morning we were woken in the very early hours and provided with a torch. For the next hour we wended our way up paths dug from the mountain by monks and arrived at the top just as the sun appeared. The view and the spectacular sunrise bathing the mountain top with flame red is burnt into my memory in a way no film could ever achieve. I felt privileged to be alive.

After my return to Jerusalem, I journeyed back across the Mediterranean by ship to Bari and by train up the centre of Italy. There Assisi, this beautiful little town set high on the side of the majestic Mount Subasio, seemed to beckon me.

Assisi, as most people know, was the birthplace of St Francis. As I walked up the steep stone path past the church built in his honour, I was reminded of an old Scots Presbyterian minister addressing teenagers from our fellowship on the glories achieved by Martin Luther and the beginnings of the Protestant Church.

'And out of the corruption that was the Roman Church and of Europe, came the plain teachings of Calvin and Knox,' he thundered. 'At last the world (and here he rolled his 'r' like a machine gun) would begin to know how a real Christian behaved.'

I had the temerity to put up my arm, stopping the magisterial flow.

'Aye, wee George,' he glowered at me. 'What do you have to say?'

'There was the Franciscan movement, sir, wasn't there? St Francis tried to bring his Church back to a life of simplicity and poverty.'

For a long moment the old martinet was stumped. He stared at me as if I had committed treason. At last he gathered his forces together.

'Aye, well now, there's nae doubt the wee mannie did a thing or two, but if a sermon to the birds and the bees is your idea of reform in the Church, then you are very easily served.'

St Francis has crossed the barriers of every sect, and remains in the hearts of every thinking human being as the man who did more than turn his back on the material world in order to meet his Lord; he fell in love with Lady Poverty and by so doing, became a universal instrument of peace.

I found digs and went on a late afternoon walk around the little town. That this was the home of the Franciscan order was evident everywhere. There was a hush, as if the town itself was a cathedral in honour of the 'wee mannie'. Except for the occasional delivery van roaring up the main street, hurrying groups of Franciscan monks and local coffee drinkers, small parties of tourists were the only inhabitants of its winding streets. As I sat on a bench in the main square bells began to peal from the many churches, and the sound carried down the mountain to the Umbrian plain below. It was a sight and sound to bring peace to any heart. I resolved to stay for a while.

Early next day I took a morning walk, which I maintained in the weeks to come. I carried a pocket guide to the town that showed the places Francis loved, and contained G.K. Chesterton's beautiful sketch of the saint's life. For days I wandered about the town and to the hill above where paths had been cut through the woods. They led to the caves where Francis and his first followers used to pray. Seats were provided nearby for those who wished to do the same. Everything in and around the town was arranged for the solitary, contemplative pilgrim. Now and then we pilgrims met, smiled and passed each other with a nod. In the month I remained in Assisi the only words I uttered were *'buon giorno'* to my landlady and a few desultory words at dinner. I became so still inside it felt at times that I was hardly breathing. The caves on the hillside and the little church of San Damiano, in the ruins of which, eight hundred years ago, St Francis had heard the voice of God ordering him to rebuild his Church, became my favourite places to sit, meditate, read, write a postcard and finally, to say 'goodbye'.

On my last day, while sitting outside the little church, I heard chanting coming from down in the valley. A young Franciscan came into view, trudging slowly up the hill. He was barefoot and exhausted, but his eyes were filled with ecstasy and his voice lifted up as he saw the church. Several monks came out and ran to him, holding him in case he fell. The young monk began crying with joy as they gently led him into the church. He had walked barefoot from his town in Germany in homage to St Francis. In Chesterton's biography I read of Francis' 'great fixed idea; of praise and thanks springing to their most towering height out of nakedness and nothing'.

Reluctant as I was to leave Assisi, I had a third destination on this pilgrimage. Taizé is a small village in Burgundy, south of Dijon, and is the home of a group of contemplative monks who call themselves *La grande communauté*. The community had been established there during World War II and was Christian but non-denominational. Their members came from all faiths and professions, composed

A service at Taizé

their own music and conducted a service uniquely their own. I had bought a book about Taizé and what I read had determined me to go there.

I arrived one blustering early autumn day and walked up the winding road towards the village. On the outskirts I came upon the tiny Romanesque church in which this community had begun its contemplative life. The interior, lit by candles, was filled with grace, reminding me of the Nityananda Temple in Ganeshpuri. A few young people meditated and prayed in the pews.

I walked further in search of the 'Welcome hut', and found hundreds of tents erected in neighbouring fields. Wherever I looked I saw only young people and wondered if there was a youth conference in progress. I walked on towards an ugly building that looked like a brick aircraft hanger. A huge circus tent was attached to the back wall. I came to a small door at the side and, hugging my backpack to me, entered. I could hardly see in the vast gloom and stood for a few moments, blinded by the light outside.

Gradually I became aware that the church was lit by hundreds of candles set quite low in the walls on three sides. At one end several steps led to an altar, on which candelabra were lit. There was no heating and the air was chilly, but what was astonishing to my eyes was the absence of seating. The floor of this cavernous church was covered only by underfelt. Near the altar many young people were sitting on the floor or on stools they had brought. A narrow area straight down the middle was made separate by two rows of what looked like low hedges.

The sound of their voices accompanied by an organ caused me to put down my bag, sit near the back and listen. It did not appear to be a service and there was no sign of a monk, but many young voices rang out, singing in beautiful harmony. Then a cello and violin joined in. After twenty minutes, without a signal from anywhere, the congregation stood up and casually filed out of the church. Perhaps they had been practising? I was left alone in the empty space with the sound of music still ringing in my ears. I had to know more.

On my way back to the welcome hut I passed groups of young people mixed, to my relief, with a number of much older adults, sitting together on benches. Sitting with each group was a monk dressed somewhat like the Franciscans who joined in the conversation. I came to the hut and stepped in. I was welcomed immediately by a German girl who spoke perfect English. I asked if I could pitch my tent for a week or two. When she discovered I spoke French she left me for a while and in her place an older monk arrived, shook me by the hand and asked me whether I would like to help arrange small groups to talk about their lives. As a concession to my age, and with the weather closing in, I would be provided with a room. Payment for the accommodation would be made by placing whatever money I could afford in a tin on the counter. I complied gratefully and he took me on a long walk to the other end of the village where I was given a room in one of a series of huts. On the way he informed me of the four daily services that took place in the church and of the discussion groups that were part of their program. With summer coming to an end, most of the young people would be leaving.

'We encourage people to go back into the world with what they discover here,' he said with a smile. 'We are going on a walk soon, to Spain, and many will come with us.' This walk took place every year to many cities, where the community took over the churches and led thousands of young people in prayer.

For the next fortnight, I sat with groups of about fifteen people from many countries, and a monk from the community who led our discussion. My first group included a nun from Montreal, a Lutheran pastor from Switzerland, several Dutch and Asian students and a Pakistani. There was no preaching here, no evangelism, only a request to tell your story and, by listening to others and understanding, to pray and contemplate these experiences. I discovered that the word 'listening' was the main resource of these monks; listening to people and then listening to their God.

As the days passed I came to love this place; the residents, their simplicity and the absence of material possessions. They had no bank account and gave away what their members earned, keeping only enough for a healthy life. For the first time I wondered about living such a life and becoming part of such a community.

Four times a day the population retired into the church to sing. The service was simple and included readings from the Bible, which the monks were encouraged to read in a language not their own. The church rang with every language; the music was simple and melodious. Many of their songs became rounds and catches, and, like the chanting in a Siddha Yoga *satsang*, went on continuously and effortlessly, expressing, by the absence of climax, that their praise was infinite.

Occasionally Brother Roger would appear and talk on the need for prayer. Brother Roger founded his community in 1940, moving there from Switzerland with several friends, all seeking reconciliation among the different Christian sects. Gradually young people from all over Europe began to come each summer to talk and pray. For him the most important idea in modern life was *reconciliation*. This word was spelled out on the church wall, above the entrance. The purpose of the community, he would explain, was to encourage people to talk with each other, to foster tolerance, no matter what race, colour or creed. If there is a group of men on earth who follow faithfully all the teachings of Christ it must be the monks of Taizé. The idea of reconciliation has taken them to many cities of the world where they set up small communities in the poorest districts. Their activities are not political, but they have protected many young people from harsh regimes. Today Taizé is known by the world as a symbol of peace.

As the weather worsened the group discussions finished and there remained only a few young people who were studying with the monks. I was reluctant to leave and applied to spend a while in their house of silence where people could contemplate. I shifted into a room in a lovely old house, adjoining six others. The guests met only at mealtimes, maintaining silence, where food was eaten accompanied by classical music. The silence penetrated every pore and forced me to look at my life as honestly as I could. Every day a young monk, Brother Emil, joined me and, breaking the silence for half an hour, we talked, read and prayed. He was a French Canadian and we spoke English as we discussed Christianity and the Psalms, taking a psalm each day as an object of study. His faith became something I both loved and feared. Such certainty left no room for doubt.

Towards the end of the fortnight he asked me if I would join the community at a meal in their main building and meet Brother Roger. This invitation immediately set up barriers within me. I confessed to Brother Emil that it was their way of life, their respect for others and their need to understand all human beings that attracted me to Taizé. For me surrender was still not possible. For me Jesus was a great Master rather than the risen Christ. I spoke of Assisi and the joy I had living there but that Francis' belief required a leap of faith I could not make. I felt that pacing my corridor before making an entrance would always be my way. Brother Emil insisted that I come and eat with them nonetheless.

It's difficult to describe the meal that day. I was awed by the simplicity and yet the power of that dining room. Brother Roger greeted me with a smile and a few words. Afterwards he invited me to talk to him about my life in the theatre and for the first time I spoke of Siddha Yoga and what it had meant to me. He loved hearing of it and, knowing of my doubt, urged me gently to join them again at Christmas. Without thinking I said 'yes,' and left the community a few days later with a strengthening feeling that with time and grace, I could perhaps belong there.

Friends from Australia would soon be gathering for a holiday in Rome and I thought I would join them there. Wandering around the splendours of ancient Rome was a distraction, but when they decided to go to Sicily I begged off and set off north to Assisi once again. Unknowingly I arrived on a special day of celebration. It was 800 years since the birth of St Francis and Assisi was packed. The streets were crowded, the churches were full and in every one glorious singing could be heard. At the end of the day not a single drunk was to be seen, only universal love for the 'wee mannie'. By now the Christ that he followed and the life I found at Taizé were drawing me close to a cliff edge. Two thoughts kept ringing in my ears. Did I simply lack the courage to leap off into space or did I draw back because of honest doubts?

The weeks that followed were spent in a waiting room of indecision. They were spent in London, which had now become a place to visit old friends and spend an occasional night in the theatre. Any ambitions I might have had were fast fading and all I could think of was Taizé and Christmas. Meanwhile my world back in Australia was trying to make sense of me. Offers were coming in for drama and opera productions but I was reluctant to sign any contract until I saw Brother Roger again. It was a sure sign of my continuing doubts about my capacity to take that leap—or my fear of it.

As I write these last paragraphs I am most conscious that Brother Roger is no longer with us. His violent death in 2005 at the hands of a poor deranged woman brought grief to his world-wide community; through it he lives on in continuing grace.

Christmas at Taizé was bitterly cold. It had snowed and Burgundian winds swept through the village like wild horses. And yet the little place was packed. On Christmas Eve, protecting our lighted candles from the fierce winds, we began to sing; faces became rapt and eyes shone as the monks of Taizé celebrated their vocation. Their assurance, Brother Emil's loving welcome and Brother Roger's words in the preparation of a young man to join the community, made my decision not easy but conclusive. I rather think this was Brother Roger's intention in asking me to return.

Psalm 125 was sung:

Those who trust in the Lord are like Mount Zion,
Which cannot be shaken but endures forever.
As the mountains surround Jerusalem,
So the Lord surrounds his people
Both now and for evermore.

A prayer was given in several languages; a hymn followed; then the young man took vows with Brother Roger that would result in a life commitment to Christ and the community. One response remains firmly in my memory:

'Will you, for love of Christ, consecrate yourself to him with all your being?'

'I will.'

The last response rang out as Brother Roger placed a ring in the hand of the new brother with the words:

'May this ring be the sign of our fidelity in the Lord.'

A hymn of praise followed this simple ceremony and I knew that such a commitment could only come about with a certainty I did not have and that I must remain in my rehearsal room doing the things I knew and loved. On my final evening Brother Roger confirmed my decisions with a smile and his blessing.

'You belong in your world and you must take your love there.'

Seven

THE ASHRAMITE

From meditating in an Indian Ashram, to wandering the shores of a *kibbutz* on Galilee, to the city of Jerusalem; onto the desert and Mt Sinai; to Assisi and the mountains surrounding the little town; I had landed on a windswept hill in Burgundy, meditating with the contemplative monks of Taizé. What did it all mean?

I had been away for six months and now at the beginning of 1980 my life resumed its full program in the theatre with plays and opera. There was very little time, perhaps thankfully, to reflect on this journey. I returned to the ashram with willing purpose. Here was the way to maintain a discipline and to receive a constant reminder that my inner guru expected the best.

At the ashram I began the sort of *seva* that the guru knew would be my best contribution. I began to introduce the evening programs of *satsang*. From this position I could see how many people of all ages came, seeking an answer, or a respite from the impossible demands life made on them. I remain astonished that Siddha Yoga found me, not only for its life-giving benefits, but for the discovery, as I talked about it at *satsang*, that it was not an evangelical religion but a means of directing us towards meditation and the path of the spirit from which both the Christian and the non-believer could benefit.

The experience of the previous two years would affect everything I now attempted in the theatre. Friends would wonder, at times, what that amounted to. 'You have not changed,' they'd say. But how can one explain shifting attitudes, thoughts and priorities which seem to be trivial and yet over the years have influenced every moment of my working life?

For a while the experience gave me the reputation of having 'found God.' But I've never thought of myself as having got religion. I do, however, see myself as a seeker. The fact that I found grace at both a Siddha Yoga ashram and the Christian community of Taizé, proves to me that grace is a gift that derives from the one source but flows through many tributaries.

In those years between 1978 and 1982 my life was a constant stream of work in drama, ballet and opera. Along with these productions, I also returned to teaching drama students through play production, this time at NIDA. It was good to be back working with the younger generation and I could revel again in the process of learning and making mistakes.

One day, after a particularly sticky session with the students, a fellow teacher fell exhausted into a chair beside me, murmuring, 'When we were young, we just got up and did it.'

The truth of these words transported me back to the learn-as-you-go methods of the Jimmie James Company. Today's theatre has become so expensive to realise, in even the most modest way, that mistakes are no longer affordable. Opening night is the night when everything must be perfect. No longer can a young actor grow into a better actor by 'doing it'. Drama school provides an answer. For some it's the perfect answer. For three years in a stable atmosphere they can expand their talent, refine the voice, extend the body and learn the history, manners and culture behind the classic theatre.

For others it can be a nightmare. Some students find their instinct rebels against the attitudes or practice of their teachers. This rebellion can bring about a quick exit or can sustain them throughout the three years by its strength and conviction. As I am not the product of a drama school my inclination lies with the rebel, notwithstanding the benefits a good school can provide.

Talent cannot be taught. Wherever talent comes from, whether from genes or grace, it lies within a good actor and only awaits the door to open for a chance to fly. Good teachers can discern that talent, though it lies beneath layers of doubt, terror, shyness or repressed anger. But they are rare. In the overcrowded auditions for a drama school it is easy to imagine how much talent is missed and how many mistakes are made in the final choices. For young actors who miss out at audition it is important they understand that it might just be bad luck or bad judgment.

Who are these people who choose? It has been a bone of contention since drama schools became part of tertiary education. Written and even oral examinations are no judge of acting potential. Many really good actors are dyslexic, so all selectors can do is rely on their experience. However, I believe the real problem lies behind that word 'institution'. The larger the institution the less flexible it becomes and the more teachers and students are required to conform or be replaced.

Very little accounting can be made for the difference in the nature of drama students—yet they are admired for their very differences. The freedom necessary for a teacher to allow the individual talent to fly is unobtainable among so many. Not so long ago I faced a personal disappointment after encouraging my talented niece, Fiona Gabb, to attend Jacques Lecoq's school, now a prestigious drama institution. She found it too restrictive and, after one year, fled. Twenty years earlier, freedom had been the very essence of this school.

My first experience of drama school was in the 1960s at the Central School of Speech and Drama in London and memories remain of the wonderful students with whom I worked. Back in Australia I began work at NIDA in Sydney, later at the Western Australian Academy of the Performing Arts (WAAPA) in Perth and the Victorian College of the Arts (VCA) in Melbourne. I was employed as a director and the teaching came through these productions. This was at my insistence, and derived from my own pattern of learning on the job.

In this process the learning of the role becomes intermingled with learning about the play and how to express it. I soon gained respect for what I call the three great rules for an actor's work in the theatre: UNDERSTAND, EXPRESS, COMMUNICATE. In order to accomplish these, something must be present within the actor: space. Space to think, to experiment and discard, space to allow new ideas to enter and be juggled, space to allow the new character to take over the body of the actor. The only way to allow all this to take place is to empty the mind of all the fears that block, any preconceptions of the role that block, and above all, the gossip of the mind.

Meditation had become a daily practice for me during the years of 1978 and 1979 and I determined that this life-giving process should be of use to the student to help them arrive at this state of readiness. After spending so many years with actors, I know that some can achieve this state effortlessly. The capacity to focus and concentrate is a blessing some have, created by having a mind ready to receive. The graduating students from NIDA in 1980 were immensely helpful in this regard. I thank them for their willingness to join me in discovering ways of using meditation to prepare the actor. I have continued to use them as the opportunities arise.

I first worked with this group of students earlier in their final year in a production of Shakespeare's *Love's Labour's Lost*. They were promising and focused and, interestingly, their average age was older than the usual drama school intake. George Whaley, then Head of Acting, had chosen these students because he felt, as I did, that previous intakes had been too young. Drama school is certainly a place for growing up, but some of this growth could be better achieved out in the world before allowing the school to take on its rightful role of preparing the actor for the theatre.

It was decided I should direct their graduation play, and we chose Galsworthy's *Strife*; an Edwardian drama about conflict in the workplace. A young designer, Deirdre Burgess, gave us a splendid set and I set about rehearsals with an idea. Every morning as part of rehearsals, we did the Circle. Seventeen students took a walk around the perimeter of the room, creating a huge circle. The walk began with chatter and a look around the room until it slowly became an inward, private, but always aware, walking meditation which led into a group run, which then took its own time to slow down to a walk again and finally, to a breathing halt, when the students stood silent, alone in the group, relaxed, and ready for work. It is a complex exercise, which takes days to begin having an effect. Persistence is the essence. It requires the students to trust and gradually learn that the Circle is a tool to clear the mind for work, and allow it to focus on the present moment. For the first few days I found it essential to stand in the centre of the circle and talk the students through the process until it became automatic and silent.[1]

---

1. See the Appendix for instructions on the Circle

For some students the Circle opened a magic door. For others it was a troubling obstacle for some time. It was important to reassure them that there was no judgment in the Circle. It was a tool to use and, if it did not work, to discard. However, with people who trust each other and are prepared to persist, it has great benefits. By the time we arrived at the opening night, the entire cast would do the circle and meditate for thirty minutes before each subsequent performance. I was intensely proud of the superb ensemble playing that resulted. I have since worked again with some of these actors and we always remember this experiment as a special time.

The usual way for a dedicated actor to prepare for a performance is to find a solitary place and with breathing exercises create a private world. To my mind this simply encourages a singular performance rather than a shared experience on stage. To prepare willingly together gives the actor an awareness of sharing that reveals itself in an ensemble performance. In future years, during my life as a film director, such ensemble sharing became a natural exercise in rehearsals.

'Where's Cliff?'

The cry went up, around the stage and in the wings. The stagehands were setting up the last act of *Don Giovanni* at the first dress rehearsal in the Opera House. I was on stage, happy and relaxed, trying to be useful. I could hardly believe I had made the journey through rehearsals with so few problems. It was April 1978, and every morning had begun with a walk to the ashram with meditation and chant, then a walk to rehearsals full of Mozart. Nothing seemed a problem as we tackled the challenges of this fabulous opera. My designers, Kris Fredrikson and Hugh Colman, and I were pleased with the setting and costumes, all light and flexible in preparation for a national tour.

The last act contained a *coup de théâtre*, and our plan was that as Don Giovanni eats his final dinner, the Commandatore would appear, standing high above him on a huge archway. He then offers his hand to Giovanni and the statues of two avenging women come to life. In a manic dance, as Giovanni sings out his torment, they tear out his heart in the form of blood-red ribbons. He then falls into the dark abyss of the archway as the Commandatore lifts his arms attached to two huge wings, which cover the stage like a triumphal, armoured angel. The elevation of the Commandatore would not permit the actual hand contact but a light change would help the illusion.

'Where's Cliff?'

Clifford Grant, who was singing the Commandatore, could not be found. I strolled around the central archway and there he was, frozen halfway up the ladder towards his position at the top of the arch. He saw me out of the corner of his eye and murmured, 'Get me down.'

I called the stage manager and we assisted the helpless bass down from his perch. The stage manager looked at me with a stricken face. The whole plan for the final act would no longer work.

'Get Cliff a cup of tea,' I said resolutely, 'and ask Kris to come up on stage.' I cut short Cliff's apology with, 'No need, Cliff, there's a really good solution around the corner. Rest and I'll be with you.'

I walked away to the front of the stage, looking back, picturing an idea. My mind was untroubled, calculating the possibilities. Within a few moments the answer was there.

'Cliff has vertigo,' I told Kris. 'So he'll sing his role on a small dais in the archway and back away into the shadows as Giovanni falls into his arms. In the meantime, find an extra the same size as Cliff, dress him in Cliff's second costume and put him up on top. As Cliff disappears we'll light above, through the gauze, and the Second Commandatore will be revealed as he opens his wings. That way we can have Cliff capable of taking Giovanni's hand and become an angel in the same instant.' This plan was put to work and it became the last moment of action in the opera. Our conductor, Maestro Carlo Felice Cillario, had to pause the orchestra while the audience roared their approval.

I tell this little story to convey my recollections of the effect my months of daily meditation was having on my work. I no longer needed the cigarette, or the headache pills, or the double scotch, to recover from a crisis like this.

Along with *The Three Sisters*, I consider *Don Giovanni* to be one of the finest experiences of my career. It gave me the opportunity of working with many Australian opera singers. They are very special people. Actors are complex creatures, constantly beset with anxiety about their talent, which to them is a mysterious something lying within themselves but in need of inspiration from text or director to reveal. Although they talk of technique, they rely more on instinct to capture the audience.

Singers, and dancers too, know much more precisely where their talents lie. They endure constant training, refining their voice and body, knowing that if their instrument fails, their career is over. It is this awareness of a finite professional life that makes the opera singer, I believe, open and willing.

In opera a director provides a context in which voices can be displayed. I discovered very quickly that every physical movement and body position first needed the approval of the conductor to ensure the voice would not be disadvantaged. Fortunately, my early training in music gave me a certain understanding of their needs. The director in the drama theatre may be king, but in opera and ballet authority is shared with the conductor or choreographer. I came to love and appreciate this sharing.

The first cast of *Don Giovanni*, led by John Pringle and Ronald Maconaghie, were Jenny Birmingham, Gregory Yurisich, Nance Grant, Margreta Elkins, Cliff Grant and Henri Wilden. The rehearsal period astonished me. Every morning I looked forward to rehearsal knowing that these singers, with their many years' experience, would join me in creating something special.

I discovered early on a clear structure within the music: two streams of consciousness. One is in the dialogue, the other in private soliloquies, sometimes a number of them at the same time. The former, both in recitative and aria, meant movement and action while the latter was still and meditative. This was the basis on which I built the production.

The many great singers with whom I worked over the twelve years of this production's life gave me new insights into the music and their roles. Over time I would ache to redirect the production.

Unfortunately, once a production is successful, its mounting is no longer the priority for an opera company. By the time a new *Don Giovanni* was mounted, I was grateful to put to bed a production that was feeling its age. Still, whenever I hear the great chords that begin the overture it brings flooding back unforgettable memories of rehearsals, singers, conductors and Mozart.

Some months after *Don Giovanni*'s opening, I received an offer from Moffatt Oxenbould, the Opera's artistic administrator, to direct Verdi's *Falstaff*. I had never seen it performed. I sat down and listened to it for the first time and was staggered by its complexity, speed and faithfulness to the Shakespearean characters. Kris and I determined to prepare an evening that would do justice to both poets.

Ron Maconaghie sang Falstaff; Robert Allman, whose work in *Lucrezia Borgia* had taught me so much, played Ford. With them came Nance Grant and Cliff Grant and other old friends like Graeme Ewer, Donald Shanks, Gordon Wilcox, Paul Ferris and Rhonda Bruce. New delights were Heather Begg and Rosemary Gunn.

Falstaff would be revived twice during the following years when John Pringle and Jenny Birmingham would join me again; two singers whom I value for their friendship and dedication to their art. Here was an opera for the singers who could act, who must act, if the work is to be achieved. From the first frantic entrance of Dr Caius, I felt at home. It was like directing Feydeau, whose music lies in the rhythm of word and pause. Verdi's score dictates exact instructions for the singer/actor and placing them at the right moment with the right gesture became a daily joy. One might have thought such a union of talents an incongruous mix: *The Merry Wives of Windsor*, written three hundred years before the composition of this essentially Italian opera, but in Verdi's score lies a witty understanding of Shakespeare's characters and outrageous plot. The melodrama of Falstaff's 'secrets and lies' suits perfectly the volatile Italian nature. Pistol, Bardolph and Ford are a troupe of *commedia* performers. I never had a moment of doubt as I plotted the women's revenges, that in playwright, librettist and composer were a perfect meld of art. On opening night, I knew that here was my best work in this art form and with Kris, our finest collaboration.

Ronald Maconaghie and Heather Begg in *Falstaff*. (Photo: Opera Australia.)

My initiation into each new form remains as clear as falling in love for the first time: my first days with the Family, directing *Blood Wedding*, rehearsing *Coppelia*, shooting the television mini-series *The Dismissal*… and a short phrase from Mozart will bring back in detail the first rehearsals of *Die Entführung aus dem Seraglio*, my first opera. I recall sleepless nights and an agony of doubt. I had no confidence in either my ideas or my rehearsal process and I had to make a supreme effort to hide such feelings from the artists. The singers of *Die Entführung* and *Lucrezia Borgia* are remembered with love and gratitude for bringing me through a difficult time.

The principal singers were Joan Carden, June Bronhill, Anson Austin, Pieter Van de Stolk, Graeme Ewer and Donald Shanks. These talented artists taught me how to work with singers. They revealed astonishing open-hearted natures, willing to try anything asked of them. Of course, before our first rehearsal began their major work was done. They had prepared the music of their role over many hours at the piano with a répétiteur. My job was to see that the complexities of Mozart were presented on stage in keeping with his intentions. I leapt into it with mad enthusiasm.

Such was their sense of fun, the singers responded. At one point in rehearsals I had the great bass Donald Shanks doing a wild Turkish dance while singing his most difficult aria. It took a gentle request from my conductor for me to unburden the poor singer from this manic cavorting and devise a reasonable shimmy. I also remember with great affection Donald Shanks and Graeme Ewer in the drinking scene, desperately trying to obey my every whim while watching the nervous baton of the Maestro. And I recall a green-room drink with Joan Carden and June Bronhill and being joined by the rest of the principals. Their gift of an inscribed silver ice bucket, now a beautiful receptacle for flowers, still sits, twenty-five years later, gleaming and polished beside me at my desk with a card drawn by Gordon Wilcox—a treasured memory.

I would work again with these singers, who became good friends, and every subsequent production became a celebration of inspired music, hard work and a great sense of humour. I have a clear memory of a joke whispered by the baritone Robert Allman during a *sitzprobe* rehearsal as the conductor took the orchestra and singers through *Falstaff.* My shriek of laughter ruined a valuable moment of rehearsal and caused me to blush, much to the amusement of the cast. Robert rose without a flicker and delivered Ford's great aria of anger and frustration.

Of all the experiences an opera director can have, the *sitzprobe*—literally a sitting rehearsal for singers and orchestra—must rank very high. For weeks the rehearsal room rings with the voices and the piano until the score is implanted in the mind; then comes the first meeting of orchestra and singer. As the pieces come together a new excitement builds for singer and director that sweeps us towards opening night. At these rehearsals the director is only an observer, but occasionally the complexities of the score will give the director a painful reminder of a forgotten moment or action on stage and urgent attention will be demanded.

It is here that the true nature of the conductor is revealed. The pleasant quiet man seen occasionally in the rehearsal room becomes a ferocious tiger, leaping at singer and musician alike. It's a performance mixed with passionate love and knowledge of the score controlled by baton-wielding power. I looked forward to every occasion. It was during the *sitzprobe* that I became conscious of the power the music has over all those who sing and conduct; music is their master and has the final say.

My undying respect goes to the backbone of the opera company—the Chorus. I have never known artists in any entertainment who work as hard, with as much dedication as the members of the chorus of the Australian Opera (now Opera Australia). They work under an assortment of directors, chorus masters and conductors and manage somehow to keep their sense of humour and their willingness to try anything. For me they expressed all that I love about the Australian artist, without pretension, with a great goodwill and skill. They also terrify as they pour into a rehearsal room, like an army ready to shoot you down if you do not deliver. Every first rehearsal with the chorus is a heart-pumping three hours until the director smells either acceptance (which means good creative rehearsals to come), or suspicion (inviting difficult times).

Over the years I came to know so many of them. Their love for opera is inexhaustible despite the fact that most will never be soloists. The love of music was paramount, beyond ambition. When they surround a truly great singer, their affection and admiration is unbounded.

The other unsung heroes of opera are those fountains of knowledge known as *répétiteurs*. They play the piano at all rehearsals, displaying an invaluable familiarity with the conductor's requirements. They will have taught the singers the score in tiny studios equipped with a piano and little else and know their vocal capacities intimately. For a director they are essential to the birth of a production. At first I was intimidated by their depth of knowledge and experience, but soon found them ready to help in every way. Such *répétiteurs* as Sharolyn Kimmorley and Caroline Lill are remembered with admiration and gratitude.

'Well,' she said, slapping her bag onto a table and facing me, 'What are you going to do with me?'

They were not the first words that Joan Sutherland had said to me, but the first of which I have an overwhelming memory. It was the opening moment of our first rehearsal together. I was terrified and in desperate need of reassurance. Caroline Lill, our *répétiteur*, was waiting at the piano. For a long moment I said nothing, only silently thankful that I had requested no one else be present at my first rehearsal with this legendary artist.

Kristian Fredrikson's design for Joan Sutherland as Desdemona in *Otello*.

'Could we talk a little, first, do you think?' I stammered. She laughed and we sat at the table.

I began talking about Donizetti, about Victor Hugo, whose story was adapted by the librettist, about the historical Lucrezia Borgia, and finally, about the character of Lucrezia Borgia within the opera. I spoke about how she had been taught to be part of the cycle of power and revenge meted out by her malevolent family. The opera begins with Lucrezia, then a notorious poisoner in her middle years, meeting with her lost son, the moment that brings about a change. The opera then becomes the story of a mother using everything in her power to protect her child. In the last moments, as Lucrezia cradles her dead son, I planned to leave the audience with the image of Michelangelo's Pieta.

I stopped talking at last, and Joan looked at me. She turned towards Caroline and said: 'Now I understand the opera.' Then she stood. 'Will I sing the first cabaletta?'

'Please,' I gulped.

Without another word Caroline began playing and the immortal voice poured out.

Donizetti is a very different experience from Mozart. *Die Entführung* and *Don Giovanni* have small choruses and require much work with principals. *Lucrezia* has a big chorus and for the first time I had to become a choreographer on a large scale. Kris Fredrikson's designs provided inspiration and I was able to arrange tableaux in the manner of a Renaissance painting.

As the weeks progressed, Joan's ease and modesty made the rehearsal work effortless. She was prepared to try anything to achieve our goal. One eccentricity that took me by surprise was her habit of 'singing out' as we explored the drama. Singing at full voice was for her a necessity in order to feel every moment vocally. A young tenor once told me that to stand beside her in performance, aware of her breathing, control and focus, was to be given a lesson in how to sing opera.

My next opera with Joan Sutherland, a few years later, was less successful. It was Verdi's *Otello*, a grand opera requiring inspiring choreography, which I found myself unable to supply. Of all the operas I have directed *Otello* was for me the least satisfactory. The huge chorus I found unwieldy and I lacked the capacity for the sweeping gestures necessary to control the great score. Nevertheless, at a rehearsal of the last act of *Otello* Joan's Desdemona gave me an unforgettable moment. After singing the 'Barbara Song' at her dressing table, she rose and continued singing, unrehearsed, the subsequent recitative in which she was joined by Heather Begg as Emilia.

I indicated to Caroline to continue playing and watched Joan sing goodnight to her maid. As the music continued she began walking away from us towards the back wall of the set. I was keenly aware that the next note would be the highest in the opera, a note of despair and terror. Suddenly she turned, opened her arms and singing the sublime note ran full tilt into Emilia's arms. The effect was so amazing that we all burst into tears.

After a few moments she said, 'Don't be silly. George, was that all right?'

Great talent in the theatre is a rare commodity. In Joan Sutherland's case it is combined with equally rare modesty and good heart.

My career in opera ended with *Otello* until a decade later when I would direct Bellini's *Norma* with the great soprano, Elizabeth Connell, the performances of which climaxed in the beautiful His Majesty's Theatre in Perth under the baton of Richard Mills. It is a noble art form capable of inspiring both artist and audience, and it has given me many unforgettable experiences.

About this time I went into the Opera House to talk with Stuart Challender, the young Tasmanian who was to conduct *Don Giovanni* in the following season. Carlo Cillario had conducted all the work I had so far done for the Australian Opera and we had arrived at a comfortable partnership. Over the many years in which he has held the baton, his brilliant work had contributed greatly to the company's high reputation. So this day I felt a little apprehensive about meeting a new conductor for this ageing production of which I was feeling less than proud. Trying to keep together any opera production, with so many different interpretations by artists who were not there long enough for proper rehearsals, caused repeated cracks in the presentation. I fervently wished I could start all over again.

It was in this mood that I met Stuart. An immensely tall young man with a large head, covered in a shaggy mane, thrust out his hand aggressively and, pumping it furiously, demanded, 'What does *Don Giovanni* mean to you?'

I began to stammer out a few phrases, trying to remember what I had felt when I first rehearsed the great work. Meanwhile, this arrogant young lion paced up and down the little room, jabbing me with questions. I was made conscious of how complacent I had become and cursed myself silently. But Mozart and Challender brought back the devotee I had once been, and I felt my heart beating again. As I rethought my intention behind this production, I became conscious that the lion had stopped pacing and when I dared to look at him, there was a broad grin on his face.

Stuart Challender (centre) with George (left) and the 1987 cast of *Don Giovanni*: Stephen Bennett, Suzanne Johnston, Malvina Major, John Wegner, Thomas Edmonds, John Fulford and Patricia Price.

'Sounds fun,' he said.

So began a friendship which could only last a few short years. The death of Stuart Challender in 1991 was a tragedy for Australian music and has left a place, impossible to fill. On one of our last meetings as he lay ill, he grinned and said, 'Well, I have not had much time but I've managed to get most things in.'

He was referring to the immense workload he had taken on in those too-short years, as his work had moved from opera to the Sydney Symphony Orchestra. He had formed friendships and gained the immense respect of singers and musicians all over the world, conducting the great music he was born to interpret. To have him at an opera rehearsal was a lesson for both director and singer. Every word, every move, every moment of drama came under his scrutiny and he was always ready to assist the singer to find the right tempo, the right intonation and the right feeling for that moment. I felt at times he would leap into the rehearsal space like a giant Arlecchino, and act out the whole drama. In the pit, the entire opera passed through his body. It was as if Mozart had taken over his soul. Later, watching him conduct Strauss and at last, Mahler, I would sit with tears streaming down my face, aware of an ecstatic transformation. The music became an expression of divine joy.

Away from music, over a drink and dinner, I discovered his interest in Zen Buddhism, and we exchanged experiences of Eastern mysticism. The outcome was his first experience of Siddha Yoga, which took him to spend time with the guru at Ganeshpuri. He later described in smiling terms his experience of standing outside in the summer rain in the middle of the guru's garden and receiving *shaktipat*.

We would spend many a dinner arguing over our shared appetite for adventure. With my caution and Stuart's eagerness to taste everything life could offer, the pros and cons would swing all over the restaurant. Having tasted opera he was anxious to move into the symphonic world and we had a great celebratory dinner when he was appointed to the Sydney Symphony. Nothing would stop him now. His entire life, his very being, was music; and in the few years he had left he devoted every moment to communicating his passion, transferring to many his love for music and revealing its beauty and its healing power.

I feel privileged to have known and loved him.

During my early years in Sydney as a teenage accountancy student, I saw ballet for the first time. J.C. Williamson's presented the Borovansky Ballet, an Australian company created by the Ballets Russes dancer, Eduard Borovansky, at the Capitol Theatre just off Railway Square. The program included *Les Sylphides*, which left a vision that lasted for many years.

When next I was in Sydney with the Australian Drama Company in the mid-1950s, I became friends with Kathy Gorham, the Borovansky Ballet's principal dancer. Occasionally I would stand in the wings and watch her dance the Sugar Plum Fairy in *The Nutcracker Suite*. I had

Kristian Fredrikson's design for *Coppelia*.

no doubt that my life was that of an actor but I loved the dance; sometimes in imagination I would be up there dancing the Prince. A few years later I made my debut as a dancer in a very different form, in the musical *Lola Montez* at the Union Theatre under the tutelage of Paul Hammond. Paul offered me classes, which I eagerly took, but we both knew it was too late for me to be a classical dancer. Instead, I went to Paris and became a mime.

On my return to the Melbourne Theatre Company I renewed by connection at the Ballet School and had a moment on stage as the Headmistress in *Graduation Ball*. But by 1978 opera had taken the place of ballet. Then out of the blue a phone call came from Peggy Van Praagh at the Australian Ballet with a proposition for Kris and myself: an entirely new production of the Delibes ballet, *Coppelia*.

I had met Peggy in 1966 during my teaching at the Ballet School. Peggy would arrive to sit and watch me turning her dancers into actors. In those days dancers were seldom encouraged to use their imagination beyond the application of their technique and timing. This is no longer true today. So, to introduce drama into the curriculum of a ballet school was, for some, odd and terrifying; but for the majority it began to open new doors. Margaret Scott was an inspirational leader of the School who encouraged me more and more to influence the young dancers towards drama. This great lady of the dance retired soon after but re-emerged years later, dancing in the superb new version of *Nutcracker* devised by Graeme Murphy and Kris Fredrikson. In one of the most beautiful nights of my theatre experience she interpreted most movingly the last days of a great ballerina.

One day Peggy raised the idea of a mime company using dancers. Most regretfully I declined; my commitment to the Melbourne Theatre Company made it impossible, but I continued to teach at the School for some years and kept in touch with Peggy during that time, occasionally giving some drama assistance to dancers in the company.

For Kris and I *Coppelia* was a wonderful idea. Ballet was Kris' principal love and would come to fruition in his partnership with the choreographer Graeme Murphy at the Sydney Dance Company. Meanwhile, for me, here was an opportunity to bring some of my work in Paris to the stage. The following months became one of the most creative periods of my life. With Peggy the two of us devised a production that has lasted for over twenty years and at the time of writing is opening another season in the Sydney Opera House.

Peggy was steeped in the traditional presentation of *Coppelia*, having danced Swanhilda herself many times with Sadler's Wells Ballet. But she was more than willing to experiment. She was eager to give the ballet a more dramatic approach, and Kris brought to our notice the original story by E.T. Hoffman, from which the ballet was devised. Instead of a foolish old clown, the character of Dr Coppelius became in our eyes a lonely, fearful figure that struck terror in the hearts of the villagers.

The brilliant dancer Alan Alder became our inspiration for this more austere character. With this as the central idea we devised a completely new second act, in which huge dolls and toys descended on Swanhilda and her friends in an orgy of destruction. One doll in particular was set up as part of the Doctor's desk; a wicked Pulcinello who obeyed his commands to terrorise Swanhilda, and Franz when he stole into the studio in search of his love. The young dancers who acted the dolls became devoted to their roles and produced real magic on stage.

For me the first rehearsal should have been an ordeal. I was not only entering into a world of which I had little experience but was interfering severely with the choreography of this famous folk ballet. But I was there to work, not worry. After several hours of rehearsal with the first act I retired to the staff room for a cup of tea. A few minutes later Colin Peasley, one of their major character dancers and instructors came in, looked at me with a small grin and said, 'You're in.' In the years to come, Colin would make the role of Dr Coppelius his own.

To ensure that the first and third acts held as much interest as possible, Peggy introduced more of Delibes' music into the score and with her new choreography, the entire Harvest Festival became the most important day in the life of the village. With the death of the life-denying Dr Coppelius, and the renewal of life in the marriage of the young people that climaxed the ballet, *Coppelia* received many ovations on opening night. I count it as one of the proudest moments of my life. Privately, I gave thanks to Siddha Yoga for being my constant companion in this work. Years later the company took the production to London and a Royal Gala Performance, where it had a splendid reception. I renew my acquaintance with it from time to time as a memento of Peggy van Praagh, a great lady of the theatre.

From time to time a play is offered which sets the adrenalin running. Close to my fiftieth birthday came Arthur Miller's *Death of a Salesman*. Linda's cry for the little man, 'Attention, attention must be paid to such a person' echoes in the mind of those of us who are fortunate enough to witness the prophetic death of an ordinary human being in the face of a world filled with indifference.

In 1982 the Nimrod Theatre Company invited me to direct the production in the York Theatre, the largest auditorium in the Seymour Centre in Sydney. It was by no means my favourite theatre and had irritating hindrances for a designer; but I could not possibly refuse. With it came an extraordinary family of actors, headed by Warren

Company B Belvoir at the Seymour Centre, 1982. Warren Mitchell, Mel Gibson and Wayne Jarrett in *Death of a Salesman*. (Photo: Branco Gaica.)

Mitchell as Willy: Judi Farr his wife Linda, Mel Gibson as his son Biff, and Wayne Jarrett as his second son Frank.

Kristian Fredrikson was the designer and we sat for days wrestling with the challenge of tailoring to this theatre the complex demands of the setting. In time Kris came up with wonderful solutions and the rehearsals began.

Every member of the cast applied themselves honestly but I had to monitor my own reverential attitude to the text. It does a play no good to be awed by it. The text is there to be explored, used and interpreted. Warren was exemplary in his exploration of the role but try as he might, he could not rid himself of memories of a previous production in which he had played Willy. There were times when I held rehearsals for Linda and her sons without him just to escape that unspoken feeling of 'I've been there before'. The cast needed their own freedom to find their truth in Miller's dialogue.

The production was a great success. It soon became difficult to get a seat for the eight-week season. Judi's performance was one of the finest I've seen in the theatre—Warren was of the same opinion.

Her humanity brought out, along with the tragedy of their lives, the humour and downright ordinariness of the family she loved. Mel and Wayne created a fraternal relationship both funny and heartbreaking, not pulling back for a single moment the stupidity and fecklessness of their characters. The tragic death of Wayne from cancer very soon after this production was felt acutely by all his friends and colleagues.

There are no heroes in *Salesman* and Warren's Willy Loman remains in my memory as the definitive portrayal of the little man. It was a humbling experience to sit among the audiences and watch great theatre take its effect. Crowds of young people who were there as fans of the young film star became silent and absorbed as Mel's Biff revealed to them their dreams, fears and horrors. Every night, in the last moment of the play, as Biff lifted his head in anguish over the death of his father and the lights slowly faded on him, the theatre remained silent for a long, long moment, filled with a thousand memories. I will never forget the sight, in the emptying theatre after one performance, of a young woman trying to comfort her sobbing father, unable to rise from his seat.

Nor will I forget the taxi driver who, early one morning, was driving me to the ashram for morning *seva*. He seemed distressed and confessed that the performance of *Death of a Salesman* he had seen the night before had so unhinged him with memories of his own father that he had been unable to sleep. I did not admit that I had directed it.

These years of work in the three major forms, opera, ballet and drama, were buoyed up by my life at the ashram and the memory of Taizé, strengthened by another visit during Easter celebrations to that windy and sacred place on the hill. The church was filled with thousands of young people, all searching for some meaning in a difficult world. Their presence gave my life the incentive it needed to continue in the profession that had supported me for thirty years, but was now growing harder for young people to enter. Competition for the smallest position had taken the fun out of it; fun which seemed, to my mind, to have been the essential ingredient in living the life of an actor.

Swami Muktananda passed away in 1982 and left behind him two followers to carry on the duties of Master of Siddha Yoga. Swami Nityananda and his sister Swami Chidvilasananda toured the world in the early 1980s, continuing to bring the benefits of meditation to many thousands. As such things happen in the affairs of men, the focus became split with two Masters and in a moving ceremony Swami Nityananda stood down to pursue his own devotions and Swami Chidvilasananda, known as Gurumayi, assumed the chair.

Whether I was teaching in a drama school, or rehearsing a play at the Opera House, my life remained centred in the Siddha Yoga ashram. It was a lovely old rambling house in Newtown, an inner suburb of Sydney, with a swami in charge and a full program of *satsangs* and meditation courses. I had rented a small flat close by but already, in my heart, I was preparing to do something unthinkable, considering the busy nature of my life. Within a few years I would move into the ashram to become an ashramite.

The step meant I saw my friends only occasionally. A social life hardly existed in the program of living I had given myself. In their place new friends arrived at the ashram *satsang* evenings. Students and actors from all over Sydney appeared and, as I became a regular master of ceremonies, I felt that my career in the theatre and film was beginning to fuse with the spiritual centre that was the ashram.

One memorable evening, seven visiting swamis sat in the audience of *Death of a Salesman*. I had informed the cast of their visit and their wish to meet the actors. Only one of the cast expressed any misgivings.

'Look, George,' he said quietly, ' I do not mind meeting them, but do not let any of them touch me.'

'Why not?' I said, a little amazed by this request.

'I do not want to get any of those nice warm feelings,' he replied emphatically.

We may have been put on this earth to suffer, but do we need to enjoy it?

By this time the ashram was becoming crowded. A larger house was needed with a hall and quarters for all those people who wished to become residents. On top of this Gurumayi was planning a tour to Australia and a stay in Sydney. We discovered an old orphanage in Dulwich Hill, a suburb a little further out than Newtown, but perfect for our new home. Hundreds of friends spent weeks preparing the new ashram, building, converting and carpeting a beautiful new meditation hall that could seat some hundreds.

Gurumayi requested that I present her programs in Sydney. There was no way I was not going to do this particular *seva*; but it was quite impossible, given that had just begun a new career as a film director. But I knew it would happen, somehow. In Siddha Yoga the impossible is quite often achieved. On the first evening after a late shoot the taxi squealed to a halt and I dashed into the ashram. As I hurried down the entrance hall, one of the monitors thrust into my hands the program for the evening *satsang*. I stripped, showered and dressed within a few minutes, at the same time trying to absorb the long list of announcements and events. With a momentary look at the madman in the mirror I was hurried into the already-packed meditation hall. I had one minute to go. I sat down by the guru's chair, took one more look at my notes, closed my eyes and surrendered my beating heart to a silent mantra. Opening my eyes I caught a signal from the door and stood, smiling and easy, to welcome the evening's guests.

As the evening progressed, the exhaustion of a difficult day receded. The energy of the ashram filled me as I focused on the present moment. Listening to the guru speak I once again learnt what it meant to be present in the now and to stop repeating self-judgment and criticism of others. At the evening's end I was re-energised.

Soon, Gurumayi would leave us to tour North America blazing new paths for Siddha Yoga and its healing work.

George Miller instructing the author during pre-production for *The Dismissal*.

THE FILM DIRECTOR

Eight

'George Miller would like to have lunch with you.'

Certain words become a point of reference. This was such a moment in 1982 when my agent, Hilary Linstead, surprised me with this invitation, which led to a mid-life career change from theatre to film.

Having established that George Miller was the filmmaker whose work with Mel Gibson had made him a star by the time I worked with him on *Death of a Salesman*. I could not resist it. What such a person might want with a dyed-in-the-wool theatre director was impossible to guess, but lunch in Hyde Park sounded pleasant.

I considered my knowledge of film. My taste went immediately towards European films from Renoir to Truffaut, and to Hitchcock. The only adventures which drew me into the cinema were the old films of Michael Powell and Emeric Pressburger. I had no knowledge of either *Mad Max* or the recently-released *Mad Max II*. The Australian film industry seemed still of small account, although Phillip Noyce's *Newsfront* had excited me. Much as I loved the movies, the theatre had been my life and I imagined that the two forms had nothing in common but actors.

But George had a sweet face, dark, penetrating eyes and the pitch black, curly hair inherited from his Greek forebears; and I listened to the story of this young man's beginnings. He had been a doctor in general practice dreaming of making movies. He and his friend Byron Kennedy were determined to break into this difficult art form and together they read Joseph Campbell's work on mythology and the hero and talked through the night as Byron drove George on his evening rounds. It was on these journeys that *Mad Max* was born. The outcome of their first success was a film company and a studio in the old Metro Theatre in Kings Cross. The last time I had walked through those doors it had been a classy theatre called the Minerva. Now in 1982 it was the home of Kennedy Miller Pty Ltd. George had seen some of my recent work and had questions about how I handled actors.

By dessert he had come to the point. They were planning to do a television series called *The Dismissal*, based on the notorious sacking of the Whitlam Labor Government on 11 November 1975. Five episodes would cover the years leading up to the event. George wanted my assistance to transform a large group of actors into the leading participants in the drama.

The chance of being part of such a scheme enthralled me. They were determined to use the best actors and give them the chance to rise to the occasion. It matched perfectly my belief that all an actor needed was background, space and time. Apart from the actual rehearsals of the script the plan was to invite politicians into the workshop to talk about this most fervent time in Australian politics. What I was not aware of was how revolutionary this idea was.

In the theatre we take rehearsals for granted—the more the better. In film the two months or more of pre-production has very little to do with rehearsals for the actors. This time is taken up preparing camera, crew and locations to shoot the film. Then the actors appear and a few days may be spent in rehearsing their positions for the camera. Any work on character is left entirely to them. I was amazed to discover that film directors generally had no idea how to rehearse actors but simply expected them to do their job. As I would learn, a film director's love affair is with the camera, not with the actor. George Miller wanted to introduce background research and character study into filmmaking. This was wholly new and would profoundly influence filmmaking in Australia from the moment *The Dismissal* was broadcast.

Over coffee George dropped another bombshell. I would direct one of the episodes. The fact that I did not know the back end of a camera from the front deterred him not in the slightest. He was determined that a man of the theatre should be involved in the shoot. It was finally decided that I should direct the third hour, having gained by then a little experience by watching George direct the first episode and Phil Noyce the second. Carl Schultz and John Power would direct the other two. I determined to learn as much as possible of the film business before the workshops began.

This proved much more difficult than I imagined. I discovered an entire language separated the filmmaker from the rest of the world. I began to wonder if film acting too had a different language and approach from that in the theatre. I was soon to find out.

The cast of fifty actors gathered each day for discussion while the writers met with Terry Hayes to co-ordinate the story and dialogue. As the intention was a documentary style with the actors impersonating the real-life characters, there would be intensive study of voices and demeanour.

It was also important that the five directors collaborate, to provide some unity while giving five different interpretations of the incidents that led to the sacking. We all knew that to establish the main actors in their roles before shooting began would provide the necessary cohesion for this complex story. Gradually we discovered ways to assist each other. However, I soon began to learn a major difference between theatre and film. Neither the actor nor the director wanted a prolonged rehearsal period on the actual script. They were happy to talk about the politics and about individual characteristics but avoided the words to be spoken on camera. This, I learned, was to preserve spontaneity at the moment of shooting. The camera despised a rehearsed scene.

With this in mind, meetings with the real politicians became imperative. The former Treasurer, Jim Cairns, studied carefully by his counterpart John Hargreaves, gave much of his time to us. There was one wonderful moment at a meeting of the cast and directors when I ventured to ask the room which Party they had voted for. Every hand shot up for Labor. With this in mind we hastily set about meetings with Coalition politicians also. John Stanton, playing Malcolm Fraser, was particularly grateful.

Work with the actors progressed easily, but alongside this familiar work was an entirely new challenge—getting ready to shoot film. George Miller spent hours of work after rehearsal instructing me on how to set out my shooting script and prepare it for the first assistant to schedule. The complex plot involved many politicians, and at times, the entire Senate.

For a theatre man, the most revealing aspect of this new career proved to be the scheduling. Rehearsals in the theatre begin at the beginning, and director and actors discover the play scene by scene from the first entrance to the last. A film shoot has altogether different priorities.

A film is shot in whatever order is the easiest, cheapest and quickest. If, as was the case, my script called for two scenes in the Senate, one in the middle of the script and one towards the end, these two scenes would be shot on the same day. Further to this, as the set had to be quickly dismantled for the construction of another, the two scenes would be shot on day one of the shoot. Drawing up the schedule of scenes was another major lesson. This preparation meant attending to every detail: when it is to be shot, how it is to be shot, and the meaning of every word and image. This was why the actors needed to understand their role perfectly before the shoot began, so that, as the chaotic schedule tore the narrative to pieces, they could still place their character in the moment.

My extraordinary good fortune continued with my first assistant director, Steve Andrews, who made up the schedule. This young man took me under his wing and showed me how to think in terms of the schedule: which scenes to shoot first and which to leave until later in the shoot. I began to see that the schedule could have an enormous influence on the final look of the episode. Without having any idea of how many shots could be achieved in one day, I followed Steve's advice and was amazed to find that his planning was perfect; that he had already got my measure and had guessed just how long I would take over each scene. (A long, long time!) It is a talent on which I would lean heavily in future projects with other first assistants.

The rehearsals and workshops took on an urgent meaning. My hour of political life came in the middle of the journey and therefore knowledge of the other directors' preparation was needed. I never inquired about their way of shooting or framing the scene. I knew that this was partly the reason George had chosen five directors—to give the series variety. But certain threads had to connect. Most of the characters lasted throughout the five hours and the actors would therefore be working with all five directors. They could not have landed with better and more amiable leaders and the outcome was a positive group attitude with which to begin the shoot—all of us charged by the political atmosphere of the time.

As I watched first George then Phil shoot their episodes, they revealed not only their work methods but their feelings about the characters. By the time my turn came we had a common point of view. In the theatre the audience has its own perspective on the drama, choosing what to focus on, sometimes watching a detail while half listening to the main action. In film, the camera selects the perspective for us; whatever it decides to focus on is what the audience sees, to the exclusion of all else. This simple distinction brought home to me that in the theatre the actor searches for the audience; in film the camera searches for the actor.

This power of choice lies in the hands of the director. 'What cover do you plan for this scene?' The language lesson continued with close-up, mid-shot, long shot, wide shot, two-shot, tracking shot, high-angle, low-angle, master shot and, 'How many "takes" will you average?' A simple scene becomes a complex quilt of shots all numbered and noted by Continuity, a highly-skilled woman (I say woman because I've known very few continuity men) who is indispensable to the making of a good movie. Having grilled me for my opinion of the best takes, she passes on her information and advice to the Editor, whose job is to sort the takes and reduce the jumble of footage to the simple scene with which we started. Jo Weeks not only had an almost frightening knowledge of the way a shot could work, but a talent for seeing the end result before it happened.

The task of 'cover' bewildered me until I met and talked to the Director of Photography (DOP), Dean Semler. This delightful, modest man who seemed to have a smile for the whole world became my mentor. It was some time before I realised that my new friend was indeed a great DOP who would one day earn an Academy Award. By the time I had finished the shoot, I was in love with film and film crews. The first assistant director, continuity, designer and the DOP became as important as the principal actors, and the teams behind them showed me what a true ensemble can achieve. The only delays I ever knew were caused by the weather or my indecision.

The one element I thought I knew about was the actor. After all, my whole life had been spent in adoration of their talent. *The Dismissal*'s treatment of actors confused and angered me until I realised just how, for an actor, standing in front of the mechanical eye of the camera, differed from standing on stage before a breathing, attentive audience. And it was an actor who taught me my most important lesson in film.

I arrived on the set for my first day as a film director, feeling sick and apprehensive. It seemed so unfair that my very first shot should involve the entire Senate. And, as if that was not hard enough, I had a crew of 35 waiting on my every word. However, I had worked hard at the preparation, and with Dean beside me, Steve ready to give signals and Jo watching every move I made, nothing (please God) could go wrong.

The first scene of dialogue involved Bill Hunter, playing the Minister for Minerals and Energy, Rex Connor. I acted relaxed, describing how I would cover the scene while Dean and his team lit the huge Senate Chamber. Steve took over the senators sitting behind Bill. My first surprise was to discover that the director did not talk to extras. If he did, they would have to be paid as actors, so all communication must go through Steve. On that day I was grateful, but in later times it became it a constant irritant. I was so used to talking to actors, explaining my intentions. At least, I thought resentfully, if I cannot do anything else I can do that.

After the camera and lights were set we were ready to go. Bill grinned at me and went in front of the camera. I yelled my first 'Action!' far too loud, bringing a smile to the faces of the crew, and Bill began.

But where was the performance? Bill was supposed to be impersonating a wily politician making a speech in Parliament but his manner had not changed from his talking to me. I was in despair as I watched him quietly ramble through the speech. He finished and I stood, staring. Steve nudged me from one side and Jo from the other and I called, 'Cut'. Dean turned to me from the camera with a look of admiration.

'Marvellous,' he said, 'What an actor!'

I was sensible enough to keep my mouth shut. I smiled and murmured, 'Another take, perhaps?'

'Sure,' Dean said, 'if you think we need it.'

Without answering I hurried towards Bill. 'Marvellous, Bill, just great. Could we just do one more?'

'Oh, struth,' Bill murmured, as he moved back, 'he's one of those.'

I hurried back to the camera, in a turmoil about what 'he's one of those' might mean. The next take was, in my opinion, no better but, as everyone else seemed to be happy, I thought it expedient to continue. As we worked through the day I asked for several takes on each shot, terrified that I was making the worst film ever made. I babbled on, chatting to actors, particularly Bill, during each set up, giving them support and hoping that someone would begin to give a performance.

The day finally came to an end and, having achieved all the shots on the schedule, the crew gave me a totally unexpected cheer to celebrate my first day on the set. I tried to be optimistic but nothing could make me feel better. I began to dread seeing the rushes the following day.

The second day was just as bad and I knew the problem must lie in myself. The crew and actors seemed so curiously pleased with it all. I concentrated on technical things and framing, leaving the acting to the actors—except for filling their heads with historical detail every break, in the hope it would inspire them to 'act'. When the second day finished, Dean said cheerily, 'Hop in and we'll go to the rushes.' The drive was one of the worst twenty minutes of my life.

I sat amazed by Bill Hunter's performance. It was hypnotic. That shambling mumble I had heard from beside the camera became riveting on screen.

The mystery surrounding Bill's performance would take years to unravel. Meanwhile I was wise enough to continue helping the actor with the world that encompassed his role and leave the 'film acting' to them. Over time, by observing the work of this large group of experienced artists I slowly picked up clues that revealed how different the skills of film performance and theatre performance were, but at that stage of my life I could not explain those differences.

One theatre habit that drove the sound recordists up the wall was cured by a formal gift of a box of handkerchiefs from my second assistant director, Chris Webb. In the rehearsal room I can become very involved in the action and react at times most vociferously. When this happened on the film set, however, my appreciative noises ruined many takes. This was resolved when, after calling 'Action,' I learned to stuff my mouth with Chris's handkerchiefs. His generous gift was repeated on a number of films we made together.

I confronted Bill one day with his, 'He's one of those' remark. He responded immediately.

'No, mate, changed my mind. You've had no more than three takes on anything. That must be a record. But even so, find a reason for each take. The actor would appreciate that.' He added darkly: 'There's some'll do twenty-three without a word of explanation.'

It was a timely warning, and over time I discovered the psychology of takes. Some actors do their best work on the first take, full of life and spontaneity, while others need several takes to gather their forces before suddenly giving their best. If actors with these two ways of working come together on the set it can provide some interesting challenges for the director.

The last day of the shoot left me bereft. Something had happened. I'd fallen for the camera and its possibilities. No, more than that. I had become aware of the power, aware that the director of a film was in the exciting and dangerous position of being able to be more than an interpreter of someone else's work. I began to understand the meaning of the word *auteur*. More than the dictionary meaning of 'author', this word meant that the artist who brought together all the elements of all the other artists could create something unique on film—something of their own.

The Dismissal had an immediate impact not only on the thousands who saw it on television but the industry itself. The Kennedy Miller partnership was famous already with *Mad Max*, but this was television. To spend such rehearsal time for television was unheard of. The future of the mini-series on the box was given a great boost as more care and more rehearsals were scheduled. I was proud to be part of it and of their next project—despite my ignorance of the game of cricket.

During the process of writing his next project, the cricket series *Bodyline*, and in keeping with his determination to find the best way of achieving performance, George Miller proposed a different sort of workshop. He wanted to go further than simply a preparation for *Bodyline*. We invited a number of writers, directors, actors and even producers to take part in a fortnight of experiment that would search for ways of writing, preparing for, and achieving an ensemble within the process of producing a film. It was a remarkable vision for the future, but not one that survived.

I devised a program of exercise and experiment to extend over a fortnight, meeting every day for a long morning or afternoon. It would involve at least twenty people, and word was sent around Sydney seeking artists who were prepared to rethink their approach to television and film. The response was extraordinary and choosing the participants was tough.

Finally the day arrived and a bizarre assortment of people stood nervously in a large circle on the vast, empty mezzanine floor of the Metro. There was only one way they would become a unit, and that was by walking the Circle. But this was different from working with students. Students are already used to following instructions in the classroom, but I was faced with people who had never done anything like this in their lives, who were not performers and who were embarrassed just standing there. However, nothing ventured, I would start with the Circle.

I began by asking them to form pairs with someone they'd never met and for a short while chat about themselves. They observed and commented on the room, until the walk became companionable. Then they separated. As they abandoned their partner and moved forward, their demeanour changed. Those who responded to the intention tended to congregate in the centre while the reluctant participants clung to the perimeter—still moving, but isolated.

The outcome was predictable. Having an actor like John Hargreaves in the centre of the group was invaluable. John, by this stage well aware of my eccentric ways, won over the stragglers by regaling them with his own tale of woe in Adelaide. The Circle continued every morning and gradually each participant found something in the experience. To those who did not I suggested they sit and watch, taking notes on what they observed. This they did and after seeing the potential, joined in again until the whole group felt the benefit.

One of the purposes of the workshop was 'scene building', studying the growing relationship between two people, using the silence that the camera loves. I devised an exercise which helped to build such scenes. I called it the Book Lift, and it proved beneficial in breaking down barriers between individuals. We collected hundreds of books, set up two tables long enough to accommodate three people side by side, and set them the task of silently moving the books from one table to the other and back. The rest of the group watched the dynamics as a work practice was established, and relationships shifted among the three.

In a subsequent discussion one writer commented that the book lift was like writing a scene with the eye. Some of the actors in the group created wonderful characters within the book game. One observer commented how some people make things happen while others have things happen to them.

Another game was called Follow the Leader. I adapted this from my work on Chorus with Lecoq.[2]

Many talks and discussions were held on the nature of the Hero/Heroine in reference to Joseph Campbell's theory and its foundation in film. We studied rhythm in film by watching old classics like *His Girl Friday* and *The Philadelphia Story*, using these rhythms for other building exercises, and every day a short seminar was held to discuss the day and its outcome. The Circle began to influence everyone, as a way of emptying out and responding to each other openly and with trust. The fortnight passed too quickly.

My introduction to film continued without a break. *Bodyline* was to be ten hours of television about the life of the young Donald Bradman and the antagonism between the United Kingdom and Australia during the Depression that came to a head in the test of 1932 when the English bowler Harold Larwood attempted to reclaim victory with a notorious overarm delivery that came to be known as Bodyline.

The writing process, of which I was part, was headed by Terry Hayes, a young journalist turned writer, now part of Kennedy Miller. He coined a phrase that has remained with me: he referred to the

---

2 These exercises are described in the Appendix.

Gary Sweet receiving direction during a *Bodyline* board meeting, 1983.

scripts as 'headline writing'. Unlike the tempo and rhythm of a film, which can afford to build slowly and poetically to its climax, television requires quicker results, with a stronger, driving rhythm that brings about climaxes at well-defined intervals.

Carl Schultz joined us again, for which I was infinitely grateful. Carl's quiet comments and advice would help me through many a hump. To complete the director team was Lex Marinos, an obsessive cricket lover and commentator, and Denny Lawrence, a young television director with much experience already behind him.

I sat for a moment in the grandstand of the deserted Sydney Cricket Ground, breathing in the atmosphere of this hallowed place. We had been given an amazing privilege: to prepare for the series we now had the chance of rehearsing for three weeks at the SCG itself.

We separated the 'Australian' and 'English' actors, giving them their own dressing rooms, practices in the nets, even encouraging the teams to eat apart at mealtimes. In this way they developed their identity first as two professional teams and then as men on a mission for their country. These young actors were all cricketers with an almost obsessive love of the game. Their coach, the spinner Peter Philpot, had stood beside the directors during the auditions, making sure that whomever we cast was already an accomplished cricketer—with one exception, Harold Larwood. Larwood had a unique way of running and bowling, which is why he was chosen by the English team to bring about the bodyline delivery that confounded the Australians. Many of the actors who auditioned were good bowlers but none proved able to reproduce this technique. Finally, my rather radical compromise was accepted: we would teach someone to bowl. I had taught Jim Holt at NIDA and knew him to resemble the cricketer—even sharing his Liverpudlian accent. Being athletic and with a fine sense of rhythm, he achieved a triumph in the role as both actor and bowler.

Hugo Weaving, whose work I had also admired at NIDA, played the charming, villainous English captain, Douglas Jardine. Others were John Walton as Woodville and my old friend from the RSC, Rhys McConnochie, as Percy Fender, Jardine's mentor. I was astonished to discover so many secret cricket devotees among my friends, including Ned Manning, who played Stan McCabe.

We travelled to Melbourne to audition another young actor who had distinguished himself in junior cricket. Gary Sweet was an instant choice for the role of Donald Bradman and the delightful young actress Julie Nihill for that of his wife. The great man himself invited Gary and me to Adelaide where he and his wife entertained us royally for a day. We sat dazzled as he reminisced about his long and triumphant career.

Throughout the preparation and shoot, it was difficult not to feel fraudulent. The dialogue, confrontations and character development were no problem, but the cricket itself was like a secret ritual from which I was excluded. As a youth at school, swimming and tennis had occupied my sporting life and cricket never came close. My confession to Peter Philpot at first brought disbelief, then laughter and, finally, an amazed acceptance that there existed a human being on earth to whom cricket was not as important as breathing.

The shooting took place at a number of ovals including the SCG. Countless hours were spent on the pitch with me concentrating on the actors' faces, Peter on their strokes and our continuity, Jo Weeks, trying to do both. Summer had never seemed to last so long. Often I would be pleased with a shot, only to find Peter shaking his head and murmuring, 'Terrible stroke, George'. Rushes became celebrations as the actors cheered the strokes rather than the performances and toasted them with a beer. I suggested one day that there might be a fine mini-series in the Davis Cup, but my voice went unheard as my producers and fellow directors practised their batting swing in every corner of their offices. Incidents occurred when Jim would get Larwood's run-up and swing perfectly but fail to hit the wicket. Then suddenly, clean bowling the wretched Australian, Jim would dance around the pitch in triumph, something the quiet Larwood would never have done.

Great marquees were constructed on the ovals for SCG members watching the test and Frank Thring presided as chairman of the board. The locations ranged all over Sydney as we searched for both Australian and English settings and the summer stretched out into the autumn. The Australian Navy gave us a ship in which to shoot the journey of the English team to Australia and we sailed down to Sydney from Jervis Bay shooting scenes on board. The historical English team had formed a choir during the trip and we found some great voices among the cast. I had a great time as choirmaster as they proudly sang the Pilgrim's Hymn for the camera.

The experience of five weeks preparing for *The Dismissal* and three weeks' rehearsal for *Bodyline* convinced me of the spectacular results group preparation could achieve. Saying goodbye to the teams on the last day of the shoot was hard. We had formed a true company of actors and crew and I believe a great sense of community and ensemble playing had been achieved. Fifteen years later *Bodyline* still held the record as the highest rating locally-made television program shown on Australian television.

For all the excitement of *Bodyline* our feelings were tempered by a tragic accident that occurred just as the shoot was about to begin. I came into the Metro one morning to find the office staff in tears and no sign of George Miller. Byron Kennedy's helicopter had crashed, killing the young man instantly.

Everyone was asked to go home and pick up the work the following morning. It was numbing news; a fine young man had been killed and a dream had been shattered. The vision George and Byron had for the Metro and the future studio came to an abrupt stop.

Only those who were close to Byron gathered to say goodbye. For the rest of us, work seemed to be the only answer. Preparations for the series went ahead but George was not seen by us for some weeks. As we began shooting, for those of us who had been able to get to know this private man, it showed in our faces and feelings and we all felt enormous sympathy for him and his vision. His whole future as a filmmaker had been mapped out in partnership with Byron.

Byron's visionary skills as a producer were already evident at the time of his death and he is greatly missed, as a fine man and one whose technical innovation was greatly influential in raising the reputation of Australian film. The Byron Kennedy Memorial Award for work in film is a yearly reminder of the contribution he made within so few short years. I felt intensely proud to be the recipient in 1988.

Mad Max Beyond Thunderdome

There I was, crouched on all fours, concentrating on the game. Forty children were in the process of inventing a way of life, finding, through their young imaginations, ways of using distant memories of a life long vanished. It was Saturday and I was conducting workshops, as I had been doing for many weeks, with those who would form the band of lost Children of the Crack in the third film of the *Mad Max* trilogy, *Mad Max Beyond Thunderdome*. George Miller and Terry Hayes watched, took notes and began to form the dialogue and rituals they would use. Their appreciative laughter distracted me for a moment and I found a tiny, three-year-old girl crouched beside me cheekily copying my gestures and noises. Her older brother was part of the gang and it had seemed natural to her to join in. This little mimic, Amanda Nikkinen, became the youngest member of the lost civilisation which would would occupy every moment of my time for the next many months.

After the intimacies of the small screen I suddenly found myself making images on a grand scale. This was to be the grandest of the *Mad Max* movies in which Mel Gibson's character had transformed from being a cop bent on revenge in a desert of dust and dereliction, into a mythical wanderer and anti-hero. Now he was to find himself in Bartertown, a feudal society ruled over by Aunty Entity (Tina

The author exhorting the Bartertown populace in the Thunderdome during the shooting of *Mad Max Beyond Thunderdome*.

Turner) with 'blood and shit'. Preparations for such a major film were demanding and complicated. Having decided that operas with a huge chorus were not my forte, what on earth had caught me up in this adventure? Excitement, of course. Every day this enormous film took shape: auditions with hundreds of actors, searching for extraordinary locations, watching Graham 'Grace' Walker design and make, with his builders, the cars, the machines and dwellings that would house the survivors of a destroyed world. Out of this chaos an infant society of lost children would emerge and Norma Moriceau's task was to design the dazzling garments its inhabitants would wear. In the same way the daily script meetings with George and Terry Hayes were occupied with a new language and new rituals for the children to perform. Workshops with the children took up my weekends.

A magical rainforest crevice in the Blue Mountains became the children's world and our first shoot. Barefoot and dressed in their desert skins, the gang froze in the September weather; but warm blankets, chanting and exercises got them ready for a day in front of the cameras. Led by their leader, Tom Jennings, and cared for by their main tutor, Philip Roope, and others, they passed the six weeks happily and their forest home was full of laughter.

One early morning I found several youngsters playing out a silent movie scene with Amanda as the heroine, tied to a tree and calling for help while the Indian warriors leapt around her. In the middle of their game Mad Max turned up and Mel Gibson began to weave his spell among these young, lost souls.

Having directed Mel in two plays on stage I was familiar with the focus he gave to all his work. I had learnt a thing or two about film acting from Bill Hunter and others so was more prepared for the relaxed manner in which Mel faced the camera. The moment 'Action' was called, he responded spontaneously and seemingly without thought. He knew intuitively the need to be surprised and that every moment must be new and unexpected. He inspired the young children around him as he worked and the life lived out in their crevice became filled with urgency. Mel's presence on set between takes was also a lesson for the young ones. Always ready and focused, his quiet friendly presence was such that you hardly noticed him until rehearsal and action.

When this episode came to an end there was no time to celebrate. We said goodbye to the children and set off for the next location. The cavalcade of people and vans sped on. Our first assistant director, Steve Andrews, was scheduling for a film that would take more than six months to shoot in no less than five major locations, each requiring five to six weeks and a crew of ninety. I would sometimes gaze at our continuity girl, Daphne Paris, and wonder how she would handle such an enormous task.

Our new location was ready and waiting: The noise of hundreds of pigs rose from an underground bull pit. This was the pigsty generating methane gas to supply power for Bartertown. It would be our home for six weeks. Standing on a platform high above the noisy floor, dressed in overalls and wellington boots, I felt nothing could be less like a film set. Disinfectant became the principal smell with which we lived as we shot hours of film among the pigs. An extraordinary railway was built through the space and onto it was placed the engine that was to provide the means of escape for Max and his small troop of followers. Since this time I've ceased to be surprised by what film designers and builders can achieve.

The pigs were a horror for the sound recordists, as the scenes we shot in the bull pit had a lot of dialogue. Whenever possible they were stowed away and an eerie and marvellous quiet would descend—and be broken by the actors raising their voices above the pig chorus that would be added to the sound track later. Saying goodbye to our pigs was not hard to do, and the entourage sped off to a huge old quarry in Homebush, which in later years would become Olympic City. In 1982 it was Bartertown.

Gasps of incredulous awe rose from the crew as we wandered around the mythical city which Grace and his team had built during the previous months and which now would be our home for a further six exhausting weeks. Street after street of stalls and makeshift huts and houses surrounded the tower from which Tina Turner would live and rule this city of barter and crime. With our camera having the ability to produce a 360-degree shot the possibilities were immense.

Our safety officers were the first to challenge this extraordinary set as the crew set up for a spectacular fall from the top of the tower. It was a salutary lesson for me to witness how exacting this one shot was. Shooting occupied the whole day, though it would last only a few seconds in the finished film. This was the first of many such shots and scenes over the next months.

In the following weeks the safety officers—or stunt men, as the public likes to call them—were more and more in evidence as the action became more adventurous. We think of stunt men as danger seekers, but in reality the opposite is true: their stunts are performed with exhaustive safety measures. Above all, their job is to see that every precaution is taken in achieving the stunt required. I came more and more to admire these little-recognised artists of the film.

Many scenes were shot in and around the town's streets, many continuing well into the night. Whenever I was free, I would walk around Bartertown, admiring the results of our designers' creation. The dwellings, clothes and remarkable mechanical objects and forms of transport were worthy of close inspection. When the day came and the town was destroyed by fire, it felt like losing a friend.

One day I heard a soft voice calling my name. I turned to meet one of the most beautiful and startling women I'd ever seen.

'I'm Tina,' she said.

With a broad smile Tina Turner entered our lives, captivating everyone with her laughter, generosity of spirit and extraordinary energy. Tina never hid her lack of film experience and absorbed every piece of advice offered. Her practice of the Buddhist way of life revealed itself constantly in her balance and consideration for others; and her last day on the shoot was hard for everyone. No one wanted to say goodbye.

A hundred feet away from the tower a huge dome, the Thunderdome, had been constructed of intertwining rope and wire and in it gladiatorial combat took place. Here the safety officers came into their own. Being the actor that he was, Mel did many of his own stunts. The safety officers stood by, watching every move: one injury and the film might be delayed for weeks. The only time I ever saw Tina angry was when George Miller refused to allow her to perform her stunts. She was not nearly experienced enough and far too valuable.

One of my most affectionate memories of Tina working was in Thunderdome when she was preparing to leap into the ring and deliver Auntie Entity's speech to the populace, who were clinging to the wire walls, screaming and shouting for blood. Our DOP Dean Semler and I were mapping out a camera movement while she rehearsed. Suddenly she beckoned and in an urgent whisper told us to move ourselves out of way as we were standing between her and her public.

'But Tina,' I whispered. 'We are the camera.'

She did a double take, burst into laughter and never gave a thought to the camera again.

Tina's companion in the film was Frank Thring, playing her aide-de-camp, the Collector. His caustic wit kept things lively on the set but even he was subdued by the night shoots when, by three o'clock, the weather closed in. We all froze. The romance of making a movie quickly vanished as we stamped around in our overcoats creating scene after scene of torrid desert weather.

I recall standing in Thunderdome at four in the morning with a loudspeaker to my mouth, urging hundreds of poor extras to give more voice and feeling to the next gladiatorial bout. George Miller was inexhaustible as thousands of feet of film were used up over the weeks in Bartertown. The day of its destruction took many more days in the planning; explosions and fire need preparation down to the final spark.

Our next location would be the desert and the summer heat, which I knew would bring me down if I was not careful. Two shoots were being planned at the same time and George and I would separate for a short while. He would advance into the desert to begin the stunts with Grace's amazing machines, while I would fly to Alice Springs with the main group of children to begin their desert adventure in search of Mad Max.

The phone rang in my hotel room very early. I had spent a week at the Alice with the children and had arrived in Coober Pedy the night before. It had been great working in the beautiful gorge that did service as the entrance into Bartertown, with the water of the lake and the green belt that surrounded it protecting us from the desert and the fierce heat. Now there would be no protection in the wasteland of the desert. Today, however, Steve Andrews had phoned to say that the shoot would be postponed because a desert sandstorm was approaching. I looked out the window and saw in the far distance an immense cloud coming rapidly towards us across the sand. It obliterated everything and the hotel battened down to escape the plague of dust.

The following day all was clear and I faced the desert. Ironically, we now had to employ huge wind machines to create the desert winds, which at least blew without so much sand. Completely covered in protective clothing and wearing desert goggles, the huge crew looked like an avenging pack from Mars.

I looked to George Miller in awe as the shoot continued. To make a film the director must keep the overview and outcome in mind even as he concentrates on the smallest detail. George managed to do this, but I was adrift. I no longer felt I had a grip on the whole and worried at times about the finished film, with so many locations, so many actors, so many stories fed into the script. George kept an iron grip on it all and even though he had insisted that I take on the role of co-director, I saw myself as an assistant who concentrated mainly on the work of the children. One exception to this was the day George gave me charge of an action scene involving all our stunt men. This was Max's hair-raising escape with the children in their small train carriage, pursued by Angry Anderson as Ironbar, on the rail trolley, and accompanied by the weird cars of 'Auntie's men'. I found myself hanging over the rail of a low loader within inches of the ground as we sped across the desert floor. I was totally without fear and felt an adrenalin rush not experienced since my first entrance onto the stage. At the rushes the following night the crew gave the shots a rousing cheer. I felt absurdly conceited.

Six months after our first day in the mountain home of the children we finally finished the shoot. It was an incredible day. It had become a way of life and suddenly it was all over. George, of course, had the edit to supervise, but for the bands of actors it was a real goodbye. While making any film, bonds are forged that are difficult to sever. The children and I had certainly become attached and in later films when I had a chance to cast some of them the reunion was very real. The edit was a difficult process as the lives of so many characters had to be followed. And it was a sad disappointment that so much of the children's superb work never made it to the final cut.

Mad Max remains a rare experience in a lifelong list of memories.

If *Mad Max* was the most adventurous chapter in my career, my association with the Aboriginal culture of Australia in the decade between 1977 and 1987 was the darkest. One day in 1977 my agency called me in to their offices to meet Robert Merritt and Bryan Syron. I was still suffering from the after-effects of my Adelaide directorship and was in no mood to fling myself into a new venture. But there was something urgent about them both that demanded attention.

Bob Merritt was Aboriginal and a writer. Brian Syron I knew as a respected drama teacher, though at the time I did not know he was

Bondi Pavillion Theatre, 1977. Justine Saunders and Brian Syron in *The Cake Man*. (Photo: Peter Holderness.)

also Aboriginal. As I listened to them talk one thought kept ringing through my head: in all these years I'd never spoken to an indigenous Australian. I knew nothing about the people whose country I had lived in for more than forty years. When it became clear that they wanted me to direct a play that Bob had written for a season at the Bondi Pavilion theatre, I pleaded a few days' grace to read it and consider.

I left the agency feeling disturbed and foolish. I knew nothing about Black Australia. My life had been spent looking towards Britain and Europe. I knew more about the myths of Scotland and the streets of Paris than any moment of Australian history. Bob's text shocked me as it poured out a simple story of poverty, degradation and deprivation from the mouths of a small family living on an Aboriginal reserve. I sat for a long time wondering not only how I could hope to understand their situation, but what right I had to be its interpreter. Finally, I rang Bob and confessed this to him.

'Good,' he said, 'this means you'll try to understand. I can't expect more. Most people do not want to understand.'

So we began rehearsals of *The Cake Man*, with Bob as a silent witness in the back row while I tussled with Brian playing Sweet

William, the drunken, despairing father, and Justine Saunders, playing his wife. I watched them painfully stripping away the white society of which they were now part and return to their roots and the tragic lives of their relatives. The dialogue was sparse and to the point as Sweet William struggled to make a place for his family outside the derelict shanty town in which they lived. When he failed and his child became a witness to his degradation, we felt the whole world should burst into tears. What future was there for this young boy? In my determination to bring alive this injustice I became harsh and demanding in rehearsals and I could feel the approbation emanating from the back row. I think the very bitterness I still felt about Adelaide helped me suppress the need that has plagued me from childhood, of wanting to please.

The audience on opening night was mainly black and the emotions were explosive. If ever I had had doubts about the power theatre can wield they were swept away that night at Bondi. The packed house could hardly sit still as they watched their story being told. Celebrations continued long after the event and when Bob introduced me to friends and family I found myself in the midst of a close community, peopled with patient elders and angry young people who were to become activists in the rising civil rights movement. That night, one audience at least listened to the voice of a deprived people.

A year or two later, Bob took me to the Eora Centre, an artists' training school in Sydney for Aborigines of all ages. I was invited to take workshops and gradually learned to relax in their welcoming environment. The students all had stories to tell. At times they were like eager children and at others sat quiet and introspective, with a look of fortitude on their young faces as if an ancient memory had passed over.

I loved to hear them speak about being in the bush, in country they not only loved, but which moulded their identity. Learning from them the stories of the Rainbow Serpent and the Dreaming, which formed their beginnings, reminded me of what Scotland meant to my parents and their forebears. As the Aboriginal legends began to share a place in my heart with the legends of the Highlands, I began to feel less of a stranger. Sometimes a raw wound would be exposed in the hothouse of Sydney living and someone would head off to the bush. Many times a student would not appear and I would learn they were attending a funeral. I became more and more conscious of the quality of sharing that exists within this nation, and the importance of family to families that have been scattered all over Australia. It was an important moment the day a student called me 'brother' as a signal of acceptance. I was grateful for the privilege but, like other white Australians, I remain in the corridor, acutely aware of the history that separates us.

In 1983, however, I found myself directing a small movie by Bob Merritt, and was witness to an extraordinary—and unscripted—event. The crew had set up around the little country church where a funeral was to be filmed. The principal actors had arrived just as the crowd of extras emerged from the tents ready for the first shot. On this day the entire cast was Aboriginal and as they gathered in front of the church the funeral car pulled up at the gate. While lights and camera were being placed, people talked together and I heard a cry of joy from the centre of the main group. I drew close and one of the boys smiled.

'Two cousins have just met for the first time.'

Even here, on a film set, indigenous people were discovering scattered families. The celebration brought a wonderful energy to the sad scene we were shooting. Bob had written the script in the years we spent at Eora and had found a producer in Ross Matthews, who became a sympathetic confidant as together we made this film about people we could not understand but to whose story we were willing to bear witness.

Bob's film *Shortchanged* followed the story of a young boy brought up by his white mother in a white Catholic community. At the age of ten he discovers his Aboriginal father and the film explores his emotional conflict and final reconciliation. In our search for a young actor a boy whose mother worked in the Department of Aboriginal Affairs was recommended and I flew to Canberra to meet him. Jamie Agius impressed me immediately. There was an innocent beauty in this boy with intelligent eyes—and something else. They conveyed something that I knew would come through on film and for which I was searching—a desperate need to belong.

The struggle for Jamie was to separate reality from the game that is a film; a struggle that many imaginative youngsters have in this strange medium. The crew responded superbly, supporting him whenever he needed sympathy and love, and refusing to give in to his need for attention. Jamie would test me constantly until he realised I would only smile and hug him, although at times I felt that we were adding to his anguish by exploiting him in this role.

David Kennedy was cast as Jamie's father. His was a sensitive talent that recognised the problems Jamie would be faced with in the future. His portrayal of the father became the anchor in the film. Bob was away making a documentary on Eora and so I looked to David's gentle nature for understanding of the heartbreaking journey the man was making, not only to find his son again but to help the boy understand a heritage he had never known. Susan Leith as the boy's mother and Ray Meagher as her father, two old friends with whom I had worked before, gave deeply-felt performances, and Mark Little gave a performance of a drunken young friend that I still remember as one of the best I have ever seen on film. It was a labour of love overlaid with the uneasy feeling that this film should have been made by an Aboriginal director, someone at home with the writer's context. Today we have such directors—among the best we have. Like so many films, once the shoot is over goodbyes are said and we all go our separate ways. Occasionally I heard of Jamie over the next few years but lost him in the crowded passages of life. I hope he found some form of happiness in the years that followed.

Not many people saw the finished film, despite its fine performances and award nominations by the Australian Film Institute. It was my first project away from the safety net of Kennedy Miller and I could not have chosen a better one to experience the isolation of a filmmaker in a business in which judgment is largely left to the box office. Making films is a wonderful, exciting adventure but when it is over, that baby you have been so proud of will only breathe and prosper if accompanied by the ring of the cash register.

Over the next decade I had many opportunities to explore the world of film and between 1985 and 1995 directed seven feature films. In hindsight, my choice is revealing; I was clearly on a journey into my past. It is true what they say about film being a personal journey for a director—and how much of myself is uncovered in the finished work.

A crewman sleeps on the beach in front of the specially-built house during the shoot of *The Place at the Coast*.

The Place at the Coast came to me from my friend Hilary Furlong. A father and daughter are spending a solitary summer in their house on the dunes. The time is the early 1960s and their beach is threatened by real estate development and the growing tourist industry. The daughter, Ellie, played by Tushka Bergen, defies authority in her desperate efforts to make the adults understand what is happening to the environment and the birds she loves. The cast of adults included John Hargreaves, Heather Mitchell, Julie Hamilton, Gary McDonald, Robyn Nevin; the young people with Tushka included Rod Zouanic from *Mad Max*, Alex Broun and Emily Crook. For me, the hero of the film was nature itself.

Turning 360 degrees on this southern beach, there was not a building in sight. We had found it: the place for our film; the place at the coast where we could shoot *The Place at the Coast*. It had taken us a long time. The eastern coast of Australia was already choking with suburbia and our search for an empty, wild landscape took us well down the south coast to a beach which still retained that welcoming isolation I remembered from family holidays as a child.

My DOP was Jeff Darling, to whom Hilary had introduced me. The birds, the beach and the forests beyond were all brought alive in Jeff's camera. When Ellie reveals her desperation over the demolition of this Eden she is echoing the beauty already established in the lingering shots over dunes and sand, through bush and over the house we constructed, which seemed to sink into the environment. The camera became the spirit of the dead mother returning to watch over her daughter in their last summer on this untouched part of the Australian coast. To see the film fifteen years later brings back the achingly beautiful location and I can almost smell the surf. I was joined by my now established First, Chris Webb, his assistant Henry Osborne and continuity Jo Weeks.

In the early days before shooting began I would see Jeff wandering over the dunes and into the forests absorbing the spirit of the place. He saw the camera as a palette on which he would paint the gently swaying brush and the mists from the surf. In the forest the camera became a small animal darting from tree to tree and climbing into the branches. The original film was to be called *The Bee Eater*, the exquisite bird that Ellie drew and loved, and I still think of it this way.

The Christmas lunch scene in the main room of the house, constructed for the film on the dunes, and with the surf sounding in our ears, took me back to summer holidays as a young boy when the family would pile into the car and head for the coast, living in a shack on the beach and picking oysters off the reef. The memories were so strong that day on the set I never wanted it to finish. The crew began to think I was crazy as I requested scene after scene around the table and at the piano after the meal. We sang songs and shot well into the night. Old-timers like Willie Fennell, Margo Lee and Eileen Britton playing relatives and neighbours loved being part of the celebration and Ray Meagher and Michele Fawdon completed the huge family gathering, peppered with a number of young children. It was my past, re-enacted.

Whenever possible I would swim in the early evenings and walk along beach and cliff, taking in memories of my father standing in the surf with trousers rolled up and a fishing line snaking out into the water. When I placed John Hargreaves in the same position early in the film I was playing back an old and treasured film in my heart.

John Hargreaves' life was going through a difficult time during the shoot, which brought on some explosive moments in our otherwise tranquil days. At quieter moments off the set he voiced his anxieties

The cast and crew of *The Shiralee* outside the boxing tent.

about the film, which he was sure would fail at the box office. He was right—a short season in the cinema and a quick fadeout. When it was shown to a selector for the Cannes Film Festival the man turned to me at the end and said quietly, 'You are a very brave man.' Later Hilary earned an invitation for the film to the London Film Festival where it was compared to an early film by Jean Renoir. An overstatement, of course, but I loved them for it. Having now suffered with the box office failure of both *Shortchanged* and *The Place at the Coast* I wondered if I still had a future in film. My spirits were to rise high in my next venture—this time, on television.

The Shiralee came about during the last weeks of shooting *The Place at the Coast*. Hilary Linstead notified me that Bryan Brown was to play Macauley in *The Shiralee* and had requested me as director. I went for a late afternoon walk along the glorious beach to think about it. I had read Darcy Niland's novel at the age of 25. It had been during my first tour of Australia, and it caused me for the first time to set aside the myths of Scotland with which I had grown up and to reassess this country. I recalled the nights of talk with Peter Kenna about what it meant to be Australian. I rang Hilary and agreed.

The moment I read Tony Morphett's script I was captured. This feeling, when it happens to any director, whether it is a play or a film script, is a rare one. It establishes a certainty that if we attend rigorously to our preparation and presentation it will be a winner. We can be wrong, of course, but very few filmmakers would disagree with the view that the quality of the script is the most important element in a film.

The Shiralee came together in pre-production with an ease that amazed me. The only problem I faced was the discovery that we did not have room in four hours of television to tell the full story. When the main actor is Bryan Brown, life behind the camera is good. His quiet, assured presence on the set affected the entire crew and I will remember him as a true artist and gentleman.

Women dominated Macauley's life and gave him love, torment and friendship along the road. Daphne Grey played the wise mother, Noni Hazlehurst and Lorna Lesley his lovers, together with Lynette Curran, Julie Hamilton, Madeleine Blackwell and Kirrily Nolan. Then there was a little girl called Rebecca Smart. This pint-sized blonde was a truly instinctive actress who knew what to do and how to do it from her very first moment on the set. Rebecca Smart and Bryan Brown held hands for a very special eight weeks, a daughter and a father destined to be together. Like a tiny angel, she seemed to hover over us, urging us on with her confident grin.

News of the series had raised early excitement but the role of Buster had been a problem: how to find a tiny girl to play this enormous role and not only carry it off but become the life of the journey she had to make? At the time I was doing post-production for *The Place at the Coast* and needed some children's voices for a scene on the beach. A number had gathered at the studio when suddenly Rebecca appeared. We took one look at each other and the connection was audible. Days later a video of Rebecca's audition was sent to the BBC, a partner in the project. 'She'll do,' was the magisterial reply. This was either arrogance or stupidity. The little 'she'll do' girl was magnificent.

Wandering through the beautiful bushland of South Australia with Geoff Simpson, our DOP, and a crew led by Chris Webb, my gentle First, I set out to interpret what the audience would see through Macauley's eyes, a man who tramped the roads, asking no charity but seeking work to feed himself and his daughter. The whole series received wonderful support from our production manager, Antonia Barnard, our benevolent producer Bruce Moir, and Jock Blair from the South Australian Film Corporation.

Kris Fredrikson came on board to design the series with a limited budget, and with our careful planning of each frame he was able to design the entire series in camera. This meant he saved money by providing design only for what the camera would see; and Anna French's clothes, so carefully researched, created beautiful images against the landscape of bare hills. Henry Osborne, our second assistant director, did much to make the many actors comfortable and happy on the set. Henry is no longer with us but is remembered with great affection by all his friends in the film world.

The older male cast was led by Simon Chilvers, Norman Kaye, Frank Gallacher, William Zappa, Reg Evans and Ray Meagher. This wonderful cast kept the story of Macauley's wanderings through South Australia full of humour. I was particularly drawn to Norman Kaye and the curious character he played—an itinerant poet who loaded his bicycle with the necessities to live out a pleasant existence on the lonely roads of the outback. There was something in all this that created a strange longing in me. Equally nostalgic was a community old-time dance that took me back to schooldays and the barn dance. I invited Keith Bain, NIDA's movement teacher, to teach the cast their paces. An enduring memory is watching Julie Hamilton teach Rebecca to make pancakes in the old way at the stove, just as my mother taught me.

Post-production was equally involving. This was my first time making post-production choices on my own. It was challenging work and over two months formed a lasting friendship with editor Denise Haratzis and composer Chris Neal. It was, I must admit, rather eerie to find myself for so many months back in Adelaide, and occasionally disturbing memories would envelope me as I passed the Festival Centre, never daring to enter. But that was already nine years ago—time to let go and move on. *The Shiralee* remains, for me, the best of times. Fortunately for my soul, Darcy Niland's story of the wanderer and his daughter was universally loved by Channel Seven, the critics and the public.

*

The new ashramite heaved his suitcase into the small neat room. A welcoming vase of flowers sat on an empty desk. Friends followed, hauling in the futon and collapsible base which turned it into a small settee, a chair and a box of books. We stood looking at each other for a moment, grinned, and intoned in a soft chorus, 'Sadgurunath Maharaj Ki Jay'. Then they left me to settle in.

I had arrived at the Sydney Siddha Yoga Meditation Centre to return to life as an ashramite. It was 1987 and *The Place at the Coast* and *The Shiralee* had kept me away on location for many months. Now work was bringing me back to Sydney and I had come to a decision. Being on location had divorced me from the life of the ashram, and now it was at the centre of my thinking. If and when I was called away, I would know this place as home.

In practical terms, being an ashramite meant rising early each morning to meditate on soft carpets, breathing in the incense curling across lit candles; chanting the morning Song of the Guru among many voices, while others cooked breakfast in the large kitchen, fulfilling their *seva*. In the evening I would be master of ceremonies at the *satsang* programs, or prepare talks, or help to tutor others as they spoke of their experiences with the guru.

With thirty Siddha Yoga devotees I lived a life of service to the guru inside the ashram while living a busy life outside, making films. Whatever it was that had led me to rent out my flat and move into the ashram can be placed at the feet of Gurumayi, my guru. The impossible idea began to work as I installed my own telephone and, with the support of my agency, would manage immediately to direct a film in Sydney and prepare to go back to the theatre for the first time in five years.

At the same time the ashram began to arrange evenings in various theatres in Sydney. More and more, as people began to understand the benefits of meditation, such evenings became easier to arrange and proved very popular, particularly for people who were reluctant to go to an ashram. I recall one such night in the Wharf Theatre, which from 1984 had become the home of the Sydney Theatre Company and in which I would direct many plays. That night it was packed with actors and workers from my own profession, many of whom later came to the ashram to take a course in meditation. The life of a Siddha Yoga devotee and that of a theatre and film practitioner began to merge.

Princess Kate became another visit to my childhood, taking me back to the music with which I had grown up. The Children's Television Foundation offered me the opportunity to direct a story about adoption. The main role is a young pianist who discovers a half-sister who is a violinist; the climax of the film is a music competition in which they both compete. My life would become a medley of Hindu chant, Beethoven, Schumann, Chopin and Mozart.

We found Ascham, a private school for girls in Sydney that had a major music department, and invited their young musicians to play for the film. Another joy was the casting. I was able to cast three of my children from *Mad Max*: Justine Clarke, Shane Tickner and Rebekah Elmaloglou. Both the girls were musicians and for weeks we enjoyed ourselves playing and listening to our favourite music. Others joined them to be part of the music school, including Claudia Karvan and Mouche Phillips. Lyndel Rowe and Lorna Lesley played the mothers with Alan Cassell and Martin Sacks, the fathers. Kristin and David Williamson delivered a beautiful script and Jeff Darling began to weave his magic. Where the environment had been the poetry of the previous film, music was the means of creating the images of *Princess Kate*. Post-production with editor Denise Haratzis and composer Chris Neal pulled all my musical and editing choices together. Film is truly a collaboration. So many people depend on so many others to make it all happen. In the dedicated hands of the producer, Antonia Barnard, *Princess Kate* was a success. Patricia Edgar of the Children's Television Foundation has my special thanks for allowing me to indulge in the music I love.

Meanhile, *seva* for the guru occupied much of my time, but occasionally, in breaks between projects, I would go to where Gurumayi was in residence to spend time in her presence. This meant several trips to Ganeshpuri, that most beautiful garden home where meditation was not so much a part of a daily program as the natural outcome of living there.

One year I visited the ashram in Upper New York State, among the forest and mountains. A glorious setting with a large, old hostel turned into a residency, provided a wonderful summer break. As part of my *seva* that summer I worked with the swamis on presenting some of the stories from *The Mahabharata*. They were a great success and it felt right that I could offer as *seva* the skills of my own profession.

A year later, a call came to me in Sydney from a principal swami in America. Would I come to New York for the summer and direct a production of *The Ramayana*? This was a most exciting prospect, but my heart almost stopped. I stood at the phone unable to speak. I was already contracted to direct a film. *The Crossing* was to begin shooting before the summer was over and it was quite impossible. I finally found my voice and explained the situation. The swami paused for a moment and said, 'It can work, George, if you think about it.'

How could it work? What did he mean?

For hours I wandered around unable to think, let alone act. Film schedules were sacrosanct and with so much money at stake preparations were already advanced. I took myself off to the meditation room to contemplate my first real work crisis as a devotee. That evening I was MC for an evening of chanting, which was always a good way of clearing the mind. By the end of the evening I knew what to do.

In the morning I rang my producer, Sue Seeary, and requested a meeting with her and the executive producer, Al Clark. This would be my first time of working with them and I was nervous but determined. As I arrived I happened to meet the author, Ranald Allen, at the door. I took him back to my car and told him what had occurred and what it meant to me.

'Just go and tell them the way you told me and it'll happen,' he said.

Feeling far less confident than he, I presented myself at the office and blurted out my tale.

'But this is important,' said Al Clark. 'Of course you must go.'

When something is of great importance to oneself, it is always an enormous surprise to find that others recognise this. The others in the room, less ready to accept the delay, were swayed by Al and I shall always be grateful for his understanding.

So I went to America and spent the summer months being busier than at any other time in my career: helping to manage and direct this story, employing hundreds of people including some very fine actors from New York. The story was performed over two nights at the end of summer on a huge constructed stage on the flat top of a hill within the ashram. It was the sort of project which would normally require a long period of rest and recuperation after the event but the supporting energy of that community gave me new life and I returned to Australia restored and ready to make *The Crossing*.

Some time later, another incident tested me in a similar way. I was in London on a visit when the phone rang late one afternoon and a Siddha Yoga friend gave me a message from Gurumayi. Could I find a choir who could sing Gregorian chant and who would like to come to India to the ashram at Ganeshpuri to celebrate Christmas there? Well, of course, this was an impossible request. It was October already and in any case, any choir worth its salt would be well booked.

It happened that a copy of *Time Out* lay on the desk in front of me and it was open at the music section. There, staring at me was an advertisement for a concert that evening in Smith Square given by a university choir from Cambridge. I grabbed my friend and we sped down to the theatre. We managed to buy two seats and sat down to a glorious evening of music ranging from mediaeval chants to Elizabethan motets.

What happened over the next few days was a fairy tale come true. The choir from Clare College and their director Tim Brown loved the idea of spending Christmas in India and immediate bookings were made. I was not at Ganeshpuri that Christmas, but I'm told that they were inspirational. Siddha Yoga has taught me not only that faith is of supreme importance in life but that it must be fed by practical action.

It was 1989. *The Crossing* was in audition mode and we breathed a sigh of relief as the interviews finished for the day. The tiny room felt suddenly claustrophobic and I needed to leave and stretch. Beside me Faith Martin, our casting consultant, was making final notes on the actors seen today. It was the first time I had worked with Faith and she would become a great friend and adviser in the years to come. I stood up and gazed out of the dirty window, a little disconsolately.

'Well,' I murmured, 'we haven't found him yet.'

Faith continued writing and said, 'Perhaps the workshop will reveal a Johnnie.'

I took up the sheet and looked down the names. Good young talents, all of them, and I looked forward to spending the day with fifteen budding film stars and a video camera, improvising dialogue and confrontation.

The Crossing was a film set in the early 1960s about a group of teenagers living in a country town in the year before the Vietnam call-up. The screenplay by Ranald Allan called for two boys and a girl to head the large cast. We were looking for fresh faces. I recalled the words of the filmmaker Robert Altman: 'Casting is 90 per cent of a film director's job.'

Already, among those listed I felt drawn to two young people. Danielle Spencer impressed me with her quiet beauty. A private world lay locked inside her eyes even while her smile lit up her face.

Danielle Spencer, Russell Crowe and Robert Mammone in *The Crossing*.

And Robert Mammone had a strongly handsome Italian face which might suit perfectly the young artist who returns home to be reunited with his girl and family. The third role, however, was more complex. Johnnie was the local boy, aggressive and rebellious, who had fallen in love with his best friend's girl. This role required a young actor who carried danger with him, as well as a passionate love for the girl.

The gang of young locals who inhabited the milk bar and roared around town in beat-up vehicles would emerge from the workshops. It was up to me to make sure they worked in action and as a group. To prepare us for that day we were interviewing the potential cast, finding from their own words where they came from and where they might belong in the film.

After eight years of working behind a camera I knew how easy it was to make a mistake in this complex business. I have known really good actors to have no feeling for the camera, and others with little experience who take to the magic eye as if born to it. Many actors do make the transition from theatre to film and back again, but they remain quite different art forms.

Faith and I were preparing to leave for the day when rapid footsteps were heard on the stairs. A young man burst into the room.

'Am I too late?' We gazed at him as he stood breathless and gasping, with his hair tousled and uncombed, a chipped front tooth and a hungry look in a pair of startling eyes.

'Russell Crowe,' he said, thrusting out his hand. 'I'm sorry—am I too late?'

Faith had already put down her books. She sat at the table with her pen poised. I continued to stand, staring at him. Do all filmmakers have this experience, just once? There was no doubt whatsoever in my mind. I knew that this young man would play Johnnie and I would witness the emergence of a star. Faith too recognised an aura about him, which we knew the camera would love and nurture. We gave him the date of the workshop and he left with a huge grin on his face. I went home cherishing the same excitement I had felt upon finding Rebecca Smart.

At the workshop the young actors danced, played games and met in small confrontational dialogues. The video camera roamed around the room capturing them at unexpected moments, so that their natural nervousness evaporated and allowed the camera to record them at ease and confident. Our expectations were confirmed and Danielle, Robert and Russell would play the three young people caught up in a small-town tragedy. It was one of the most satisfying days I have ever experienced in the film business. My producers, Sue Seeary and Al Clark, were equally delighted.

For all of us, the town was of supreme importance. After driving for days, Sue and I discovered Junee, a forgotten town that had once been a great railway junction. Junee had no parking meters or any other intrusive modern street furniture. It required only simple dressing to take it back thirty years to those days of emerging teen music and rebellious youth.

Jeff Darling joined me again as DOP and we made exhausting preparations in Junee and the surrounding district for the thousands of shots the film required. At one location we were standing in a paddock filled with Patterson's curse that gave us both such blinding hay fever we ended in hospital.

Then, as shooting dates were being fixed the telephone call came from America. Everything was set and I now wanted it to stop. What was I thinking of?

I often think back over that dramatic time—to the ready agreement of my producers and the understanding I received from crew and cast. To find among my friends and work colleagues such ready respect for views they did not share was astonishing.

As autumn began I was back at my post. Chris Webb and Jo Weeks joined me once again in Junee. Our production designer Igor Nay dressed the streets and pubs with inspired memories of a time now gone and Katie Pye's clothes made this film a real celebration of the 1960s. Armistice Day was the most important event in the life of the town and I persuaded the Canberra Pipe Band to come down for the day and lead the march. Among the pipers was my nephew, Bruce Ogilvie, and I felt an inordinate pride in having him in the film.

As the shoot progressed, the leading trio grew into a formidable team, despite their lack of experience. And the more I saw of Jeff's work at rushes, the more I knew that the town too was becoming a leading character.

Russell displayed immediately his empathy with the camera. His whole world became the film. He absorbed everything, remained focused and determined to give his best, expecting me, his director, to do likewise. He knew at once that working in front of the camera was his natural habitat and he gloried in it. His demanding presence unsettled some of our crew; but I was grateful for the young artist's dedication and searched for the right words to release his talent.

Not far from town we found the railway crossing needed for the tragic climax and State Rail agreed to its use. Robert Mammone was found to be not just a good driver but an expert, even impressing our safety officer, and he was looking forward to the car races that precipitate the tragedy. His disappointment was very real when he discovered that for the dangerous shots the car would be mounted on a low loader. However, as we discovered, he proved much more relaxed when in control. Our safety officer, Zev Eleftheriou, kept his eyes wide open during this part of the shoot but there were no accidents. It meant time and tremendous care with the set up of each shot. The car races reminded me of the memorable day of stunts on the *Mad Max* shoot. Again we needed hundreds of shots to catch the excitement, and the final collision of car and train needed nerves of steel and much patience throughout long night-shoots.

The film opens with the town commemorating Armistice Day—still, in the early 1960s, an emotional memory. George Whaley and Les Foxcroft, Jacqy Phillips, May Lloyd and Patrick Ward joined me to give the film a strong foundation. Daphne Grey came from Adelaide to play Russell's alcoholic mother and her performance made these difficult scenes very moving. The entire population joined in the shoot. When the pipe band marched at the head of the old soldiers the whole town was there to cheer. One chap was so keen he attempted to be in every shot. Jeff's camera made poetry of the tragedy in the older faces and the hope in the faces of the young people. It became a dissertation on love from the first scenes.

Jo Weeks and I had worked together since *Bodyline* and I had come to depend on her film craft as continuity. Her observation was particularly accurate with young actors making their first film. She recognised immediately the nerves which beset a newcomer and helped me to relax them and shoot more takes until we achieved the performance we needed.

It became a daily necessity to view rushes with our editor, Henry Dangar, and, as the shoot continued, to see sections of the film cut together. It gave sense and direction as the story took shape. Jeff's images were so beautiful we kept lingering on them; and the final film, when cut together and released, would earn him an AFI award.

We were now well into the shooting and one matter had still not been resolved in my mind. The film's resolution kept nagging at me. All along I had felt the young people's actions were carrying them to disaster, but the script had a happy ending. At the end of the third week I rang Al and asked him to come to Junee with the other associates and talk before I went any further with the shoot. They arrived late one night and I put my arguments to them once again. But this time the film was in jeopardy. I reminded them that Ranald's original story had had a tragic ending and argued that the story, as we were telling it, called for the death of the young artist. To play the last scene with Danielle and Russell meeting at Robert's grave, Russell already in uniform for Vietnam, seemed to me the inevitable conclusion. They finally agreed and we set about bringing the story to its climax.

Such was the modest film that began Russell Crowe's fabulous career. The later marriage of Russell and Danielle brought us together one more time as I read a passage in the church and wished them a long and happy life. The film also remains with me for the exquisite images Jeff Darling conjured out of this country town, and for the fierce encouragement he gave me I will always be grateful to my executive producer Al Clark for making this shoot such a powerful experience.

Armistice Day, with which *The Crossing* begins, also made an appearance in *The Soldier Settler*, a story by Peter Schreck set at the end of World War II. It had been an important day for my family too, all of whom attended every year, some playing the pipes in the Highland band. When my two young sisters joined the Navy we were even closer to the marchers and the ritual.

Jim Holt had been in *Bodyline,* and I knew he would be perfect to play the returned soldier who receives a selection of land from the Government, but no help to farm it. Cast with him was Sue Leith, who had also worked with me in *Shortchanged.* The 13-year-old Ian Tongue joined them to play their young son, Jack. Ian proved himself to be an intuitive actor for the camera in the few weeks we had to shoot this little television film.

The Soldier Settler was one part of a series about great Australians compiled by Michael Willesee, and it pleased me to think that an unknown soldier was to be included. There is probably no family in Australia without one of the unknown somewhere in their family tree. I was fourteen years old at the time of the soldier settler scheme and remember nights of discussion between my parents and friends caught up in the scheme. High hopes led to even greater anxiety and struggle as the young soldiers and their families sought a living from poor ground and hard living. With Sue and Jim we relived their hopes and disappointment in three intense weeks.

The family's hope was invested in an old windmill and we spent many days shooting around this broken and rusted object. When finally we made it work it was as much a triumph for the crew as it was for the soldier and his wife. Other things were more familiar: the small objects collected in their new weatherboard home reminded me of my childhood in the few rooms behind our shop; and the joys we experienced with the smallest Christmas treats were re-enacted in the film.

During *The Soldier Settler* shoot we had one of those occurrences that plague the life of a film director on location. It was the middle of summer, which proved perfect for most of the film. However, we needed a scene of torrential rain in which Sue, with the help of her son, had to cover the newly-stacked hay in the paddock before the rain ruined it. We had large water trucks to provide the rain but nothing could be done about the dazzling blue skies. In a big-budget film a wait for cloudy skies is possible, but for us it was imperative to finish on time and on budget. For my DOP Jan Kenny it meant shooting the drama of the scene without once catching a glimpse of the sky. We somehow managed it but no wide shots were possible. In the edit we added some footage of a stormy sky.

The campsite for *The Battler*.

I began this story with memories of my parents and their struggle to survive the Great Depression. Six years after *The Soldier Settler*, I began research and preparation for *The Battlers*, Kylie Tennant's famous story of those times. *The Battlers* became my tribute to Cissie and Stewart and their life together, in the hope of recreating something as a lasting record of the battlers of that era.

The Battlers had once again the South Australian Film Corporation and Gus Howard at the helm. I have had tremendous good fortune in my film producers with people like Bruce Moir for *The Shiralee*, and Antonia Barnard, with whom I have worked since *Mad Max*. Antonia and Gus have rare talent for bringing the right people together to make a movie. The relationship between director and producer is absolutely crucial. The return to Adelaide recalled happy memories in film and the Corporation could not have been more welcome or supportive.

My parents' experience during those terrible years of the 1930s became the background to my thinking as our film crew and cast followed the homeless Snow and his dog down country roads and by riverbanks. Many new people joined me on this shoot, mixed with old friends. Our DOP, Roger Dowling, came from Adelaide; our designer, Richard Roberts, from Melbourne; and our first assistant, Toby Pease, from Sydney. Old crew friends like Karan Monkhouse, Graeme Shelton, Robbie Morgan and Zev Eleftheriou helped to create a close community as we wandered through the South Australian winter.

The casting process became a long drawn-out business, frustrated by television executives who demanded a say in the choice. Over the years I have more than once walked away from a series because of their insistence on what I believed to be bad casting. But I was determined to stick with *The Battlers*, and after weeks of argument Gary Sweet and Jacqueline McKenzie were cast in the roles of Snow and Dancy.

The first day of the shoot arrived, in a beautiful setting by a river under enormous gum trees. Snow's van sat under the trees and a fire was lit for his damper. His horse grazed nearby and his blue heeler sat obedient, waiting for food. Gary Sweet and I stood looking at it as Roger set up his camera for the first shot. It had been a decade since we had worked together on *Bodyline* and we somehow knew this would be a good one. Moments later Jacquie arrived on the set dressed as the bedraggled waif Dancy and the story of two outcasts began. There were many weeks of hard work ahead, outdoors in all weathers, and many night-shoots to endure, but I knew at that moment I would love every day and night of it; and I did.

My father's stories accompanied me as we shot scenes along the roads full of the homeless, who created a fellowship of sharing. The adventures of these characters brought us in touch with a number of wonderful eccentrics. The talent of South Australia filled these roles as they brought the times alive in camera. One complaint that came from the network early in the shoot was that the cast were too clean to be living on the road. It displayed their ignorance of the people and the times. These were respectable citizens brought to their knees by economic disaster.

Peter Yeldham's script was carefully adapted from the novel. At the centre of the drama was the makeshift town built by the homeless, which brought back memories of driving down to the Goulburn River with my father to give away bread. This extraordinary, living, breathing, world was the triumph of our designer Richard Roberts. Anna French clothed the hundreds gathered around their tents and campfires, and Roger's camera caught unforgettable images.

Theatre actors and directors are always aware of the artificial nature of the stage setting. On film, the same façade is constructed but sometimes, as it was in Bartertown in *Mad Max* and now in *The Battlers*, the camera needs to explore every corner of the location. The design and construction of the refugee camp had to convince us, walking through, that we could be living there ourselves. Along with a good designer and construction crew this requires an expert in the craft of scenic art and in John Haratzis we had the best. John transformed canvas, wooden structures, brick walls, and applied his art to countless wagons and other forms of transport. To create the old from the very new and make it seem real is a rare art and John is a rare artist.

In post-production there is time to relax a little and watch the editor at work. My editor, Denise Haratzis, once again joined me and weeks of work were spent in the editing suites of the SAFC. When cutting the love scene between Snow and Dancy, Denise suggested a song should accompany their lovemaking. I found the words in a book of poems by Elizabeth Barrett Browning, and within days Carl Vine, our composer for the series, had written the beautiful song that accompanies the pair before they headed off down the road again. It is a song that is often heard on radio and takes me back to those days. Gary and Jacquie provided me with eight weeks of focused work, supported by mutual respect and accomplished with laughter and ease, a perfect mix.

The Crossing was set in the late 1960s, *The Place at the Coast* in the early sixties, *The Shiralee*, the fifties, *The Soldier Settler*, the forties. Now in the 1930s with *The Battlers*, it was like tracing my life backwards to the point of its beginning.

Nine

THE OLD LEGEND

Two actors were recently heard discussing a production I was due to direct for the Sydney Theatre Company.

'Isn't he that old legend?' one of them asked.

What the other replied is not recorded.

In March 1991 I celebrated my sixtieth birthday. In Siddha Yoga a birthday is an important day and the ashram gave me a royal ceremony. I had already returned to my first love, the theatre, directing productions in Sydney and out west at the Q Theatre in Penrith. Working in the theatre is a much more leisurely and far less intense business than making either film or television. A 'comfortable' rehearsal schedule gave me adequate time to explore character and meaning.

It also allowed me to continue my *seva* in the ashram, where excitement was mounting on account of the imminent arrival of our guru, Gurumayi. She would be spending some weeks in Sydney and give nightly programs at a huge hall in Darling Harbour. As it was my responsibility to act as her master of ceremonies, it was vital that no other work commitment coincided with her time in Sydney.

The advance party arrived, bringing with them a number of swamis. Their ability to reveal the benefits of Siddha Yoga in talks and stories and above all, their joy in life, revealed them as men and women on a journey of light. But with them came a contingent of young Americans determined to show us how to prepare the way of the Guru and what to say when she arrived. Their insistence made me more and more uneasy as the time approached. As I made notes of their demands the first flickering symptoms of irritation embedded themselves in my heart. I remembered something my mother said many years ago when talking of my father. 'He could never work for anyone, you know. Had to be his own master.' Was this true of me? Was this the reason why I became a director, the one in charge? Certainly, Adelaide had made me contemptuous of bureaucracy and, in particular, resentful of being told what to do by people who had authority but lacked understanding or ability to persuade.

Gurumayi arrived and on her first night at Darling Harbour I peeked out from behind the curtain and saw an immense sea of people waiting. This was no longer our small ashram speaking to our small community; this was a huge industry. I heard the signal to walk to the microphone and my heart gave a leap. Almost mechanically I stepped forward and walked the twenty metres across the stage. As I did so, I saw in my mind my first photo of Baba, waving and smiling just for me, and I remembered my advice to actors: 'Enter stage and perform for your favourite auntie in the back row who is there just for you.' I smiled at my auntie Jean in New Zealand and began the program. Gurumayi appeared and everything settled into perspective. What mountains we make of our fears. Standing near her, making announcements and introducing the chant, I let it all go and began to enjoy myself. This was *seva*, I thought, and I forgot about how I might look, or how others might see me.

So it continued for the Sydney tour. Mornings were spent going over the evening schedule, making changes and adjustments to the program, learning to manage large crowds, most of whom were there for the first time. Every night crowds enjoyed the benefit of Gurumayi's wisdom and grace, learning how to apply to their lives the meditation which lay at the source of Siddha Yoga. And in Canberra I took the opportunity of introducing some members of my family to Gurumayi.

At the end of this part of the tour I fell ill with influenza and was unable to follow Gurumayi to Melbourne. But by then I was grateful to be out of the public eye. I was at last beginning to take serious account of something my theatre work had been teaching me for many years, and that E.F. Schumacher had put into words I never tire of re-reading—that in the things that really mattered to me 'small is beautiful'.

Whether it be a play, an opera, an audience, a theatre and even the home I live in, small is beautiful. I've a horror of crowds, of rallies, which remind me of Fascism. Once an idea becomes an institution, power structures arise and the source of its beauty is too often suffocated by bureaucracy. By the time St Francis was dying his followers were numberless and a structure became imperative. The freedom he had always advocated now had to be controlled. So, acknowledging the need to turn back to the smallness of immediate surrounds and to take stock of the 'real' me, I retired from the public life of Siddha Yoga. I also took the step of shifting back to my small flat, simply to be alone to think and work out these feelings. I continued to learn from the source of Siddha Yoga and to meditate on the inner guru. And I continued to go to *satsang* as part of my weekly program. In the years that followed, Gurumayi, like Baba before her, spoke often of leaving the big issues alone and of focusing on the inner self. By so doing, by searching for the truth within ourselves, everything else falls into place. Contemplation of the past became an important and daily occupation in the following year. The daily act of commiting to paper my recollections of a long professional life has been an important part of that ritual process of contemplation.

Perhaps surprisingly, I had never directed a Shakespeare play until 1973. Since then, however, I have had the pleasure of directing eight of them, several of them twice. Some of these productions have been with students, others with actors in the major state companies, but all of them, however painful the process might occasionally have been, have been extraordinary journeys of discovery and self-discovery. Three stand out in my memory: *The Comedy of Errors* (1973), *Pericles* (1987) and *King Lear* (1995). Perhaps it was out of feelings of terror—unworthiness, perhaps—that I had put off the experience for so long. But, when we put together the program for the second season of the newly-formed Adelaide company, I decided to include *The Comedy of Errors*. Why this one? Probably because it was an early play, one of the great man's 'less mature' works, but also because its

Sydney Theatre Company, 1995. Frank Whitten as Gloucester and Helmut Bakaitis as King Lear. (Photo: Tracey Schramm.)

farce and physicality were performance styles with which I felt most at home.

In 1987, although still very much involved in film at the time, I received an offer from the STC's artistic director, Richard Wherrett, to direct a production of *Pericles* at the Wharf Theatre. I almost jumped through the phone on my ashram desk, and danced around the reception hall chanting '*Sri Ram, Jai Ram*'. Why should *Pericles* be the Shakespeare play that has most fascinated me? Its very flaws have contributed to my continual appraisal of the text, trying to reach the truth within its eccentric construction.

Scholars insist that the first two acts have very little to do with Shakespeare, while conceding that the final reconciliation scene between Pericles and his daughter Marina remains one of the glories of Renaissance English drama. Pericles, like Job of the Old Testament, is on a journey of obedience, a journey in which everything is taken from him: reputation, kingdom, wife, child and friends, only to receive all back in his old age with the blessing of the Goddess. It is the story of the seeker, which makes this romance unique among his plays.

Richard Wherrett's offer also gave me the chance to work with Kristian Fredrikson again and we conceived a modern setting this time, because *Pericles* is a fairytale set in a non-existent world that could be as modern or as old as we felt it to be. Kris's dazzling white tropical world disguised the secret horror of a Pol Pot killing field. From there. Simon Chilvers' gentle narrator took us on the journey into a tyrannical regime that banishes Pericles into life-long wandering, revealing on the way the ambitions, cruelty and corruption of our present world, together with its beauty and love. It is this production that in memory is my memorial to Kristian Fredrikson, who in 2005 died suddenly in the middle of designing a great ballet. For forty years we worked together and his friendship and knowledge became an essential part of my life.

When I was invited in 1995 by the Sydney Theatre Company to take on a studio production of *King Lear* in their Wharf 2, I baulked at the idea. Who would play the role? Why mount a production of this of all plays, unless the right actor is in your sights? We are blessed in this country with a range of actors capable of encompassing such a role—except in voice. Lear requires an extraordinary vocal range if he is to make that long, arduous and tragic journey. Helmut Bakaitis has such a voice and I put him forward as my candidate for the role. Much humming in the ranks later, we set about studying this great work. An American film company later discovered Helmut's voice and cast him as the Architect in *Matrix III*.

To study and rehearse *King Lear* was like opening out my whole life and seeing the selfishness, the hopes, the ambitions, the greed and compassion that we all experience on our journey. I was shocked to discover just how modern this great play is. I was reminded daily of the news of boardroom quarrels, corporate takeovers, suicides, and employees being sacked as scapegoats. The identification of every member of the cast with the characters was the easiest part of the process; the most difficult, the verse itself. Our task was to communicate the here and now that we had discovered in the text and at the same time give it the heightened power that blank verse demands if the audience is to be carried into the rafters of breathless drama.

It was a tough and exciting adventure and Helmut, accompanied by his clown and familiar, Tom Weaver, with his family of daughters, friends and enemies, have my gratitude and love for their total commitment. It was a particular joy to sit in the daily performances and see the absorption of the student audiences. They sent in letters full of questions and compliments and made the season of *King Lear* one of the most absorbing periods of my life in the theatre. For me *King Lear* was the pinnacle of my work with Shakespeare and this great play continues to haunt me as the years of my life lengthen. I pick up a copy often and yearn to have the chance of one more attempt. It gets more complex with each reading, revealing more of our common humanity.

Performing Shakespeare makes enormous demands on both actor and director. First, the humility to submerge oneself into the character and become part of the journey each play takes; secondly, a certain showmanship to display the bravura inherent within the words; and thirdly, a strong technique which can master the heightened but always natural speech of this poet-playwright. The problem facing most Australian actors is that they so rarely get the chance to play Shakespeare. Only the Bell Shakespeare Company provides regular productions. With so little experience in speaking blank verse, the actor is bound to take short cuts in order to try and make the language sound natural. But by doing this he loses the heightened quality which gives the verse its inspired rhythm. Great voices are rare in the theatre today. Film does not need them, or television, or many modern dramas. Such voices are becoming rare even in Shakespeare's homeland. There is no longer much virtue attributed to a beautifully modulated voice that can seduce an audience with the range of an opera singer. Those days are gone and I miss them. Our lifestyle has changed too. The young Australian actor is a highly physical being, who loves to run, move and use the body in adventurous ways, but the voice is not one of our great achievements. Nevertheless, some modern Australian plays, as well as the classics, have the capacity for lyricism, and few actors will take the leap necessary to reveal the beauty of such a text.

The French are intensely proud of their language. To speak well, fluently and with a certain dash, is considered right and proper. But for the Australian student to begin to study the voice is like entering foreign territory. They are willing, but do not see it as essential to their careers. To handle Shakespeare's Elizabethan English requires not only vocal range but a good breathing technique, in the way an opera singer finds essential if they are to express the musical language of a score. I have known a famous opera singer to study a major role for ten years before attempting a performance. It is shameful that really good voice teachers are available to the student in this country and are so little used. The tragedy is that it means the slow death of the classic theatre and our enjoyment of it.

The dream of building an ensemble company of actors, a dream that people like Kris and Helmut had once shared with me in those early days of state-subsidised theatre—and one which we almost made come true—had disappeared by the mid-1980s. Film and television had created a rival profession offering money that no actor could afford to ignore. These actors who came together in *Pericles* had no time to even begin to trust each other or to feel they were sharing the same goal. Each one worked according to their own rhythm and practice. With time we could have created a company to reach the sky.

It is most regrettable that companies such as we had at the Melbourne Theatre Company no longer exist. We have new theatres, new actors and new directors, but neither government bodies nor corporate sponsors are capable of seeing the relevance of the true ensemble such as exists in France or Germany, for example. Today our subsidised companies have come to resemble those of the commercial world I remember from *Conduct Unbecoming*, and for which only enough money is supplied to get the plays on. Ensemble life can produce a level of performance unachievable by any other means, and the Australian theatre would be the richer for it. It goes without saying that I applaud the Sydney Theatre Company's commitment to the notion of ensemble companies. In 2005, thanks to some financial help from an enlightened NSW Government, they were able to give a guaranteed life-expectancy of five years to an ensemble of twelve actors.

Twelve actors is just about the right number, I think; if that was enough for Shakespeare or Molière, it would do for me. As I have already said of both companies and the spaces in which they work, small is beautiful. Which thought takes me back fifteen years, to the moment I first saw the auditorium of the Q Theatre on Sydney's western outskirts. As a building it was easily missed: it looked like a small, dark warehouse stuck between the railway and a huge car park in the unfashionable end of town. And today it is no longer there, the site having been 'developed'. But I fell in love with it the moment I walked into it. Of all the theatres I've worked in, this one remains my favourite and if I ask myself why, two related answers assert themselves: intimate spaces and what the Polish theatre guru, Jerzy Grotowski, memorably called 'poor theatre'. My life as an actor began as I entered a dark little hall in Wales. Now as I look back over the experiences of fifty years, that experience of living with the Family, touring with them, playing on an assortment of inadequate platforms, wearing hand-me-down clothes against a background of painted canvas, has journeyed with me all my life. Their way of doing things became, for me, a natural way to live the life of an actor.

It is the intimacy I have loved: some of the most exciting theatre I have helped create has been in small spaces—Russell Street, the Hampstead Theatre Club, the NIDA studio, the STC's Wharves 1 and 2, the Q. And when the experience has been one of working in a small space with very few people—as when I directed Willy Russell's one-woman *Shirley Valentine*, at both the Wharf and the Q, with my beloved Julie Hamilton—what more could I ask? The same can be said of some of my most treasured memories of visits to Stratford-upon-Avon—not the spectaculars in the company's main house, but productions such as Deborah Warner's *King John* and *Titus Andronicus* in the confined space of the large Nissen hut that is The Other Place.

Like a faithful apprentice, I've learnt my trade in the theatre's school of hard knocks, where improvisation and compromise were all, and where 'leave it to the actors' was the catch-cry. No wonder the little Russell Street Theatre in Melbourne gave me such unbearable excitement. Today, as I walk past it, I ache for its shuttered doors to be re-opened. It is for this reason, too, that I have so enjoyed working with students and facing the challenge of working within such constraints and with reduced means. I have precious memories of productions of *Twelfth Night* and *Pericles* with the students of the VCA in Melbourne, *A Midsummer Night's Dream* and *Love's Labour's Lost* at NIDA, and *As You Like It* at WAAPA in Perth.

The Q Theatre was like a small, rough diamond, economically designed without either flies or wing space, but with a soft descent from audience onto a thrust stage, which gave the audience the feeling that they could physically touch the drama being played out. Such theatres are made to be managed by people who have an unconditional love of theatre and are ready to risk everything. My five years there began in 1991, shortly after I left the ashram, at a time when my life needed a renewed sense of purpose. From then until 1996, under Helmut's artistic directorship, the Q took me back to my dedicated days with the Family.

If I say that the first work I did at the Q—a *Twelfth Night*, designed by an old Russell Street colleague, Anna French—was the best I had done for many years, it is because we were both working as we had in our old Melbourne days, within restricted means. Perhaps at the Q we were even more restricted: our budget limited us to a cast of ten, and Anna was desperate about every cent spent. It helped, of course, to have had what I believe to be to the best female trio I've ever seen in this play: Jacqueline McKenzie as Viola, Rebecca Frith as Olivia and Michele Fawdon as Maria. Moreover, our work also benefited from being carried out in relative isolation: Penrith may only be an hour's train journey from central Sydney, but this was enough to build a creative working environment well away from the city's usual distractions. It helped that over the several weeks of rehearsal we spent the first hour of every day singing together and learning Elizabethan songs for the play. This chorus work not only prepared the actors for the day's work, perhaps more importantly, it helped bring them together and mould them into a comfortable and harmonious unit. As I have found so often in my work, this is the indispensable ingredient of good theatre work. My love for poor theatre lies in my love for the actor. To say that theatre can dispense with everything except an actor, an audience and the space they share, and that it is the actor who gives meaning to everything that happens on a stage, is a truism, of course. But it's one I hold dear. From the first moment I was aware that there was such a thing as a performance, I have been in love with actors, both as a breed and as individuals. If, as the guru says, all life is an illusion, then actors, in celebrating and heightening that illusion, are able, on occasion most wonderfully, to reveal the truth that lies behind it. Just as the brush strokes of a great painter surpass his materials and give the viewer a glimpse of something mysterious, so I have seen expressions of rapture on the faces of an audience and been made aware that they were sharing an ecstatic experience.

Theatre does more than reflect back to us the world in which we live, it presents us with a mirror in which we can see our own lives and recognise our innermost selves. For me, looking into *King Lear* with Helmut Bakaitis had been just such an experience. Directing a new play by a friend of long-standing, actor-director Nick Enright at the Q in 1992 was another. The play was *St James Infirmary* and in his program note Nick wrote: 'Though the play is far from autobiographical, certain connections are undeniable.' I could have said the same, for *St James Infirmary* struck an immediate chord. The memories the play uncovered from my own life were so vivid that by the end of rehearsals I had begun to commit them to paper. So began the exercise which became this book. I have to thank Nick Enright and his *St James Infirmary* for this.

It is a play about a boy growing up and, although the setting is a private school twenty years later than my own exciting and terrible years at state school, the connections were unequivocal. The world I grew up in was one in which adoration of 'maleness' prevented any compensating sensitivity from being expressed and, in so doing, produced what Nick describes as 'brutal, unreflective and emotionally inarticulate human beings'. The play showed me that it was thought no less eccentric for a young boy to have 'artistic tendencies' in the 1960s than it had been twenty years earlier. Such young artists found themselves just as isolated. It took me many years to understand that every human being is composed of essential 'masculine' and 'feminine' traits, which together create balance and harmony.

As Nick sat beside me during the early rehearsals, I was careful to implement his vision of the text. In my experience, Nick Enright was unique amongst playwrights: not many would have insisted on the actors and I telling him everything we thought was not working in the text, and helping him inject the right words and feelings into the script. Our four young actors—Glenda Linscott, Felix Nobis, Damon Herriman and, in the leading role, a new NIDA graduate, Sam Wilcox—responded in a sympathetic and knowledgeable way. With my old pal Ronald Falk to complete the cast, rehearsals were totally open experiences for us all, exactly what rehearsals should be. It is the director's job to create the environment in which that can happen.

I was to work alongside Nick twice more, with his sharply-observed comedy *Quartet from Rigoletto* for the Q and the Ensemble, and his *A Man with Five Children* for the STC in 2002. It was through working with him that I came to acknowledge a lot about my own practice as a director and about my views on the relationship between the director and the actor. Casting, for example, has traditionally been a matter of choosing the right person for the role. My preference, however, has always been to seek out the best actor *for the play*; and *for the rehearsal process*, someone whose contribution to the whole will culminate in the best interpretation of the play. The two are not necessarily the same person. There is an important distinction to be made here between directing in theatre and working in film. In the theatre my priority is and has always been the play. I see myself as a servant and interpreter of the author's text, and my job is essentially to bring it to life according to the author's intentions. It is therefore important to me to cast a play with actors who will inhabit their role, rather than use the role to express a talent uniquely their own.

Incidentally, I believe that the designer's job is the same as the actor's, namely to interpret the text visually, rather than to use it.

As working in the cinema soon taught me, on screen it is the director who rules, not the actor. Except in special circumstances, the actor is not an active collaborator in the creative process of filmmaking. Indeed, he or she is utterly dispensable in film, a visual medium in which the camera is the be-all and end-all. Similarly, the screenplay, like the footage, is only material for the director's vision. In the theatre it is the author's words that take precedence, in film it is what the camera sees. Looks and silences between people can be made more eloquent than any amount of text. Most filmmakers soon discover that the creative process consists, at least in part, in deciding which—the image or the word—will be allowed to win the struggle. An experienced screenwriter will have learned this and accept the process as part of the natural order. Nick Enright had certainly learned it. In 1992 the film industry rewarded his talent by nominating for an Oscar his screenplay of George Miller's *Lorenzo's Oil*.

The passing of moral judgment is another issue which, I believe, may be important for producers in theatre and film, but which I, as a director, find anathema in the rehearsal room. Nick Enright's *A Man with Five Children* illustrates the point well. It tells the story of a man of influence—an influence exerted by the power of celebrity—over the hopes, dreams and ambitions of a group of young people and extending over almost three decades. As someone who has had influence over the lives and career of young artists, I felt very close to it.

Gerry is a television-documentary maker who, not unlike Michael Apted, creator of the celebrated *Seven Up* series, has arranged to film one day each year in the lives of five children, from the age of seven to twenty-one, then, subsequently, thirty-five. As the drama progresses, encompassing all the good fortune and tragedy the characters experience, Gerry becomes more than a passive observer and begins to influence the course of their lives—with the best of intentions. Here was a play in which a premature early moral judgment could easily be made. Gerry could so easily be portrayed as an unfeeling professional, only concerned with the impact on television. My job was to ensure that the audience be allowed to judge for themselves.

The moral judgment issue is one that both actor and director would do well to understand at the outset. It is too easy for an actor to begin to add to, or condemn, their character in keeping with their own ideas of morality and social significance. This will colour their interpretation, often to the detriment of the play. The outcome can be even more devastating should the director make a moral judgment about a script in advance. He or she will, almost unconsciously, take that piece in a different direction from the author's intention. I know that for many of our young directors today the author is dead and that it follows, therefore, that texts, especially historical texts, can only mean what they mean to the reader. I know that to these young people I shall seem old-fashioned, but I firmly believe that it is the actor's, director's and designer's job to be an interpreter, not a creator. A musician does not play Mozart in the way that he feels it should have been composed. He may put his own dynamics into the work, but he leaves the notes alone. This becomes just as important when considering the audience. To make a judgment on the play is to tell the audience how to think. Let them be the judge of the author's work if the director thinks it is worthy of production.

A Man with Five Children was a big, complex production, a far cry from the 'small and beautiful' work I generally prefer. However, when every single person working on a production is in love with the play and the idea behind it, opening night floats in like a dream. This opening night was a triumph and Nick's generous speech at the curtain call was one to remember with respect and love. This was to be Nick's last play: his death from cancer in 2003, at the age of only 52, robbed me of a dear friend and Australia of an extraordinary talent.

At the beginning of 1997, my mother quietly left this world. Her presence had kept the whole family anchored in Australia and my regular visits to see her were excuses for huge family get-togethers. Now, with her gone and no offers of new work in the offing—'You're getting on, you know, George,' she would have reminded me—an idea took root in my head.

It had always been a disappointment to my mother that none of her children had gone to university. So, at the age of 66, I left Australia in order to take up residence in London and begin study for a degree at the Open University—all the while continuing to record these reminiscences. Crazy as the whole idea seemed to most of my family—my young nieces and nephews all thought it 'cool', of course—I spent a wonderful year studying and writing. It might have continued into a second year, had not fate stepped in. The stress of too many years of hectic living, to say nothing of the damage caused by having smoked far too many cigarettes for far too long, culminated in an angina attack. It happened while I was back in Melbourne, doing a couple of months' teaching at the VCA, and I was given a quadruple by-pass on the spot.

When I left hospital I entrusted myself to the loving care of my brother Jim and his wife Rita. But I was determined to complete at least one dream of my life and, late in 1998, to the astonishment of my dear carers, I returned to Europe and bought myself a flat in Paris. The day I moved into my new place, a tiny apartment in the rue de la Roquette in the 11th *arrondissement*, it felt like coming home. Not that it was ever my intention that my career should come to an end: there would be planned working (and family) visits back to Australia each year. But for much of the time I was going to be able to walk the streets of my beloved Paris every day and to revisit all those places that had been so dear to me for so long. I quickly settled in and, surrounded by my boxes of memories, I sat down to complete these memoirs. It was whilst I was trying to do just that, in June 2001, that the telephone rang: the Sydney Theatre Company were offering me Nick Enright's *A Man with Five Children* to direct for the following January. There was no question of my saying 'no': the script arrived, I read it, I put these memoirs instantly aside, I packed and I flew back to Sydney to work with Nick on his final draft.

In March 2001 my twin brother Jim and I stood together, facing the two beautiful cakes that one of his grandsons had made for us. How proud my father would have been of their baking! We were celebrating our seventy years and brothers, sisters, nephews, nieces and grandchildren

Jim and George at seventy.

all gathered round to sing 'Happy Birthday'. Jim took up the cue and, quietly and simply, spoke a few words in reply, thanking our huge and wonderful family for the gift of all the years gone by and of those yet to come.

I gazed around, feeling welcomed and part of it all. But at the same time I also felt alone. Like a speeded-up camera I saw the years of watching others, sitting apart. I remembered the countless opening nights when I would wander around the theatre, no longer part of the community I had created and listening to actors and audience getting to know each other. I'm not the first theatre director to confess just how painful it is, once the show has opened and the actors have taken over, to admit that you are no longer required, and to let go. My brother finished speaking and I realised that I too would have to say a few words. So I did—in French. The youngsters gazed at me openmouthed, until nephew George suggested that I'd only been ordering a bag of croissants! For a moment they must have wondered who this strange foreigner was. Did he really belong to their family?

Well, yes, he did—and then, again, no, he didn't. I had watched from a distance as brothers and sisters took hold of life and shaped it according to their own hopes and dreams. I was away on some distant stage when my father died so many years ago, and shooting a film on some far-flung location when finally my dear mother drifted away at the age of ninety-two. I was in London when a young brother suffered a stroke and, despite its crippling effect, battled back into life. Again I was abroad when Robert, his twin, died suddenly, and I was preparing another film in Sydney when a young nephew let go of life, leaving the family grieving and bewildered. It seemed wholly appropriate that I should continue my role as the uncle who occasionally paid a visit as he ricocheted his way around the world.

Families! From this distance in time I could look back and see that our family had experienced everything large families go through—the business of being human. And because we were so, all this grief was mixed with laughter and love.

Living in Paris enables me to revisit old friends in Taizé, and to contemplate the world from that sacred place; and on my regular visits back to Australia, both to work and to see brothers and sisters, I am able to keep in touch with my Siddha Yoga friends at the ashram. The working part of my visits takes a variety of forms: directing episodes of the much-loved and soon-to-be much-missed TV series, *Blue Heelers*, with my old friend Gus Howard; teaching at one or another of our growing number of drama schools; and directing the occasional stage play. To see the purpose and joy in the faces of students just beginning their journey into the world gives me some small cause for optimism.

As I look back on fifty years in the business, I readily acknowledge that my own passion and perseverance have been amply rewarded. In 1984 I was awarded membership of the Order of Australia for my work in the theatre. In 1988 I received the Byron Kennedy Memorial Award from my peers in the film industry, and in 1994 one of the Australian Artists Creative Fellowships introduced by Prime Minister

Keating. These may have been short-lived, but mine enabled me to take some time off work and to make headway with the writing of these pages. Moreover, and most importantly, I have made numerous life-long friends—and in 2002 a cardiologist gave me new life in which to make many more. But perhaps my most sincere debt is owed to a wise guru from Ganeshpuri who many years ago woke up my spirit. It is with his words that I finish this story:

'To see God in everyone is the sign of true humanity.'

Appendix

The Circle

The Circle is a relaxation exercise used to warm up a large group of artists before they begin a day's work together. The leader instructs the group by quietly saying these words, or a variation of them.

THE WALK. Quiet reigns: Continue to walk and slowly quieten down inside. To observe—to think—to slowly let go all thoughts—to feel your body move—to feel the motor through your hips—to feel free—to loosen the body—the bare feet—the knees—the legs—the pelvis—the chest—going forward—to meet the future with wonder and excitement—to empty in order to be filled—to let the stomach and face be loose—relax the jaw—let the motor take you with spring in your heart—going forward—always forward—with hope and expectation—see everything—180 per cent—like a tidal wave move forward—seeing all but letting the particular focus go—don't focus our eyes on anything—see without looking the motor quickens—be as one—become part of the whole—lose yourself as you sweep around—let the whole sweep you into a run—an avalanche—NOW—without thinking CHANGE DIRECTION—just go—turn—twirl—skip—sidle—twist—jump—dance—be there—don't look—just see—everything—let the whole take you—let the whole be you—the whole will then ever so lightly begin to slow down—be part of the whole—slow down with it—don't do anything—let the whole do it for you—keep moving—keep the energy up—but slow down—the really difficult part—slow down but keep up—up with the wonder and joy and expectation but slow down physically—don't go to sleep as you slow down—become more, more, more—don't collapse—keep alive—as the whole slows to a walk—to a slow movement—to a shuffle—keep alive—don't begin to focus—180 per cent always—become more vibrant as the body slows—slower—slower—together you stop—close your eyes—hear your heart beat—listen to your heart—breathe—listen to your breath—stand still—feel the vibration of standing still—stretch out your hands—keep your eyes closed—find other hands—hold hands—lightly but firmly—breathe—breathe.

THE SOUND—hold together—a sound begins as you breathe—a good sound—a serene sound—hear the sounds—make more sounds—sounds that go with the other sounds—a chorale of sound—breathe the sound—open your mouth—use your stomach—let the sound out—join the sound—celebrate the sound—like a cathedral—gothic—let the sound go—soften the sound—sweeten the sound—lower the sound—whisper the sound—into silence—calm and empty.

The Book Lift

The Book Lift enables the participants and the onlookers gradually to develop a scene for film or stage. It allows development between characters established within the exercise and reveals, for both performers and scriptwriters, how the dynamic of drama is created, and how it can be created without the use of words.

For this experiment we need hundreds of old books, for use without worrying about damage, and two tables long enough for at least three people to stand in a row in front of them. We spread them out, piled up in a mess on one table while the other is placed, empty, on the other side of the room. Three players are then asked to shift the books between the tables, arranging them in careful piles. This simple task is conducted in silence as they move loads of six or seven books at a time from one table to the other and back.

Meanwhile the observers take notes on the three players' way of working and discuss it when the players are asked to stop. The first objective for the players is to create harmony, to focus easily and comfortably on their job. The observers see the trio becoming absorbed in their task so that they work without tension or diversion. They display harmony of movement and attitude, their rhythm never mechanical but like music, without dynamic or drama. It is important that the participants smile and be in contact with each other, knowing that nothing will break the rhythm of, or devotion to, their work.

This then is the basis of work and anything that intrudes into this harmony creates drama. Perhaps two of them become aware of each other in a way that has nothing to do with the work, and some new element intrudes as the third becomes conscious of their attraction to each other. Or perhaps a fourth character joins, who is new to the work and must be helped to establish a new harmony—but things go wrong and different rhythms intrude. A thousand small things can be suggested from the nimble minds of those who watch and many scenes can be built. Drama occurs because harmony is broken. Establish the harmony first a nd drama and comedy naturally follow.

The book lift is a perfect exercise in power, as victims and bullies emerge from the simple task of shifting books. Once a particular scene is established, words might enter the script and the complexity of the situation grows. New scenarios emerge as the writers expand the relationships in further sessions. With the busy minds of the participants in flight it is essential to control the detail as it pours in, and protect the simplicity of the original idea. In this way it becomes apparent, when too much is added, how easily scripts can become overcrowded.

Follow the Leader

Follow the Leader is a way of revealing to the actor, director and the scriptwriter the meaning of power on stage, and the responsibility leaders must have for their followers. It develops an understanding that power is bestowed, not taken.

The company is divided into small groups, with an appointed leader, and the action—without words at the start—ranges over a number of settings from a hunting party to an art gallery. The leaders choose the scene and the group is required to be totally subservient to the leader. Whatever the leader does, or to whatever they react, the group duplicates this reaction. By watching each group, observers begin to see that power is given, not taken. By changing the leadership, a different dynamic is established. Some leaders are tyrannical, others benevolent. The leaders begin to realise the group is dependent upon them, and that a leader needs followers. Some followers begin to wish they were leaders. Thus the drama begins.

Here is an example. As one group walks around an art gallery echoing the likes and dislikes of their leader, a dissenting voice suddenly offers a different opinion. The resulting shock within the group can produce some marvellous drama. Sounds and words may then be introduced allowing both sides to express their opinions. Once two groups are well established, they might confront each other and set a complex dynamic in action. The building of a scene, of a character, continues. This game, over time, can become very inventive.